# STEADFAST 2027

# STEADFAST

## 365 DAYS OF DEVOTION

ABINGDON PRESS | NASHVILLE

2027

# STEADFAST 2027

## 365 DAYS OF DEVOTION



978-1-7910-4358-2 (print)
978-1-7910-4359-9 (epub)



Cover description: Towering giant sequoia trees reach toward the sky in a sunlit forest, with the title "Steadfast" in large white text across the center. The subtitle "365 Days of Devotion" appears in smaller light orange type beneath the title with "2027" at the bottom in a green banner.

MANUFACTURED IN THE UNITED STATES OF AMERICA

# CONTENTS

# Introduction

When I was a child, my father would read a chapter of the Bible to us every night. He went in order, from Genesis 1 all the way to Revelation 22, and when he finished, he'd start all over again the next night. There is no telling how many times I heard the Bible in its entirety before I got to be "too old" to be read to before bed, nor how many times I've read the Bible on my own since then. I suppose you could say I'm a bit of an expert on the Bible by now.

But when I was compiling the devotions for *Steadfast 2027*, I came across parts of the Bible I had forgotten about. Other devotions gave me the opportunity to see scriptures in a new way. After finishing one series on a particular Old Testament character, I told the writer it was the best, most eye-opening look at that character I've ever seen.

And that's the amazing thing about scripture. Even if you know it all, you don't know it all. There are more depths to be plumbed, more heights to soar to, and more ways these words from, to, and about God can reveal Truth to us. I hope that these devotions will broaden and enrich your knowledge and understanding of the Bible, and of the God our scriptures reveal.

Jarrod S. Davis,
Editor

# JANUARY

## Contributor:

*Sue Mink*

*January 1–31*

## Friday, January 1

# Comfort for God's People

### *Isaiah 40:1-11*

**How has God enabled you to find a way "home"?**

The Hebrew people had been in exile, punished for their lack of faithfulness to God. But in the first verse of the second half of the book of Isaiah, God called the heavenly hosts together. "Comfort, comfort my people!" God told them. God was ready to bring God's people home.

It seemed like a lot of work to call these people home. People are short-lived and easily forgotten. They don't always deserve the blessings of God. Why would God even make the effort? It was because this call home was not based on who the people were, but who God is. God's word is eternal and always based on righteousness and mercy.

This invitation from God has been issued repeatedly to broken people. John the Baptist claimed this passage, telling the people that once again, the way to the heart of the Lord was being prepared for all people. Through Jesus Christ, the barriers to a relationship with the Lord would be removed and the people of God could come home again to the comfort and mercy of God. Like a shepherd with vulnerable lambs, God would carry God's people back to a place of wholeness, and they would know the true joy of salvation. There was a way cleared to the heart of God, and because of that, a way to the home that all of humanity longs for.

O Lord, thank you for clearing the pathway to your heart so that I may find my true home in you. Amen

## Saturday, January 2

# Change Your Hearts and Lives

### *Luke 3:1-8*

**Why would John insult those who came to see him?**

When people trekked out into the desert to hear John the Baptist speak and to be baptized, he was very demanding and even insulting. Didn't we just read the passage in Isaiah yesterday where God made the rough places smooth so that people could enter into a true relationship with God? What is going on here?

In Isaiah, the prophecy was written for the Hebrew people who had suffered under exile and who realized their sins. They had repented and wanted to humbly make their way back to the Lord. Their repentance was real and visible, and visible repentance was exactly what John was demanding. Without it, his baptism meant nothing.

A person can be raised in the faith, attend church every Sunday, tithe, and read the Bible, but if their life doesn't reflect a dedication to Christ, then their actions are worthless. The good news is that while God calls people to a life of faithful discipleship and reformed lives, the grace and mercy of Jesus Christ enables us to continue the journey to salvation even when we inevitably stumble along the way.

Lord, humble me so that I may see my sins, lead me to repentance and teach me to live as your disciple. Amen.

## Sunday, January 3

# The Fruit of Repentance

### *Luke 3:9-18*

**How would I change if I lived a life of repentance?**

Israel in John's time was under Roman rule, and corruption was rampant. Many people took advantage of others. When the people asked how repentance would affect their lifestyle, John called for honesty and fair treatment. John was even more demanding of those who had more than they needed. According to John, another's poverty is a reproach to those who have more than they need.

John illustrated judgment as dividing the wheat and the chaff. It's easy to read this as the godly people being separated from the bad, but every wheat kernel is made up of the nutritious inner seed and the tough, inedible outer hull—the chaff. We all have behaviors that need to be culled in order to be pleasing to the Lord.

And so this passage invites serious self-examination. How do we fail our neighbors, and in so doing, fail God? When do we take advantage of or withhold from others? What parts of our behaviors, beliefs, and attitudes need to go into the fire in order to be a more godly person? It is through this self-examination that we can truly prepare ourselves for the saving grace of the Lord Jesus Christ.

Lord, open my eyes to the ways I fail you, and prepare me for your transformation of my heart. Amen.

## Monday, January 4

# Good News Coming

### *Isaiah 29:17-21*

**When have you been surprised by God?**

This passage is a response to Isaiah 29:15-16, which is about people who think they know better than God. This is great and wonderful news, at least for those who struggle in this world. Those who think they can outsmart God by lying, cheating others, and plotting evil won't last. Often, it seems as though those who cut corners and are corrupt come out ahead. But God can change all that in a flash.

We shouldn't be surprised to be surprised by God! When human tradition favored the eldest son, God called the youngest to his service (Joseph, Jacob, and David). When society shamed barren woman, God blessed them (Sarah, Hannah, and Elizabeth). And when those who wanted to rule by status and power killed the Son of God, God raised Jesus Christ to life again. The "truths" we think we know about the world aren't truths at all in the hands of God.

And so we can dare to imagine a world different from those who think they know better. We can look forward with hope to a world with no more tears and where all are treated with dignity and live to their full potential. We can trust the way of God and deal with others honestly and with justice. If others laugh at our faith in a God who calls us to mercy and righteousness, we can rest in the knowledge that we worship a Lord of surprising reversals, and that God's way will, in the end, prevail over all.

O Lord, prepare me for your glorious surprises
as you mold the world to your will. Amen.

## Tuesday, January 5

# Walking on the Holy Way

### *Isaiah 35:1-10*

**How do people find the comfort and healing of God?**

For the Hebrew people exiled in Babylon, God gave them their freedom and all of creation rejoiced. God cared for every need, tenderly shepherding them back to their home and their place in God's heart. Scripture speaks of God's highway to salvation, the beautiful Holy Way created exclusively for God's redeemed people. The Holy Way was a path of singing and rejoicing as God's people made their way to freedom, hope, and healing.

Wouldn't it be wonderful to follow a highway full of celebrants to the very heart of God? But there is a Holy Way today, created by God and kept clear and smooth by the salvific actions of Jesus Christ. It's a way out of the slavery of sin to the kingdom of God. Every person is invited to follow its path, but only those who are dedicated to the way of the Lord can remain on it. It winds through our lives and brings us closer to God's vision for the world, which will one day be reached when God's kingdom comes to stay on earth. Meanwhile, this pathway offers us glimmers of the world to be, strength for the journey, and hope for the future. Together with the rest of God's redeemed people, we can walk the Holy Path to freedom and wholeness. God has created a way for us to enter a place without grief and groaning, a place within the heart of the Lord.

Lord, keep my feet on your holy pathway and my eyes on the coming of your kingdom. Amen.

## Wednesday, January 6

# Jesus Raises a Widow's Son

### *Luke 7:11-17*

**Have you ever seen a hopeless person's life turn around?**

When Jesus passed the funeral for the widow's only son, he was witnessing hopelessness. With no male relations, a widow had very few resources, so besides dealing with the grief over her son, she was most certainly looking at a life with no good future. But Jesus excels in hopeless situations! He commanded her son to get up. The young man stood, began to speak, and in that moment, Jesus turned around the future of the widow. Her life had meaning again.

Jesus was sent to be the Savior of the world, and the world has huge, global issues to solve. Yet Jesus made sure that this hopeless woman had hope and a future. She was probably unknown to him, and her well-being didn't affect anyone he knew. But Jesus came to bring hope and mercy to the world, and that meant to every person, no matter how unimportant to the rest of society. The future of a destitute widow mattered to Jesus.

And as followers of Jesus Christ, the lives of all who are hopeless need to matter to us too. Christians are in the business of restoration, renewal, and hope. We are future-bearers, following the Savior who brings us the hope of eternal life! What a wonderful message to bring to all, and even better, what a wonderful message to demonstrate to the hopeless of the world!

Lord, help me to be your servant to the hopeless. May I show your future to all who are hurting. Amen.

## Thursday, January 7

# The Good News Seen and Heard

### *Luke 7:18-23*

**Is Jesus Christ the kind of Messiah you expected?**

John was bold and demanding in his preaching and had gotten himself arrested for calling out the sins of Herod. Yet Jesus wasn't challenging the authorities like John was. Instead, he was healing the slave of an enemy Roman centurion, curing the blind and lame, and had caused an inconsequential widow's son to rise. Meanwhile, the Romans were still in power, John was still in prison, and God's people were still oppressed. John wondered, "Is this the Messiah we've been waiting for?" Is it any wonder he asked?

Jesus' answer was to quote the Scriptures. How would someone know who the Messiah was? The blind would see, the lame would walk, lepers would be healed, the deaf would hear, the dead would rise, and the poor would hear good news. Jesus was doing all of that.

If Jesus was the Messiah, the world would see what God thought was important through his work. And if we claim to be people of God, then in Jesus Christ we see what is important for us to be doing. It's caring for the least, the helpless, and those without a future.

Jesus knew that many would take offense at him. He wasn't their kind of Messiah. Maybe they would look for another or re-create Jesus into their idea of a Messiah. But Jesus' work is what was prophesized and is what God desires in the world today.

Lord, may I serve who you are, and not
what I want you to be. Amen.

## Friday, January 8

# Jesus and John the Baptist

*Luke 7:24-30*

**What makes a spiritual leader legitimate?**

Jesus questioned a large group of people who had followed John into the desert to listen to his preaching. Jesus was not condemning John, but he was questioning his followers' motives. Just what was it that they were looking for? If they were looking for a prophet, then not only had they found in John a true prophet, but they'd found the greatest prophet yet born.

Yet this great prophet was but a messenger of greater greatness to come. As profound as John was, he was just introducing a new kingdom that would outshine anything that had ever been on earth.

Thus, the best reason the crowds should have gone to the desert and see John was not to become followers of the newest thing, yet another prophet who had caused a buzz in the area; it was to fully commit their lives to the call of God. It was to forge a relationship with their Creator, not to become a disciple of yet another mouthpiece who claimed to be a way to enlightenment. John was pointing them not to himself, but to God. He was about opening people's eyes to the dawn of the kingdom of God, a kingdom brought to earth by Jesus Christ, the Son of God.

O Lord, may I never confuse a relationship with a spiritual leader to a true relationship with you. Amen

## Saturday, January 9

# Critics of Jesus and John

### *Luke 7:31-35*

**Why are people often blind to God's work in the world?**

Jesus was comparing those who were waiting for the Messiah to cantankerous children. Neither John nor Jesus fit their idea of a Messiah, so they weren't going to "play along" and join in the work of building the kingdom of God.

Jesus contrasts himself and John in the way that they ate. Israel was an occupied country, and customs around meals and food were one of the few ways that they could preserve their cultural heritage. But John didn't eat with anyone, and so he was supposedly rejecting the people of the covenant. Jesus, on the other hand, would eat with everyone, and so was supposedly rejecting that which made the Hebrew people unique. Neither one was following the social construct, so their critics maintained that neither was acting the way a Messiah was supposed to.

It's important to remember that God doesn't always work in ways that we expect. In fact, God rarely works in conventional ways. Because God isn't bound by convention, there's no limit to the creative and unconventional ways that God works in the world. As people of God and followers of Jesus Christ, we should expect the unexpected, being open to a call that may sound strange or uncomfortable, but that just might wind up being exactly what we were hoping and praying for.

O Lord, help me to see your hand in unexpected
and unconventional places and people. Amen

## Sunday, January 10

# Bringing the Good News and Healing

### *Luke 9:1-6*

**How are Christians to minister to others?**

Four times in the Book of Luke, Jesus sent his disciples out into the world to minister to the poor, the sick, and those who needed to hear God's word. They were not permitted to stay in their comfortable place at the foot of Jesus. While time with Christ and time with other Christians is an important part of living faithfully, Christianity is not only inward-looking but outward-looking. And so, Jesus sent his disciples out into the world to serve others.

Jesus didn't make it easy for them, either. They were to depend on the hospitality of others for every need. By travelling with nothing, not only were the disciples standing with the poor they would be serving, but they were also allowing others to serve them. Setting out with nothing showed their faith in God to provide.

This passage instructs us on both how to be givers and recipients of the word of God. As givers, we are to leave our comfortable places to offer the word of God to others. In doing so, we trust the providence of God and accept the gifts of those who offer them to us. As recipients, we are to recognize the great gift we are given in hearing the word of God and respond with generosity in caring for those who bless us in that way. It's an act of trust on both sides and an exchange of the beautiful grace of our Lord.

Lord, as I follow your command to minister to others,
help me to trust in your providence and to practice
hospitality to others who serve you. Amen.

## Monday, January 11

# Wait for the Lord

### *Psalm 131:1-3*

**What is it like to rest in the peace of God?**

Although not every commentator agrees, many suggest that this psalm was written by a woman, because the writer was caring for children. At the very least, it is based on the image of a mother calming her child, written in the first person.

The psalm begins by rejecting arrogance and destructive pride. The "great or wonderful" things could mean overly ambitious activities or things beyond her ability (v. 1). But in other parts of Scripture, this phrase refers to God's great works. Therefore, it could mean that the psalmist did not attempt to figure out why things happened as they did, but accepted God's will and trusted in God's wisdom. Like a child who trusts her parents and their care, the psalmist did not question the wisdom, love, and protection of God.

On our journey through our lives, we will certainly have moments of stress, worry, and anxiety. But we are all God's dearly loved children, and just like a sleepy toddler can rest secure in his or her mother's arms, we can put our worries aside and rest in the arms of God. We can trust in God's wisdom and lay down the problems of the world, at least for a while. And when we confront them again, it can be in the knowledge that God knows all about our troubles, and like a loving parent, will hold us fast and that the peace of God can surround us no matter what we face.

Lord, teach me to turn the stresses and worries of the world over to you and rest in your peace. Amen.

## Tuesday, January 12

# Paul's Hope in God

### *Acts 24:14-16*

**How does our faith heritage reflect our hope in God?**

In today's passage, Paul was accused of being an agitator, running a disruptive religious sect and trying to defile the Temple. Paul admitted without hesitation that he was part of "the Way," an early name for Christianity. But along with his confession, he explained that he was not as different as they thought he was. Paul accepted "everything set out in the Law and written in the Prophets" (v. 14). His hope was the same as those accusing him, which was a hope in the one God of Israel. Paul celebrated the resurrection of Jesus Christ, but the same God promised resurrection for everyone.

Paul devoted his life to spreading the word of Jesus, but he never denied his Jewish roots. Christianity is based on the central affirmation of Judaism, which is a faith and trust in the one God who surrounds everyone in *hesed*—never-ending, all-encompassing love.

Our belief as Christians is that this love was best demonstrated by the life, death, and resurrection of God's Son on earth, Jesus Christ. It's the hope of the love and mercy of the Lord God, our Creator, and the life everlasting that we are promised.

Lord, help me to live a life rooted in your love and share the hope that is found only in your love. Amen.

## Wednesday, January 13

# The Blessed Hope

### *Titus 2:11-15*

**What is the "blessed hope" that Jesus promised?**

Titus referred to the tension for completion as "the blessed hope" (v. 13). It's the certain knowledge that completion will come, but it's just not here yet. We are living between when Jesus introduced the glimmers of the kingdom of heaven to those of us on earth and the time when he will return and heaven and earth will become one.

When Jesus came, he brought the grace of God to all people. It is our charge to follow the Spirit's guidance while we wait for the day when Jesus Christ returns. We're living in that tension-filled in-between state. We belong to Christ, yet the story is not complete. We need to live as faithful followers, building our lives in Christ as we eagerly await his glorious return. We are to be examples of godliness.

Today, we often don't think of Christ's return as a motivation for godliness. Instead, our motivation is usually going to heaven or about affecting the world for good. But it is important to remember that the same Jesus who came to earth as a humble infant will one day return in glory as "our great God and savior" (v. 13). This world, even in its incompleteness, is his. And we, even in our incompleteness, are his also. The glorious hope, which is the certain knowledge that we have been promised, is that Christ will return to claim that which is his. And when that day comes, the incomplete will become whole and complete.

O Lord, help me to live a sensible, ethical, and godly
life as I wait with longing for your return. Amen.

## Thursday, January 14

# Hope in Christ

### *1 Thessalonians 1:2-10*

**What helps Christians to persevere in their faith?**

By the time Paul wrote his first letter to them, the Thessalonians were already facing difficulties from outsiders. Paul never spelled out the nature of their persecution, but we know that this young church suffered (v. 6). Yet they grew so strong in their faith and practice that they were held up as an example to other churches. How was this small group of new Gentile believers able to stay so strong in the faith?

First and most importantly, they were loved by God, and they knew it. They had allowed the Holy Spirit to change them, and they lived wholeheartedly for Christ. Secondly, they had deeply committed teachers. These teachers prayed for them, lived with them, and continued to guide them through letters such as this one. Paul also wrote how their perseverance came "from hope in our Lord Jesus Christ" (v. 3). They were waiting for Christ's return and were secure in the grace he offered them.

Every day, Christians can draw on the power of the Holy Spirit and know that Jesus Christ is our Savior and Advocate. The promise of Christ's return and the ultimate healing of creation tells us that despite all that is happening today in the world that is evil or tragic, God will win. We can rest in the certain knowledge that history will end with the triumph of our Lord and Savior and our salvation as his people.

Lord, help me to persevere in my faith through
knowledge of your love, support from your
teachers, and a hope for the future. Amen.

## Friday, January 15

# Standing Your Ground in the Lord

### *1 Thessalonians 3:6-13*

**How does your faith help others?**

The Thessalonians were being persecuted for their belief and Paul was concerned that they would be tempted to leave the church. But that church's faith and perseverance changed Paul and the other leaders as well. The church became an example for others. Paul, Timothy, and the other leaders gained joy, hope, and comfort through the church's faithfulness. "For now we are alive if you are standing your ground in the Lord," Paul wrote (v. 8).

We often think about how a pastor or other faith worker inspires or encourages the church. But when people in the church respond to their teaching and truly live within the word of God, the blessings from that life of faith flow to their leaders as well.

Thus, while they waited for the final blessing of Jesus Christ's return, both the leaders and the church members had blessings they could give to one another. In the midst of this nurturing was the Spirit of God, working through both parties, strengthening and giving confidence so that all of them might grow in their faith, until the day of Christ's return. By drawing together on the power of the Holy Spirit, they could endure the persecutions and disappointments and grow in their faith until they would become fully transformed and whole in the Lord.

Lord, strengthen my faith so that my example may strengthen others. Amen.

## Saturday, January 16

# Living That Pleases God

### *1 Thessalonians 4:1-12*

**How can we take steps toward holiness every day?**

The most repeated word in this passage is *peripateo*, the Greek word for "walk." Most translations have used the word "live" or "behave" instead, but "walk" connotes a journey with a path to travel. Every day was a step forward toward holiness. Those who adopted the faith needed to learn how to walk in the Word with perseverance.

The Thessalonian church was already known for its love, but Paul challenged them to love even more. Their goal was to demonstrate the life-changing effect of the Holy Spirit to both other churches and other Gentiles. To do this, Paul first told them to live a quiet or restful life, meaning a life that didn't invite drama or crisis. That related to Paul's next challenge; to mind your own business. The third challenge was to work with one's hands. Perhaps because they believed that Christ would come soon, some of them stopped working. But if they were to be an example to others, they needed to walk the path of honor and be self-sufficient.

Of course, there are many other aspects to walking in the way that pleases God. But everything in this passage can be reduced to cultivating an enduring love for others. Paul taught the Thessalonian church to walk in the path of harmony with one another and devotion to God.

Lord, guide me in cultivating an enduring love for
others so that my walk may please you. Amen.

## Sunday, January 17

# Believers Who Have Died

### *1 Thessalonians 4:13-18*

**What promises can we rely on when a loved one dies?**

Paul instructed the Thessalonian church on how to live for God. But they also had a lot of questions about dying. Some Bible scholars think that they had believed Christ's second coming would happen before any of them would die, so when some of them did, they were deeply distressed. What would happen when Christ returned and loved ones had already died? Would they miss that glorious day? Would they see each other again?

Paul assured them that they would. Christ's return would not only be a joyful reunion with Jesus, but a reunion with all believers who had died. The trumpet of the Lord would cause the dead to rise, and then those who were alive would join them. Everyone, both the living and the dead, would join in celebration with the Lord.

Because Jesus demonstrated that death no longer has power over believers, death no longer separates them forever. It is merely a pause in eternal life for all believers together with God. And for those of us still alive, these words remind us that for believers, death ultimately won't affect us, either. Something glorious waits beyond. The wonderful banquet of the Lord waits for all those who believe in the salvation of Jesus Christ.

Lord, thank you for the promise of eternal life with
you and all believers. Come, Lord Jesus! Amen.

## Monday, January 18

# The Lord Lets Me Live in Safety

*Psalm 4:1-8*

**What allows you to sleep peacefully each night?**

Where is your safe place? For this psalmist, the safe place was with God; the most reliable safe place of them all. Things were not going well for the writer of this psalm. But the psalmist had called on God before, and God had set him free from his troubles. And so in trust and faith, the psalmist called on God's help again.

Some commentators think that the people being addressed in verse 1 were looking for material gains. They would be willing to worship God if God gave them something of worth for it. But what is worth more than riches and abundance? The psalmist had joy, peace, and comfort (vv. 7-8). He could sleep at night without anxiety, knowing that God was with him, and that was worth more than any riches. Living a life of righteousness created his safe place with God and gave him a peaceful heart.

Trust in God is the key to a life of true treasure, a life of safety, security, and well-being. Physical possessions and worldly influence alone will not allow anyone to sleep in peace, but you can rest with joy knowing that you are safe in the arms of the Lord.

Lord, teach me to trust in your care and rest
peacefully in your embrace. Amen.

## Tuesday, January 19

# Hope During Persecution

### *1 Peter 3:18-22*

**How did the early churches persevere in persecution?**

The believers that Peter wrote to in this passage were suffering persecution, but Peter told them not to worry. Peter pointed to the example of Christ, who suffered persecution for everyone in order to bring the world closer to God, only to be vindicated and raised from the dead (v. 18).

Peter gave hope to the small churches of Asia Minor by mentioning how few people were saved by Noah's ark (v. 20). Their faith, not their numbers, would keep them safe. Noah's flood, he wrote, was a precursor of baptism; as those who boarded the ark trusted themselves to God, so in baptism we entrust our salvation to Jesus Christ.

For these tiny churches, Peter's words of hope helped them withstand their persecution. Yes, they were suffering, but Christ suffered too, and he achieved victory over and through death. Yes, there were only a few of them against the world, but God saved the few who were obedient to God during the floods of Noah's time. And since they had committed themselves to God through baptism, they had the power of Christ behind them—Jesus Christ who rules over angels, authorities, and all other powers. They had nothing to fear!

O Lord, strengthen my confidence in your power to protect and provide for your churches. Amen.

## Wednesday, January 20

# Humble Yourselves Before God

## *1 Peter 5:5b-11*

**What does it mean to be humble?**

Peter wrote of acting with humility with other church members, but even more importantly, one should be humble before God. Humility before God is actually the route to peace. When one wrestles with anxious thoughts, knowing that God holds all the answers is a great relief. One can rest in God because God has the power, and God cares.

Yet that does not mean, Peter wrote, that the churches could become complacent. They were being persecuted, and evil was lurking like a lion. Many believers were suffering, and so they needed to stand firm to be an inspiration to one another.

Everyone who claims salvation in Jesus Christ can look forward to eternity in glory with God. For all those who have suffered, God will restore, empower, strengthen, and establish them (v. 10). Restoration means being made whole and healed. Empower and strengthen means that believers will be supported and built up in faith. Establish means that they will have a firm foundation in Christ. All these things are the hope that enables perseverance in faith.

And because believers stand together looking toward God in hope, none is standing in his or her own power, but in the power of God. Humility before God is recognizing that it is God's grace, mercy, and love that guides us, protects us, and strengthens us.

Lord, may I always treat others with respect as your valued children and stand humbled before you. Amen.

### Thursday, January 21

## Not Ashamed of the Gospel

*2 Timothy 1:8-14*

**How do you respond to those with bad reputations?**

Christians worship one who was shamefully and publicly executed as a criminal, and whose story was spread by a man—Paul—who spent time in jail. To align oneself with a convicted, executed criminal and obey the teaching of a jailbird went against every societal norm. How could anyone adopt Christian beliefs when it all came from such discredited roots? It was all quite embarrassing.

Paul's answer, written from prison, was that the roots of our faith come from God. From the beginning, God called people to a holy life. Jesus Christ was the fullest revelation of this call, which was shown by the way he lived, and by demonstrating God's power and love in destroying death itself. Christ's shameful death was used by God to turn the world upside down and demonstrate the power of holiness.

This is why Paul wrote that he was not ashamed of the gospel (v. 12). Jesus' teachings, life, death, and resurrection were a direct challenge to society's shame-and-honor system. Jesus preached that the last would become first, and that the hungry, the poor, and the meek would be blessed. Christians can afford to be scorned, reviled, and even persecuted on earth because they have eternity to look forward to, when their pain will become glory.

Lord, thank you for the honor of being a
disciple of Jesus Christ, an executed criminal
who lives now in eternal glory. Amen.

## Friday, January 22

# Our Suffering and Our Hope

### *Romans 8:18-25*

**How will the world change when Christ returns?**

This beautiful world, which God pronounced as "good" at the moment of Creation (Genesis 1:31), is suffering mightily under the weight of sin and human destruction. But it won't always be like this. Believers long for Christ's return because their suffering will end and they will be with Christ in glory. But the same thing is true for all of creation. The end of the world as we know it does not mean the end of the world altogether. Just as all believers will be made whole and healed, so will creation

This new world is a promise that began in the life, death, and resurrection of Jesus Christ. Paul compared our present time to labor pains (v. 22). And as creation waits for her transformation, so do believers. Our current forms are but a pale shadow of what we will become.

So what does that mean for us living in the time in-between? We know that it's not just about our individual salvation, but the salvation of creation. As Christians, we are called to live with a heart and mind to this future. That means that we are to be the heralds of this healing, bringing glimmers to the world that we live in today of the Kingdom yet to be. We are to show the hope of a transformed world to the rest of humanity. We must strive to give creation a foretaste of God's justice and healing by being harbingers of justice and healing in this broken world today.

Come Lord Jesus! As we wait in breathless anticipation, may we be harbingers of your hope. Amen.

## Saturday, January 23

# The Spirit Helps Our Weakness

### *Romans 8:26-30*

**How can we be part of the glory to come?**

I find I sometimes just sit quietly with an emotion, sharing it with God, not even attempting to put it into words. But I don't have to worry. The Holy Spirit is my translator, so God knows my heart.

The Common English Bible translates verse 28 as "We know that God works all things together for good for the ones who love God, for those who are called according to his purpose." Things don't just happen for the good of God's people. Instead, Paul's meaning was that God crafts the long-range outcome of events to bring the world to completion, to the ultimate glory of God. From the beginning of time, God foretold the existence of a people who would love God, and God knew that their story would end in glory (vv. 29-30). Paul was writing this for suffering church members, not describing how they had become Christians in the first place. This passage does not say that God made an arbitrary choice as to who would be saved and who would not. God knew that there would be the elect (v. 29), but God did not will who would be among them. Paul's words were to assure believers that God would not allow anything to separate them from God's love and ultimate plan.

God knows the end of the story of creation, and we can be confident that we are part of it; those of us who love God now can rest in the promise of the glory to come.

Lord, as I sorrow for the world today, comfort me
with the knowledge of the world to come. Amen.

## Sunday, January 24

# God Is for Us

*Romans 8:31-37*

**How does knowing the end of the story change things?**

God is totally committed to human salvation, so much so that God sacrificed God's own Son. Paul was writing to Christians who were suffering persecution, so he was not promising them an easy life, or even an easy death. Paul was reminding them that anything that could possibly happen is temporary, a dramatic turn in a story that has a joyful and triumphant ending. Paul stood trial, as would many other Christians. But who could possibly condemn them? The only one who has that power is Jesus Christ, and he died for all believers and stands before God in humanity's defense. Because we can trust the love of Christ, we are safe from condemnation.

Paul's great truth in this passage is that there is nothing in all of creation more powerful or greater than the love of God. Each person who accepts that love and lives by it has a promise of the coming kingdom of God, a new world order, that nothing on earth has the power to thwart.

And because of that, there is nothing that truly needs to be feared, because we know the end of the story. Anything else that happens between now and then will be healed and made whole when the kingdom of God comes to earth and there are no more tears or pain, and those who are the children of the Lord will be more than conquerors in Christ.

Lord God, may I never forget the end of the story
and your great love when I face difficulties. Amen.

## Monday, January 25

# Coworkers with the Truth

### *3 John 1-13*

**How do you practice hospitality in faith?**

John wrote to his dear friend Gaius, pleased that Gaius and his church had been hospitable to traveling Christian evangelists, even though they were strangers to them. It was common in the first century for churches to offer hospitality to traveling evangelists, but Diotrephes was creating problems and refusing hospitality to the travelers.

Diotrephes wanted to be in control and didn't want to listen to other church leaders. His divisiveness was making it difficult for the evangelists to fulfill their calling because they depended on the generosity of the churches they visited when they travelled. John states the reason for his letter by recommending Demetrius to Gaius. Demetrius was probably one of the evangelists who needed hospitality from churches. John wanted to be sure he would be welcomed, despite Diotrephes' meddling.

Think of what Gaius' church would have lost if they had turned Demetrius away. They would have forgone the opportunity to welcome another in Christian love. They would have lost teaching and insight. They would have been un-Christlike while professing to be a Christian church. Perhaps because he was afraid of being taken advantage of, Diotrephes not only turned from Christlike behavior but condemned others who did so. In guarding what he had, he lost so much more.

Lord, may I open my hands and heart to
those who do your work. Amen.

### Tuesday, January 26

## Worshippers Gathered from the Nations

### *Isaiah 66:18-24*

**Who will be saved when God's kingdom comes to earth?**

The Book of Isaiah is very concerned with foreigners and those who don't know God. In this last chapter of Isaiah, God tells the people of the intention to send ambassadors to all nations to tell of the divine glory. God will send a covenant sign. The sign will enable people to respond with praise and offerings and find their place in the family of the Lord. No one will be prevented from righteousness or devotion to God. The knowledge and blessings of the Lord will be available to every human being on earth.

But what of the last verse of the passage? It says that those who reject God will experience the agony of death over and over again. It is such a horrifying verse that Hebrew tradition demands that verse 23 be repeated after verse 24 in an oral reading so that the great Book of Isaiah does not end with such a distressing image. After this wonderful song of inclusion for all, it's shocking to read of the agony of those who would ultimately turn from God.

But if God is the source of life, then turning away from God means nothing but death. God offers salvation, wholeness, and life to all who would come to the Lord. Refusing that call is a self-condemnation into darkness. There can be no other answer than to choose the light and the life that the Lord offers us.

O Lord, thank you for your gracious offer of
salvation for all who will hear you! Amen.

## Wednesday, January 27

# Waiting at Home

### *2 Peter 3:7-13*

**How can we trust that Jesus will return after 2,000 years?**

At the time that 2 Peter was written, early Christians had doubts about Christ's promised return. It was taking way too long—so long that the promise must not be true. False teachers were telling Peter's churches that it had all been a lie. But these "teachers" were seeing events through human eyes, not realizing that they were dealing with the ways of heaven. God's delay in sending Jesus back to earth is actually an act of mercy, Peter explained. By waiting, people have more time to come to repentance and accept the salvation of Jesus Christ. But have no doubt, Peter wrote, Christ will come, and when he comes, it will be sudden and unexpected

And so Christians cannot be complacent, even though it's been over 2,000 years since Jesus was born. God is eternal, merciful, and desiring our salvation above anything else. To those who know God, the promise is absolute.

This passage teaches us three things. The first is that God is patient and God's promises are real. What has been assured to us will happen. Second, that God's will is that all will find salvation, so much so that the world waits in anticipation for sinners to find Jesus Christ. And third, that no one knows or will be able to predict when the final day will come. It is the ultimate risk to wait another day for a sinner to find salvation.

Lord Jesus, may my heart and soul be
ready for your return! Amen.

## Thursday, January 28

# The Final Judgment

### *Revelation 20:11-15*

**How can we interpret the difficult Book of Revelation?**

Apocalyptic literature is not meant to be a literal accounting of end times, but rather a deeply symbolic and coded message for believers. Despite the difficult reading, the core of the message is simple—God wins! Those who align themselves with God will triumph. Those who oppress, who are hypocrites or turn from God's ways will suffer in the end. It's a song of hope for all believers.

This passage tells of the last judgment of humanity. God is described as seated on a great white throne, white being the symbol of victory. All who have died are resurrected and summoned before God's great throne to be judged. In the end, it's not what you say you believe, it's how what you believe has impacted your life. Those who claim Christ with words only will be in for a rude surprise. God sees through hypocrisy into each person's heart. Those who live as God intended will be in the Lamb's Book of Life (Revelation 21:27 KJV).

There are ample questions about the exact meanings in Revelation. We don't know the answers to these things. It's easy to get caught up in trying to analyze symbolism or cultural references, but the most important thing to remember is that this is a story of hope and victory. The faithful can look forward to a glorious future.

Lord, thank you for the assurance of your final victory, and may I be worthy to be a part of your celebration. Amen.

## Friday, January 29

# A New Heaven and a New Earth

### *Revelation 21:1-5*

**What will it be like to live in God's new creation?**

The old heaven and earth are swept away. God's new vision for the future descends from heaven, the community of humanity is made new. God will live among the people of the world. What an amazing scene!

It's important that God descends to earth in a city. While each of us individually have and will continue to have a relationship with God, this is also a healing of humanity. The world will be God's society. There will no longer be oppression, selfishness, or greed. People will deal with one another with love and compassion, and everyone who lives in the holy city will be a valued part of God's community. God will not seem distant or unapproachable but will be right in the center of the people, knowing them and seeing them face-to-face. God will truly be with us.

The Book of Revelation is about the end of the world, but it is also about the beginning of a new world. This passage is a celebration of this new world to come, but it is also a reminder of how much the world has to heal to become this new kingdom of God. Jesus showed us a vision of how the world is to be. As Christians today on earth, it is our duty as children of this new kingdom to show glimmers of the world to come to those living in the world today.

Thank you, Lord, for the promise of your
future kingdom on earth. Amen.

## Saturday, January 30

# The Victorious and the Faithless

*Revelation 21:6-8*

**What do God's people look forward to in the Holy City?**

God began the history of the world with creation and now will bring that phase of creation to an end. Water, which was always valued and scarce in Israel's desert climate, will be available to all, without cost. The ancient promise made to King David of inheritance in the family of the Lord is offered to everyone resting there with God. The trial is over.

Tragically, there will be some who will not make it to that resting place. It is a solemn warning for us to take God's word seriously and to live each day doing justice, loving mercy, and walking humbly with our God (Micah 6:8).

Because there will no longer be a division between heaven and earth, those things and behaviors that cannot stand before a holy God must be banished. This is not the work of a vindictive God, but of a God who will re-create the universe for the greatest joy of the faithful ones. If we claim Jesus Christ as our Savior, then we also claim citizenship in the New Jerusalem, even as it waits to come to earth. As people of the kingdom of God, our call is to be the light of this new age, even as the creation continues to struggle with the effects of sin and death.

But we know that there will come a day when we can put down our burdens, when God will whisper, "It is finished," and we can rest forever with our Lord.

Lord, help me persevere until the day that you tell me that it is finished and I can rest in you. Amen.

## Sunday, January 31

# Jesus Is Coming Soon

### *Revelation 22:12-15*

**What relevance does the Book of Revelation have today?**

In this passage, Jesus tells the people that he will reward all according to their deeds. But how do we prepare ourselves? Revelation 7:14 gives us the entry requirements: "favored are those who wash their robes," in the blood of the Lamb of God. Washing our robes in the blood of the lamb is the only way that we will really be ready or even able to stand before God. It's all because of the sacrifice of Jesus Christ.

This is the central message of the Book of Revelation. It's tempting to analyze it and apply its symbols to present-day events, using it to predict the future. But the reason and significance for the prophecy is to broadcast the good news that God will create a new heaven and a new earth. Because of the death and resurrection of Jesus Christ, those who accept his offered salvation and strive to live by his word can enter into this new creation. The task for us now is not so much to try to decipher the strange symbolism but to accept the grace of Christ and to devote ourselves to living as his disciples.

Revelation tells us what we as Christians are up against, but it also gives us a vision of hope and wholeness for all of creation. It tells us how crucial it is for us to hold firm to our faith and to practice it in our daily lives. And finally, it tells us how each one of us are part of God's great plan for the future, when we will rest in God's glory with all the saints for eternity.

Lord, may I be a worthy resident of your
holy city. Come Lord Jesus! Amen.

# FEBRUARY

## Contributor:

*Michael Whitcomb-Tavey*
*February 1–28*

## Monday, February 1

# Give Justice to the Lowly

### *Psalm 82*

**What is biblical justice?**

To many people, justice connotes judgment against those who have committed a crime or some wicked deed. However, another definition of justice is just behavior or treatment toward others. According to the Old Testament, justice is the state or quality of being fair to all people.

Justice is the subject of this entire psalm, which was written in a time when the people of Israel were tempted to worship other gods, as neighboring peoples did. Israel's God did not want this for the chosen people, as was forbidden in the Ten Commandments (Exodus 20:3-5). Psalm 82 depicts the Lord standing in a divine council, passing judgment on other gods for acting unjustly and failing to "maintain the right of the poor and the destitute" and "rescue the lowly" (vv. 3-4).

We should not assume that Psalm 82 declares that other gods actually exist. Rather, the psalm starts where the people are: In their minds, the other gods are real and contend for their worship. So, the psalmist starts there and doesn't argue the existence of these rivals. Instead, the psalmist depicts the Lord as adjourning the divine council and decreeing the death of the other gods.

The message for us is in the subtext of this psalm. Just as the false gods are judged for acting unjustly toward those in need and "granting favor to the wicked" (v. 2), so we, too, will not be looked on kindly for similar behavior.

Dear Lord, thank you. You are perfectly just. Open my eyes to see. Give me hands to help. Amen.

## TUESDAY, FEBRUARY 2

# God's Justice for All

### *Deuteronomy 16:18-20*

**What does it mean to pursue righteousness?**

Many passages in the Old Testament describe aspects of Israel's legal system, and today's text is one such reading. In it, the Israelites were commanded to appoint judges and officials throughout their lands. The judges and officials were to be held to high standards, so that people who came before them were judged fairly (v. 18b). Specially, the judges and the officials were to adhere to four specific divine instructions:

First, they were to not delay justice (v. 19a). If legal redress is available for a party that has suffered some injury, but is not forthcoming in a timely fashion, it is, in effect, like having no redress at all. From this reading in Deuteronomy, it's clear that God values speedy judgment in legal dealings.

Second, these judges were to render just decisions for all people with favoritism toward none, regardless of social standing or lack thereof (v. 19b). Third, the judges were commanded to refuse bribes and reject all forms of corruption, specifically, "because bribery blinds the vision of the wise and twists the words of the righteous" (v. 19c). And finally, they were to "pursue righteousness" which, in this context, means standing in for God and rendering justice as God would (v. 20).

Throughout the Bible, we are commanded to emulate these behaviors. To treat all people with equality, fairness, and moral goodness will probably not come naturally to all of us, but it is the divine standard toward which we should strive.

Dear Lord, may I treat all people with equality,
fairness, and goodness. Amen.

## Wednesday, February 3

# Happy People

### *Luke 6:20-26*

**What are some indicators that God has favored you?**

The word Jesus used in this passage for "Happy" is, in New Testament Greek, *makarios*, which is translated in many Bible versions as "blessed." The word denotes a happiness that transcends life despite care, labor, or problems. In the Greek culture of the time, it described the happy state of the gods who were above earthly, as well as the wealthy, whose possessions gave them a good position in life, and those who were free from tribulations, who were honored and famous.

You may sometimes hear a nonbiblical theology claim that wealth and health are indicators of being blessed by God. The problem with such a perspective is that it implies that those without it are cursed or forgotten by God. In this passage, Jesus inverts that concept. According to Jesus, the blessed and happy are those who are poor, hungry, weeping, hated, excluded, reviled, and defamed. In a crude way of paraphrasing it, "Blessed are those considered losers by earthly standards." Jesus creates an implicit contrast to those regarded by the world as blessed.

We can find comfort in this passage. It reminds us that there are gifts of God that problems, pains, betrayals, and brokenness cannot steal. Some might interpret these statements of Jesus as blessings delayed until the kingdom of God comes (Revelation 21:1-8). But note that Jesus stated them in present tense. The kingdom of God is yours, Jesus said, *already*.

Help me, O Lord, to perceive your blessings,
even when surrounded by loss. Amen.

## THURSDAY, FEBRUARY 4

# False Teachers

*Jude 11-19*

**Are we better to rail against religious leaders who have it wrong or listen to those who help us grow in spirit?**

The occasion for this letter from Jude, which was written to an unspecified Christian community, is stated in verse 4: "Godless people have slipped in among you." While Jude called these people "godless," they probably would not have thought of themselves that way. Rather, they were probably people who drew conclusions about what it meant to follow Jesus that were different from what the apostles had taught.

Jude's understanding of Christianity was in line with the apostolic teachings, however, and so he wrote this letter to warn his readers away from the version of the faith being advocated by these teachers. Judging from Jude's comments in verse 4 about these interlopers turning "the grace of our God into unrestrained immorality" and his reference in verse 7 to Sodom and Gomorrah, it's likely that these traveling teachers were saying that Christian freedom meant that Jesus' followers were relieved of responsibility to behave morally and ethically. Jude warned about the dangerous teachings of these people. In verses 17-19, he reminded the letter recipients that the apostles themselves had warned of "scoffers" who would come and create "divisions."

Jude then encouraged his readers to "build each other up on the foundation of [their] most holy faith" (v. 20) and wait for the Lord's mercy, which "will give you eternal life" (v. 21).

Help me, O Lord, to build others up in faith. Amen.

## Friday, February 5

# Instructions for Elders

### *1 Timothy 5:17-25*

**What qualities and attributes exist in an upright leader?**

Paul addresses how church elders should behave and lead within the congregation they serve. The implication is that a church leader not only leads and protects the congregation, but also represents God and God's message to the congregation. This is a weighty responsibility.

Paul expects church leaders to be of good character and instructs them in their duties. One instruction is to discipline anyone who is actively engaging in a sinful lifestyle and to do it publicly as a warning to others (v. 20). This would be part of the protection duty. Just as justice should be dispensed without favoritism, as we saw in earlier readings this week, so discipline should be given "without playing favorites" (v. 21).

Paul also instructs Timothy not to appoint a leader too hastily (v. 22). By the proximity, Paul may be implying that before being appointed, candidates must first show that they can function without bias and favoritism (a subject of verse 21). Lastly, Paul commands Timothy and the elders to remain pure, and not to participate in the sins others may do.

Some might argue that these commands apply only to elders. However, Jesus calls all his followers to reflect the character of God in all areas of our life. All Christians, especially those within church leadership roles, are called toward equal treatment of all, insofar as we can see our biases.

Dear God, help me to reflect your character in my life and to learn from both my successes and my failures. Amen.

## Saturday, February 6

# Do Not Show Favoritism

### *James 2:1-7*

**What do your biases reveal about your faith?**

James begins with a bold accusation against those practicing favoritism. After making this declaration, James explains that favoritism is rooted in evil attitudes, perceptions, and thought patterns (v. 4). Moreover, such actions are antithetical to the character and actions of God. If God shows any favoritism at all, is for the weak and the poor (v. 5).

James is essentially making the point that our actions reveal our level of commitment to the Lord. In more specific terms, the ways in which we treat each other tell about our faith in Christ. Some people reject this perspective because they think of faith as an intellectual exercise, practiced in the realm of mental assent. However, "faith" denotes commitment, active trust, and a willingness to follow the commands of the individual to whom you pledge loyalty. Thus, Christians who have "faith" are those who pledge loyalty to Christ and willfully, to the best of their ability, live in obedience to him. Those who put their faith in Christ try to be like him in character, compassion, and fair treatment of others.

This understanding calls into question one's faith in Christ. And it is a good question to ask. Are you really putting faith in Christ if you show favoritism to certain groups of people? If you are called to emulate the character of Christ, how should you treat other people? If God shows no partiality toward people, should you? Good questions to ask indeed.

Dear Lord, may I treat all people in fairness and equality. Help me to emulate your character. Amen.

## Sunday, February 7

# Judged by the Law of Love

### *James 2:8-13*

**How specifically do you "Love your neighbor as yourself"?**

In today's passage, James also focuses on keeping "the royal law": "Love your neighbor as yourself." This is a law for God's people in that it is a primary way in which one practices holiness, and it is the basis for life in the kingdom of God. It is an expansive law, giving room and reason to embrace others.

In verse 9, James says that to practice favoritism is to commit a sin, a sin exposed by the very law of God's kingdom—"Love your neighbor as yourself"—that one is ignoring. James next talks about the Mosaic law that stands behind the royal law. He argues that keeping only part of God's law is like disobeying all of it. That's because one does not sin against a commandment, but against the God who gave it. James says in verse 11, that the God who said, "Don't commit adultery" also said, "Don't commit murder." Thus, although one may not murder, if one commits adultery, one is still a transgressor against God. And James is implying the same about failing to love one's poor neighbor by being partial to one's better-off neighbor. In that case, one is still a transgressor against God.

James defines how one shows mercy to one's brothers and sisters—by loving others as oneself. He makes it plain that one also shows mercy through the equal and fair treatment of all people: rich and poor, weak and strong. Favoritism, then, is the antithesis to mercy, as well as against the law of God.

Dear Lord, assist me to love my neighbors as I love myself and thereby fulfill the royal law. Amen.

## Monday, February 8

# The Characteristics of a True Prophet

### *Matthew 7:15-23*

**How do you distinguish a true prophet from a false one?**

Jesus contrasts two trees, distinguishing them by the fruits they produce. A person who is a "good tree" produces "good fruit"—integrity, honesty, compassion, and the like. The rotten tree produces "bad" fruit. This bad fruit is morally reprehensible in the sight of God and dangerous to humans.

As metaphors, these trees are stand-ins for true and false prophets. The latter are not those who misunderstand some aspect of holy living or who misinterpret God's message due to immaturity of thought. Rather they are those who deliberately disguise themselves so that they appear to be something other than what they are. The key to distinguishing between true and false prophets comes not by looking at what they appear to be, but at what they actually teach, advocate, and do.

People can speak the language of commitment to Jesus—"Lord, Lord" (v. 21) and still be far from the kingdom of God. People can even perform dazzling miracles in the name of God but still be wolves in disguise (v. 22). One has to actually do the will of God to be people of God's kingdom.

God is concerned with how we treat each other—something Jesus stated just a few verses before today's passage: "Therefore, you should treat people in the same way that you want people to treat you; this is the Law and the Prophets" (Matthew 7:12). In short, a true prophet is one who loves others, and a false prophet is one who primarily loves oneself.

Dear God, help me to treat others the way
I want them to treat me. Amen.

## Tuesday, February 9

# Abraham Obeys God

### *Genesis 22:1-18*

**What do you know about God now that you didn't know five years ago?**

In ancient cultures surrounding Abraham, sacrificing children to a deity was a religious practice. To people who experienced loss due to natural occurrences like storms or drought, appeasing the god thought to be in control of nature seemed to be the only way to prevent further troubles, and one's child was the most precious gift a person could give.

Following God's instructions, Abraham led Isaac to Mt. Moriah and prepared to slay his son. It was only the interference of God that stopped Abraham. Here's what Abraham learned about the God he served: this God provided the needed sacrifices (v. 13), whereas the other deities demanded gifts; this God did not want children sacrificed.

This story is part of the progressive revelation of God's character and actions, whereby God reveals God's self continually to the people of God and is wholly different than expected. The story teaches that through obedience, Abraham came to know God in a new and more profound way.

Such truth stands applicable to us as well. God calls us toward obedience and trust. And through obedience and trust, we come to know God in new and profound ways. We learn more about what God expects of us and more about what God abhors. The challenge, of course, is how we conform our lives to what we learn about God.

Dear Lord, reveal to me what you want me to know, and help me to serve you. Amen.

## Ash Wednesday, February 10

# People of Faith

### *Hebrews 11:17-31*

**In what way is faith in Christ forward looking?**

The reading for today is a list of people who "by faith" acted in ways that revealed their trust in God; the whole chapter is a roll call of the faithful. This chapter conveys that faith is what we have now, instead of what we believe will come eventually. But faith is reality in that it populates our imagination with the promises of God and inspires us to hold on to those promises through even the worst things that happen to us before the fulfillment of our faith. In other words, faith is forward-looking.

The writer lists Abraham, Isaac, Jacob, and Jospeh as men of faith who trusted God with future realities they would not live to see. Notice, too, how the writer describes Moses in verses 24-29. Called by God, Moses made choices, refusing to rely on his Egyptian citizenship to instead "be mistreated with God's people," trusting that "the abuses he suffered for Christ were more valuable than the treasures of Egypt" (vv. 25-26.) In those verses, "trusting" equals "forward-looking." The Hebrews writer understood redemptive history as a single narrative oriented toward a future completed in Jesus Christ, and thus presented the forward-looking Moses as participating in the reproach Christ would experience.

Each of the people named in Hebrews 11 died before the full actualization of their faith. But their faith was the reality that gave meaning to them and that is ultimately fulfilled in the life to come.

Lord, may the conditions of my life not dictate my faithfulness toward you. Keep me looking forward. Amen.

## Thursday, February 11

# Faith Working Through Love

### *Galatians 5:1-6*

**What prerequisites, if any, must precede our salvation?**

When some Jewish-Christian missionaries arrived in Galatia, they insisted that Paul had it wrong. Paul had *not* told the Galatians that to become followers of Jesus, they first needed to be circumcised and put themselves under the Mosaic law. But these later-come missionaries insisted that they must. This was the occasion for Paul's letter to the Galatians, to insist that what God had done in Christ was sufficient for their salvation. There was no need to first adopt a Jewish way of life and the Mosaic law.

Paul was saying that the demands of the law were like slavery to those who have been offered freedom from sin through Christ. Though Paul warns the Galatians against circumcision, he's not so much talking about the actual medical procedure as what the act represents in Judaism: a declaration that one is under the law of Moses. Paul's claim is that when one anchors the condition of their salvation to the ways of Old Testament legalism, they will eventually fall from grace and become subject to the yoke of slavery.

Paul writes that neither circumcision nor uncircumcision have any real power to bring about salvation (v. 6a). What does have power to save, however, is "faith working through love" (v. 6b). In order to be saved, one's faith must be rooted and anchored in Christ Jesus. True faith is evidenced through faithful action.

Lord, thank you for my salvation in Christ. May my actions evidence my redemption. Amen.

## Friday, February 12

# Love in Action

## *1 John 3:13-18*

**How are our perceptions and beliefs shaped?**

Our passage opens with John boldly asserting that Christians have assurance of salvation "transferred from death to life" which is shown "because we love" (v. 14). That is to say, the actions of love testify to one's justification and sanctification. Ideally, this type of mutual love for all should exist throughout society as a whole, but John is calling for it *within* the faith community. He likely recognizes that such love cannot exist more broadly in the world because the necessary mutuality cannot exist there. The worldly reality is incompatible with the reality of the kingdom of God. This is why John states that Christians who hate their brother or sister do not evidence eternal life—the reality of salvation—in their lives.

John pleads for us to love in both truth and action. Doing this, implies we treat others according to the standards set by Christ, not by the world. This ought to challenge all of us. Hidden racism, sexual objectification of others, ageism, xenophobia, and much more all exist because people treat each other within the world's standards.

This day, we should not let the ways of the world define how we view and treat others. We must reject division and egotism. This day, choose to treat your Christian siblings, as well as everyone else, according to the standards set by Christ. In the church, of all places, mutual care ought to be in effect, helping the person in need.

Lord, prompt me to treat people based on
the standards you have set. Amen.

## Saturday, February 13

# Faithful Activity

### *James 2:14-20*

**How are faith and faithful activities related?**

By its very nature, faith *is* works. In more pithy terms, works are the activity of faith and faith is the energizer of works. James makes that point clear in today's passage. In fact, James is emphatic, claiming that "works" are necessary for faith to have "life." Without the "works," faith is *dead*! That is, such faith is akin to a corpse: it does nothing, produces nothing, and is good only for burial or cremation.

Works, in this context, as well as many other Scripture passages, include deeds of charity. These works are the expression of one's faith and commitment to Christ. Rather than being one's pursuit of salvation and self-righteousness, works are the evidence of faith. If works are included in the character of faith, then those who have faith in Christ will naturally act in a redemptive manner within the world.

Some Christians find this perspective troubling. They believe this might lead to "works-righteousness," where people seek salvation through their works. That is, they must strive, via their own merit, for salvation. Such a claim is untrue. "Works" are the natural evidence of salvation, not its prerequisite. Thus, a changed life, manifested with Christian charity, evidences true faith. We are not perfect. But our works not only are evidence of our faith, but they can help assure us of it too.

Does your faith seem dead? Remember that our Lord is the God of resurrection!

Dear Lord, through my life, may others see my
faith and how you have redeemed me. Amen.

## Sunday, February 14

# Righteous Through Faithful Actions

### *James 2:21-26*

**How is justification different than redemption?**

In today's reading, James argues that faithful actions validate faith. Some people see this passage as standing in tension with other Scripture verses that declare one is justified through faith alone, such as Galatians 2:16a: ". . . we know that a person isn't made righteous by the works of the Law but rather through the faithfulness of Jesus Christ." Is one justified by faith alone, or are "works" needed as well?

In many Christian circles, justification implies redemption and salvation. However, "justify" means that one is made to be right. This perspective is an ongoing theme throughout James. Through works, righteousness is evidenced. Righteousness is a gift of God and righteous is a descriptor of action that is obedient to God's will. The core elements of faith are belief and obedience. One assents to God's declarations and then obeys God's direction associated with those declarations.

Such an understanding redefines how we comprehend "morality." Good and excellent morality is not "doing good things." Rather, true and proper morality is a facet of one's belief and obedience (i.e., faith) but is manifested in faithful actions.

Lord, let my actions be consistent
with my faith in you. Amen.

## Monday, February 15

# Correcting Rebellious People

### *Titus 1:10-16*

**When does church correction of others go too far?**

Though today's passage begins at Titus 1:10, the whole epistle is a letter from Paul to his "true child" Titus (v. 4). Paul left him behind in Crete (v. 5a) to oversee development of congregations there. One of Titus' duties was to appoint elders to lead the churches on the island (v. 5b). Verse 9 mentions two specific duties elders should attend to: they were to reliably teach the gospel message with "healthy instruction," and they were to "refute those who speak against" that message and instruction.

Our reading for today is an elaboration on that second duty, for apparently there were "rebellious people" (v. 10). Paul wanted Titus to instruct the elders to silence those who insisted on that Jewish-first path to Christ, so they wouldn't "upset entire households" of the congregation (v. 11). We don't know the whole story in the churches of Crete or what prompted Paul to write what he did here. He seems especially frustrated in his words. Unfortunately, Paul's words, here and in other places, have been taken out of context and used to justify hatred, bigotry, and greed.

It is easy to give in to our frustrations and to say things that can be used to cause harm. Scripture itself has often been taken out of context and used for evil in this world. This is why it is important for us to be open to correction ourselves and also to test our understanding of parts of Scripture against other parts of Scripture, so that we have a full and broad understanding of God's grace in and through Jesus Christ.

Lord, let my speech reflect your values. Amen.

## Tuesday, February 16

# Destruction on the Horizon

### *Jeremiah 14:1-14*

**What religious practices do you conduct, and why?**

Today's passage begins by describing the suffering of the people of Judah during a long-lasting drought. The people cry out to God for deliverance from the drought, but God does not listen to them (vv. 8-9). Verses 11-12 indicate that no amount of religious piety will save them; God refuses even their burnt offerings. God cares more about justice and right and faithful living than religious works and pietistic practices. This does not mean that religious works and pietism are useless. Rather, that devoid of right living and right faith, such acts of religion are "dead."

We, too, have religious practices. We go to church. We pray. We read Scripture. We receive the Lord's Supper. We tithe. Yet, devoid of right living and faith, our actions are dead. To please God, we need to live righteously and love our neighbors as ourselves.

The Jeremiah passage includes God's warning about false prophets who offer "worthless predictions, and deceit they have made up on their own" (v. 14). What makes them worthless is that rather than call their hearers to love God and love neighbors, they essentially say, "Everything will be all right. You don't have to make any changes in how you treat others."

Don't believe it.

Dear Lord, may I seek justice, love kindness,
and walk humbly with you. Amen.

## Wednesday, February 17

# Change Your Heart

### *Joel 2:12-17*

**How does forgiveness relate to repentance?**

Joel is not condemning pious actions—in fact, he's calling for active fasting (vv. 12, 15), but he is saying that there must be a vital connection between the inward attitude and outward action, as well as seeking a renewed relationship with the Lord. The call to repent has five aspects: First, it involves returning to God with "all your hearts" (v. 12). That is, it must be sincere, not just going through the motions.

Second, the call to repent involves fasting. Fasting is the act of denying oneself something precious, usually food. It is an act that declares that one's relationship with God is the most important thing in life. Third and fourth, this call involves weeping and mourning, which signify remorse and regret.

Finally, the call to repentance involves "tear[ing] your hearts and not your clothing" (13a), referring to the ancient practice of ripping one's clothing as an outward sign of sorrow and a desire for a change of circumstance. Instead of that outward show, have true sorrow in your heart. The outcome of that inner rending of the heart should be that one "Return[s] to the Lord your God, / for he is merciful and compassionate, / very patient, full of faithful love, / and ready to forgive" (v. 13b).

Doing these acts turn rituals into a pathway toward reconciliation with God. Indeed, it is only through the redemptive power of God that one is reconciled with God. Seek God's forgiveness with all your heart, and God will grant it.

Lord, I seek you with all my heart. I repent with fasting, remorse, and sorrow. Please forgive me. Amen.

## Thursday, February 18

# Answering the Bethel Delegation

### *Zechariah 7:1-13*

**How might one's lifestyle affect one's prayer life?**

A delegation sent from Bethel came inquiring if they ought to continue the twice-yearly fasts as they had during their exile in Babylon. The exile had ended and they'd been allowed to return to their homeland, but they wondered if perhaps they should continue the fasting anyway, so God would bless them.

They are asked just who they were fasting for, for God or themselves? What the Lord says indicates two truths: First, God listens to those who are godly in character, but not to those who are only godly in form. Second, God does not bless people because they act "religious." Rather, God's blessings accompany those who act justly and who live righteously.

These truths are not absolute. Jesus suggests that God's blessings sometimes fall even upon those who are evil (Matthew 5:45). Yet, the principles behind the two truths are consistent throughout the Bible: what God wants is that we "Make just and faithful decisions; show kindness and compassion to each other! Don't oppress the widow, the orphan, the stranger, and the poor; don't plan evil against each other!" (vv. 9-10).

Sadly, in Zechariah's day, this delegation "turned a cold shoulder and stopped listening" (v. 11). Nonetheless, let us heed the text. Let us be godly in character. Let us be just, kind, and compassionate. Let us be faithful and charitable, and serve the Lord wholeheartedly.

God, help me never to turn a cold shoulder
and stop listening to you. Amen.

## Friday, February 19

# Fasting Disconnected from Righteousness

### *Isaiah 58:1-7*

**When have you thought of yourself as a hypocrite?**

The passage opens with God informing Isaiah to accuse the Judahites of committing crimes and sins against God. The wrongdoers ask for righteous judgments and closeness with God, but don't receive it. They fast but God seems not to notice (vv. 2-3a). The answers are obvious and implied within God's questions themselves (vv. 5-7): God does not answer their beckoning because of their crimes and sins. Moreover, the fast that God actually calls for is one of godliness and holy living.

This scene hints at a problem that persists to this day. It was one that Jesus spoke against in the Gospels. In Matthew 6:1-8, Jesus spoke against "look-at-me religion," calling its practitioners "hypocrites." In the Greek, this word means "mask," and was a common term to reference actors. The connotation of the word is that of "show." The implication, then, is that "showy" religion is an insincere act.

The same is true within today's reading. The text suggests that they fasted in a superficial sense. In other words, their everyday actions proved that the sincerity of their religious devotion and practices was lacking. Although we are separated from this event by millennia, the problem persists in the people of God. We sometimes act out our religion more than live it out. This text calls us away from that. To be sincere in our practices and devotions means that we act holy and godly in our everyday lives.

Dear God, I pray for forgiveness for the ways
in which I have been a hypocrite. Amen.

## Saturday, February 20

# The Fast God Chooses

### *Isaiah 58:6-10*

**How is fasting related to caring for your relatives?**

Today's Scripture passage starts with verses 6-7, which were also included in yesterday's reading, and the main idea in them—that true religious practice should help others—has been a theme of other readings as well this month. But note that verse 7 has something we've not encountered in other readings: that true fasting includes "not hiding from your own family."

We can understand that better by listening to something Jesus had to say in Mark 7:11-12, where he chided people who said their to their father or mother, "Everything I'm expected to contribute to you is *corban* (that is, a gift I'm giving to God)," and thus I'm no longer required to care for you. We also hear something like that in the fifth commandment: "Honor your father and your mother so that your life will be long . . ." (Exodus 20:12). Throughout Leviticus and Deuteronomy, God's teachings emphasize caring for the needy—widows, orphans, resident aliens, and even your own relatives. The biblical Hebrew phrase translated as "kinsman redeemer" describes our responsibility to do whatever it takes to help our family members in bad situations.

Our reading from Isaiah today reminds us that there can be no true religious practice that does not benefit others. That includes those in our own families who need help. Only then will we be the people God calls us to be, a light to the world.

Bless my family members, O Lord, through me! Amen.

## Sunday, February 21

# Like a Watered Garden

### *Isaiah 58:11-14*

**How has God blessed you? Why has God blessed you?**

In yesterday's passage, God commands the people to be charitable, generous, and munificent. Here, God promises them flourishing and sustained prosperity if they act in that way. The implication can be summed up with the phrase "blessed to bless." That is, God does not bless us with prosperity, provision, and protection so that we might hoard it and keep it only to ourselves. Rather, God blesses us so that we can be a blessing to other people.

God's call to honor the Sabbath is another reminder that proper religious observance benefits all. God tells the people to "stop doing whatever you want on my holy day . . . seeking what you want and doing business as usual" on the Sabbath (v. 13). For the Sabbath to be beneficial to all, we must be charitable, generous, and munificent, so that even the most needy might be free enough of worry to receive the blessings of the Lord's day.

Such an understanding has implications for us. Some argue that God has blessed us with abundant prosperity and material goods. Considering the immense wealth and power we possess, especially compared to most of the world, that might be the case. The real question, however, is not if God has blessed us, but what ought we do with the bounty we have? If God has blessed us, then it is so that we can be a blessing to others. Therefore, go and be a blessing.

Dear God, I am blessed to bless. May I
be a blessing to others. Amen.

## Monday, February 22

# The Lord's Temple

### *Jeremiah 7:1-11*

**Where does God abide? Where do you find God's presence?**

Some people in Jerusalem thought of the temple as something like a good-luck charm, warding off national troubles. In those circumstances, the word of the Lord came to Jeremiah, telling him to station himself near the temple gate and deliver the message that the temple was no insurance against calamity (vv. 1-2). The prophet chided his audience for chanting "this is the LORD's temple" (v. 4) as if it were an incantation to protect them.

Jeremiah announced that the presence of God would dwell amongst them if they worshipped rightly *and* behaved rightly (vv. 5-7). Jeremiah declared that judgment would come upon the people of Israel and God's presence would depart because they worshipped wrongly (i.e., idolatry) and behaved wrongly (i.e., wickedness). Such a departure of God will occur even though the Israelites have the temple of God in their midst. In many pagan cultures, it was common to believe that temples "housed" the gods, and that in some mysterious way, the "gods" were bound to them. Our text, however, teaches that that does not apply to the Lord. God is not bound to a temple made by human hands. Rather, God can depart from the Temple . . . and will do so if the Israelites do not return to right worship and behavior.

This truth is applicable to us. God wants to dwell with us, and we should live so that we reflect God's glory.

Dear God, may my worship be right.
May my actions be right. Amen.

## Tuesday, February 23

# A House of Prayer for All People

### *Isaiah 56:1-8*

**Who does the church tend to treat as "outsiders"?**

Today's text begins with a call to remain faithful to the righteous standards of the Law. "Salvation is coming soon" for those who "act justly and do what is righteous," the Lord declares (v. 1). That should have been no surprise to the people of Judah. What may have been surprising was the assertion that this also applies to "outsiders," specifically two groups considered outside God's covenant: immigrants and eunuchs.

Immigrants included anyone who was a non-Israelite. Eunuchs are men who accepted castration to advance into official circles in court life. Many Judahites considered eunuchs cursed and outside the covenant of God.

Yet, according to the Lord, immigrants and eunuchs who keep the Lord's commands will receive an enduring name and be brought to the Lord's holy mountain. Such terminology reflects salvific promises. That is, if these "outsiders" obeyed the laws of God, then salvation would be given to them as well.

This perspective was a radical view in Isaiah's day. It was a radical view when Jesus paraphrased verse 7 in his time when he cleared the temple (Matthew 21:13). And, this perspective is still a radical view in modern church culture, where some Christians want to exclude other people, deeming them as outside God's covenant. But that is not what our text teaches us, and it's not our decision to make. God's house of prayer, the text says, is for all people.

Dear Lord, you welcome all people into your salvific promise, even "outsiders." Praise be to you. Amen.

## Wednesday, February 24

# Jesus Enters Jerusalem

*Matthew 21:1-11*

**Where in your life do you desire to have control and power?**

Once Jesus came, some people, including his disciples, began to wonder if he might be the Messiah. When Jesus entered Jerusalem riding on a donkey, crowds laid palm branches on the ground in his path and shouted praise, both practices commonly used to welcome a conquering general or a king. The implication was that these crowds were welcoming Jesus into its gates as their savior and leader.

We might wonder what Jesus' disciples thought, for they, too, had concluded that he was the Messiah (Matthew 16:16-17). Did they like thinking of Jesus as powerful? The incident in Luke 22:24-30 where the disciples argued over which of them should be regarded as greatest reveals that at least some of them were interested in having power themselves,

A closer look at Jesus' entry into Jerusalem, however, shows that his focus was not on gaining power. Jesus rode into Jerusalem not on a war horse, and not as a conquering hero, but on a donkey, a symbol of no power. He had come to serve others and to die for all.

The disciples would get a clearer picture of this later in the week when, at the Last Supper, Jesus washed their feet (John 13:1-15). At that time, Jesus also told them "I assure you, servants aren't greater than their master, nor are those who are sent greater than the one who sent them. Since you know these things, you will be happy if you do them" (John 13:16-17).

Teach me, O Lord, humility and service. Amen.

## Thursday, February 25

# Jesus' Disorderly Conduct

### *Matthew 21:12-17*

**Who can receive the grace of God?**

In today's passage, Matthew records three significant events that occurred after Jesus entered Jerusalem:

First, Jesus cast out the sellers and buyers within the temple. These business people daily sold animals for sacrifice in the temple, and exchanged Roman currency, seen as idolatrous because of the image of Caesar, for currency acceptable in the temple tithes. Second, Jesus healed the blind and lame in the temple. The lame and blind were considered impure and were not allowed within those walls. Jesus broke protocol by healing these persons there. Third, Jesus accepted the praise of children. The specific phrase they used—"*Hosanna* to the Son of David!"—signified their belief that Jesus was the foretold Messiah of Israel (v. 15).

Jesus had disrupted the affairs of the temple. He had allowed the impure to enter a restricted area. He had allowed children to declare him the Messiah. All of this threatened the religious leaders' status and role, both within the temple and over the Jewish populace.

By these actions, Jesus signified a restoration to God's intent for the temple. The temple was designed for all people. The sacrificial system was to be open to all, even the poor. The temple blessings were to be poured out upon all Israelites, including the lame, sick, and blind. This speaks to a reality that is reiterated throughout Scripture: the grace of God is for all.

Thank you, God, that your grace is open to all people, including me. Hosanna, in the highest! Amen.

## Friday, February 26

# Jesus' Authority Questioned

### *Matthew 21:23-27*

**Why is the source of Jesus' authority important?**

The priests were the ones authorized by the law of Moses to oversee the religious practices of the Israelites. Their question implies that they saw what Jesus had done the previous day as a direct challenge to their authority—which, of course, it was. So, their question about Jesus' source of authority to act as he had wasn't a sincere inquiry. Rather, it was more in the sense of "Just who do you think you are?" with the implication that Jesus was treading where he had no business going.

Jesus didn't answer in the ways they had anticipated. Instead, he put *them* on the spot with a question of his own: "Where did John get his authority to baptize? Did he get it from heaven or from humans?" (v. 25a). The leaders immediately recognized that Jesus had turned the tables on them. In the end, they settled for a weak "We don't know" (v. 27).

We can admire Jesus' mental acuity, but that's surely not the only reason Matthew included this story. Rather he wants us to recognize that Jesus has God's authority and that he acts as the agent of his heavenly Father in bringing God's call and divine redemption to us. Jesus is more than a good moral teacher or philosopher, and his authority is the very same as the Creator of the cosmos. It would behoove us, then, to be mindful of what Jesus says and does, particularly when he is interrupting our status quo.

Lord Jesus, thank you for bringing God's salvation
to me, carrying God's full authority. Amen.

## Saturday, February 27

# You Are God's Temple

### *1 Corinthians 3:16-23*

**In what ways is your congregation (the people, not the building) a temple for God to dwell in?**

In the times in which the apostle Paul lived, people who worshipped other gods built temples for those deities. It was a common belief that these gods dwelled within their respective temples. It is in that cultural context that Paul makes his important statement in verse 16 of today's reading: "Don't you know that you are God's temple and God's Spirit lives in you?" Although this verse is often taken to mean that one's own body is a temple of God, and thus should be treated as such, in this context, it refers to the local church community.

Paul is intending the metaphor as applying to the Corinthian congregation rather than to the individual believer or the universal church. This becomes clearer in verse 17 where Paul speaks of people whose actions "[destroy] God's temple." Paul is writing here with the kind of concern that a clergyperson might have for a church she or he formerly pastored that was now being ripped apart by contentious members.

The unity that Paul wanted for the Corinthian congregation was the kind that united over faith in Christ. Maybe Paul was being unrealistic and not taking into account the diversity of human personalities, even among Christians. Nonetheless, Paul knew that if we can at least agree about Christ, we can be a redemptive force in the communities where we live.

Lord, amid the human diversity of Christians,
help us to concentrate on our commonalities
rather than our individualities. Amen.

## Sunday, February 28

# A Temple Dedicated to the Lord

### *Ephesians 2:17-22*

**What does "family" imply? What does "family" require?**

Virtually all the first believers, and Jesus himself, were Jews. Thus, at the time of the Ephesian letter, there was still a belief among some that for Gentiles to become followers of Jesus, they fist had to become Jews.

This helps us understand verse 17, where Paul speaks of Christ as the one who brought "good news of peace" to both those who were "far" (the Gentiles, the "outsiders"), and those who were "near" (the Jews, the "insiders"). Both groups have access to God through Christ (v. 18) and they both are a part of God's household (v. 19). In other words, the Jews and Gentiles are family through the atoning work of Christ. This family is the temple of God, God's chosen dwelling (vv. 21-22).

Such a bold declaration was a radical claim in those days. Many of the Israelites believed that the Gentiles were outside God's chosen people and could never be included into the "family" of God. But Paul argues otherwise. Christ is available to all people, and all who accept him are now among God's chosen people. It is difficult for us today to grasp how radical that viewpoint was during the time of Paul. However, we still have some sense of "outsiders" and "insiders" as we think about who we do or do not welcome into our congregations.

We should praise God for including us, and we must continue to welcome the outsiders in our life to be a part of the family of God.

Dear God, thank you for including me in the family of God. May I welcome those on the outside. Amen.

# MARCH

## Contributor:

*Clara Welch*
*March 1–31*

## Monday, March 1

# Everyday Holiness

### *Leviticus 19:1-10*

**How do you live a holy life every day?**

After the Israelites escaped from Egypt, God gave them instructions about what it meant to live in community as God's people. God commanded them, "You must be holy, because I, the Lord your God, am holy" (v. 2). Holy means "set apart." We are holy because we are set apart for God. We are not holy on our own. We are called to live in a way that witnesses to God's faithful presence and love.

God gave the Israelites specific commandments to teach them how to live holy lives. The first one in this text is "respect your mother and father" (v. 3). It seems that a holy life begins with our relationships with our families. The second command in this text is "you must keep my sabbaths" (v. 3). Sabbath is a time to take a break from our work and chores and remember our "set apart" relationship with God. A holy life extends to caring for all God's children including "the poor and the immigrant" (v. 10). The Israelites left some of their harvest and grapes in the fields for the hungry to gather. How do you show compassion for people in need, even those you do not know?

God commands us to "be holy" (v. 2), set apart for God. How do you embrace this call in your daily life?

Holy and loving God, help me to always be mindful of your holy presence as I serve others in your name. Amen.

## Tuesday, March 2

# Love Your Neighbor as Yourself

### *Leviticus 19:11-18*

**Why do you love your neighbor?**

God's command, "you must love your neighbor as yourself" (v. 18) is at the heart of living a holy life, a life that is set apart for God. This passage gives us guidelines for loving our neighbor. These include honesty and respect toward neighbor and toward God, and fair treatment of all. Verses 14-16 command us to extend kindness and fairness to others and not take advantage of people who are vulnerable or experiencing hardship.

We live a life of holiness, a life set apart for God, when we obey the commandment to love our neighbor. Jesus said this is the second commandment. The first is "*You must love the Lord your God with all your heart, with all your being*, and with all your mind" (Matthew 22:37). The command to "love your neighbor" may seem burdensome as we look at all the rules and regulations listed in the Book of Leviticus. Yet when our love for other people grows out of our love for God, it is not burdensome at all. Our natural response to God's love for us is compassion and kindness toward others. We find joy in the opportunities we have to offer our resources and time to serve others in the name of Christ. In this way we embrace God's call to live a holy life.

Loving God, open my eyes to the ways I may answer your call to love my neighbor. Amen.

## Wednesday, March 3

# Holiness Applied

### *Leviticus 19:19-32*

**What actions set you apart as holy for God?**

It is fairly easy to apply the instructions in Leviticus 19:1-18 to our present day lives. Today's text is a little more difficult. We must remember that this text was written to address specific concerns at a specific point in history. The Pentateuch, the first five books of the Bible, were compiled and canonized many centuries after the events they describe. Guided by God's Spirit, the writers of these books addressed concerns that were relevant at that moment but seem less so at other times. But what lies at the heart of these specifics? In today's passage, the prohibitions—from crossbreeding livestock to fortune telling and cutting our bodies "for the dead" (v. 28)—are ways of setting apart God's people from the pagan societies around them. It must have been hard for the Israelites, especially in the years of the Exile, to live set-apart lives; yet repeatedly God reminds them "I am the LORD" as the reason for this set-apart living.

Leviticus 19 is called the "Holiness Code." If you were to write a code for living a holy life today, what would you include? How would God's command to "love your neighbor as yourself" (v. 18) be at the heart of your code? In what ways do you hear God saying, "I am the LORD"?

Holy Lord, open my heart to the ways you call
me to live a holy life set apart for you. Amen.

## Thursday, March 4

# Acting Justly

### *Leviticus 19:33-37*

**How do you love others with acts of justice?**

The people of Israel knew well the life of an immigrant because they had been "immigrants in the land of Egypt" (v. 34). They moved to Egypt to find food during the famine and received a warm welcome because they were related to Joseph. Joseph was highly regarded in Egypt since God had given him the wisdom to interpret Pharaoh's dreams and oversee a plan to store food. The Israelites also experienced oppression and injustice in Egypt when, years later "a new king came to power in Egypt who didn't know Joseph" (Exodus 1:8). This king feared the powerful numbers of the Hebrews and enslaved them to do forced labor.

As I write this, immigration is a divisive and challenging concern in our country and around the world as both church and government leaders consider what it means to act with justice. The Lord says, "When immigrants live in your land with you, you must not cheat them. Any immigrant who lives with you must be treated as if they were one of your citizens. You must love them as yourself" (Leviticus 19:33-34). How do you put these commands to treat others with justice into practice as you respond to God's call to live a holy life?

God of love and justice, open my eyes to the ways you call me to treat others with love and justice. Amen.

## Friday, March 5

# Separated to Be God's Own

### *Leviticus 20:22-27*

**How do you live set apart for God?**

In the Scripture for March 1, we read God's command, "You must be holy, because I, the Lord your God, am holy" (Leviticus 19:2). In Leviticus 20:26 this command is worded a little differently: "You must be holy to me, . . . I have separated you from all other peoples to be my own." We do not live a separate, holy life for the sake of holiness. We live a separate, holy life for the sake of God and our relationship with God. We express our love for God when we embrace this separateness.

As Christians we do not follow all the rules and regulations that God gave to the Israelites. Instead, we follow Jesus and live according to his example. Jesus summed up the law by identifying the two greatest commandments—love God and love our neighbor. When we do this, we fulfill God's command to be holy. The world encourages us to live a self-centered life, but Jesus shows us a God-centered life.

What have been your experiences of living "separated . . . from all other peoples" (v. 24) because of your love for God? How does God's command to "be holy" influence the way you interact with other people, the places you go, the words you speak, and the choices you make?

Loving God, help me remain strong in my faith as I obey your commandment to live a holy life for you. Amen.

## Saturday, March 6

# The Most Important Commandments

### *Matthew 22:34-40*

**How do you obey the two greatest commandments?**

Jesus cited Deuteronomy 6:5 as "the first and greatest commandment" (v. 38). Jesus said, "*You must love the Lord your God with all your heart, with all your being,* and with all your mind" (v. 37). Deuteronomy 6:5 also includes "all your strength." Jesus cited then Leviticus 19:18 as the second greatest commandment, "*You must love your neighbor as you love yourself*" (v. 39). We explored this commandment on March 2. It is included in the Lord's instructions about what it means to live a holy life.

Jesus said, "All the Law and the Prophets depend on these two commands" (v. 40). His listeners knew "the Law and the Prophets" referred to the Hebrew Scripture. We must read and study Scripture through the lens of God's love if we hope to truly grasp its meaning.

We love God with an all-encompassing love so complete that it spills out and influences our actions toward others. Our love for God is our response to God's love: "We love because God first loved us" (1 John 4:19). How do you express your love for God with all your heart, being, mind, and strength?

Loving God, I love you. Open my heart that
I may love you even more. Amen.

## Sunday, March 7

# Your Life Hidden in Christ

### *Colossians 3:1-14*

**How have you put on your new nature in Christ?**

Paul tells us, "Take off the old human nature . . . and put on the new nature" (vv. 9-10). This new nature includes "compassion, kindness, humility, gentleness, and patience" along with tolerance and forgiveness (vv. 12-13). Love binds all these together (v. 14). Love defines our character and directs the way we treat other people. Love binds all believers together in Christ. No one is excluded (v. 11).

We continue to live in this world, but now we live differently than we did before. Paul encourages us to "Think about the things above and not things on earth" (v. 2). We no longer look for fulfillment in the secular world. Instead, we focus on God and allow God to conform us into the divine image (v. 10; see Genesis 1:27). Through Christ, our sinful nature dies and we are raised to new life.

When we put on the new nature, we know our lives are safely "hidden with Christ in God" (v. 3). We have the assurance of God's forgiveness for our sins. God's promises of salvation and eternal life are trustworthy and sure. When we "put on love" (v. 14), God's love directs our way of living with others. It is a joy to know that we are hidden in Christ. We are precious to God and God holds us close.

Loving God, thank you that my life is safely hidden with Christ, and that in Christ I am holy and loved. Amen.

## Monday, March 8

# A Stone Laid in Zion

### *Isaiah 28:14-20*

**Where do you look for security during the storms of life?**

Judah's leaders responded to Isaiah's warnings with contempt and defiance. They blatantly turned away from the Lord and looked instead to Egypt for protection against the Assyrians. Isaiah called their alliance with Egypt "a deal with death" and a pact "with the underworld" (v. 15).

Isaiah compared Assyria's power to that of a flood. Isaiah accused Judah's leaders of naively saying, "When the overflowing flood passes through, it won't reach us" (v. 15). But people cannot safely hide behind lies or find security in a shelter built on falsehood. Judah was seeking protection from the false and powerless gods of foreign nations instead of from the one true God.

In contrast, God provides security and safety for God's faithful people in a shelter that is constructed on "a tested stone, a valuable cornerstone, a sure foundation" (v. 16). We know this "sure foundation" to be Jesus Christ. God's shelter for us is built with "justice" and "righteousness" (v. 17). We nourish holiness when we seek shelter in Christ. The foundation stone that God laid is for all God's people, including us!

Thank you, God, for sheltering me with your faithful love through all the storms I face. Amen.

## Tuesday, March 9

# The Message That Bears Fruit

### *Colossians 1:3-8*

**How is God's grace bearing fruit in your life?**

The church in Colossae was founded by Epaphras, and though Paul did not visit Colossae himself, when he and Epaphras were in prison together he listened as Epaphras told him about the young congregation. He then penned this letter to the Colossians to offer his compliments and encouragement.

Can you imagine spreading the gospel throughout the world without modern technology? The message grew through word of mouth and the witness of changed lives. The number of faithful believers grew as new converts grew stronger in their faith and welcomed others into the fellowship of the churches. Paul wrote that "the good news" (v. 5) was also "bearing fruit and growing in the whole world" (v. 6). In what ways is the gospel bearing fruit in your life? How have you experienced and demonstrated God's grace?

The world needs to hear the gospel message today as much as it did then. How is God calling you to nurture the message of love and salvation in your own life and in the lives of others? How is the ministry of your congregation bearing fruit in your community and around the world?

Ever-present God, help me live my life in a
way that bears fruit for you. Amen.

## Wednesday, March 10

# Grow Into Christ

## *Ephesians 4:11-16*

**How does your church help people grow in faith in Christ?**

The tumbleweed has shallow roots. They dry up and are blown off the shallow root by the wind, then tumble about wherever the wind takes them. Ephesians 4:14 reminds me of tumbleweeds: "We aren't supposed to be infants any longer who can be tossed and blown around by every wind that comes from teaching with deceitful scheming and the tricks people play to deliberately mislead others." Instead, we must mature and grow in Christ.

In his letter to the Colossians, Paul expressed joy that the message of the good news of Jesus Christ was "bearing fruit and growing" (Colossians 1:6). In his letter to the Ephesians, Paul identified gifts that Christ gave to the church to contribute to this growth. Paul described the church as the body of Christ and Christ as "the head" (v. 16) of the church. He wrote, "The body makes itself grow in that it builds itself up with love as each one does its part" (v. 16). The church "builds itself up" by helping its members grow from infancy to maturity in the faith.

How is your church helping you grow from infancy to maturity in your "faith and knowledge of God's son" (v. 13)? How do you participate in this ministry to help others?

Loving God, help me mature in my faith as I serve others to build up the body of Christ. Amen.

## Thursday, March 11

# Press on to Maturity

### *Hebrews 5:12–6:2*

**In what ways are you pressing on to maturity in your faith?**

The audience for Hebrews, "should have been teachers by now," but instead needed, "someone to teach you an introduction to the basics about God's message" (v. 12). They should be eating "solid food" by now but instead they were still drinking the milk of babies. Ouch!

The author of Hebrews suggests that the difference between immature and mature believers is "practice" (v. 14). Mature Christians exercise their faith and apply the Christian teaching to their daily lives. Their "senses are trained by practice to distinguish between good and evil" (v. 14).

Having a mature faith means that we are better able to trust God through crises and hardship. It means we live each day with peace and assurance that God will provide everything we need to weather life's storms and journeys. One of the ways we grow in maturity is through "practice" (v. 14), through experiencing God's presence and provision when we feel fearful, discouraged, or lost. These experiences equip us to be "teachers" (v. 12). We are better able to teach others about repentance and forgiveness when we have experienced it. We are able to invite others to place their faith in God when we have done so ourselves.

Holy God, help me to continue growing stronger in faith. Show me the ways I may teach others about you. Amen.

## Friday, March 12

# Grow in Grace and Knowledge

*2 Peter 3:14-18*

**How can you be patient and grow in grace while you wait?**

The author of 2 Peter wrote, "Therefore, dear friends, while you are waiting for these things to happen, make every effort to be found by him in peace—pure and faultless" (v. 14). The phrase "these things" refers to the second coming of Christ, the final judgment, and the fulfillment of God's promise. The instruction "make every effort" is a call to remain faithful and active in Christ. This period of waiting for Christ's return is not a time to sit back and become lazy in the faith.

While we are waiting, we are called to "Consider the patience of our Lord to be salvation" (v. 15). This time before Christ's return is to be used for proclaiming the gospel. People who are weary of waiting may be tempted to listen to false teachers who lead unsuspecting believers "off course" (vv. 16-17). Instead, we should embrace times of waiting as opportunities to "grow in the grace and knowledge of our Lord and savior Jesus Christ" (v. 18). Seek God's gift of "peace" (v. 14) in all circumstances. Pray that God will use your faithful witness to influence others to "change their hearts and lives" (3:9) for Christ.

Loving God, thank you for being patient with me. Help me continue to grow in the grace and knowledge of Christ and be a witness that draws others to faith in you. Amen.

## Saturday, March 13

# Now You Are God's People

### *1 Peter 2:1-10*

**How do others know that you are one of "God's people"?**

Peter was writing to Gentile Christians, and he declared, "Once you weren't a people, but now you are God's people" (v. 10). Unlike the Gentiles, the Jews already understood themselves to be God's people. They shared the history of God's deliverance. Peter told Gentile believers that they too were "God's people" (v. 10). He applied images from Jewish religious life to Gentile believers, calling them "a chosen race, a royal priesthood, a holy nation, a people who are God's own possession" (v. 9).

In Christ, God was doing a new thing, bringing together those inside and those outside of the old covenant and making a new people with a new way of life. As God's people, we do not continue to wear the old sweater, if you will, of a nonbeliever. We "get rid of all ill will and all deceit, pretense, envy, and slander" (v. 1). We wear a new sweater because we are new people. We have experienced God's goodness and mercy. We want to nourish our new life of holiness with "the pure milk of the word" (v. 2), the good news of Christ. We wear new sweaters of honesty, compassion, and love.

Merciful God, thank you for including me among your people. Continue to nourish my life with your word so that I may grow in holiness and reflect your love. Amen.

## Sunday, March 14

# Living Honorably

### *1 Peter 2:11-17*

**How do you live a holy life in an unholy world?**

Do you ever find it challenging to resist temptations of the world around you in order to live the life of holiness to which God has called us? We have the impression that "worldly desires" exerted a strong pull on first-century believers. Peter wrote that these "desires . . . wage war against your lives" (v. 11). We may feel as if we are indeed doing battle as we strive to "live honorably" as Christ's followers in a nonbelieving world (v. 12).

In verses 13-17, Peter instructed believers to have respect for the governing institutions and leaders. Peter stressed the importance of getting along with both believers and nonbelievers. He wrote, "Honor everyone. . . . Honor the emperor" (v. 17). We nourish our lives of holiness when we treat everyone, from the lowliest to the highest official, with respect. Peter wrote, "Love the family of believers" (v. 17). Choosing love for others combats the self-interest that the world around us teaches. Most important of all is our relationship with God. Peter instructs us to "Have respectful fear of God" meaning reverence (v. 17). How do you nourish holiness within your relationships?

Holy God, give me courage and wisdom to remain faithful in the face of the world's temptations. Amen.

## Monday, March 15

# Out of the Heart . . .

### *Matthew 15:1-2, 10-20*

**How do the thoughts and words reflect your love for God?**

The "Pharisees and legal experts" approached Jesus with a complaint that his disciples were not following the "elders' rules" for ritual purity because they did not "ritually purify their hands by washing before they eat" (vv. 1-2). These rules were guidelines handed down, intended to keep adherents well within God's laws. Jesus reprimanded these religious leaders for being more concerned with strict adherence to these rules than with a relationship with God.

Jesus explained that whatever is eaten will follow the same natural course of digestion through the body, whether or not a person washes their hands. In contrast, "what goes out of the mouth comes from the heart" (v. 18). Our thoughts and words come from our heart and determine the way we live. We "contaminate" (v. 20) ourselves before God when "evil thoughts" (v. 19) and words emerge from our hearts and lead us to sin. To truly honor God, we need pure hearts, not strict rules. We cannot purify our hearts on our own; we need God's help! We embrace physical holiness when, through prayer and repentance, we offer our hearts to God. We pray with the psalmist:

"Create a clean heart for me, God; put a new, faithful spirit deep inside me!" (Psalm 51:10). Amen.

## Tuesday, March 16

# Be Children of the Light

### *Ephesians 5:1-11*

**What does the world see in and through you?**

Paul's readers faced challenges as they obeyed God's command to live a holy life in a self-centered society. Paul described Christ's followers as "light" and the pagan culture as "darkness" (v. 8). The words and actions of "children of light" (v. 8) produce "fruit that consists of every sort of goodness, justice, and truth" (v. 9). In contrast, "the unfruitful actions of darkness" (v. 11) are harmful to both those who commit them and the victims of these sins.

The "children of light" have two responsibilities regarding darkness: "don't participate in the unfruitful actions . . . [and] reveal the truth about them" (v. 11). This is not always easy.

We practice physical holiness when we follow Jesus' example of love and sacrifice (v. 2). We show Christ's love when we act on behalf of victims of sexual immorality, verbal abuse, bullying, and greed. We help bring an end to darkness when we "reveal" the sin and share the good news of Christ with the sinner. How do you share the light of Christ with your words and actions?

Loving God, thank you for loving me as your child. Let my words and actions bring your light to the people you place in my path. Amen.

## Wednesday, March 17

# The Dangers of Adultery

### *Proverbs 6:27-33*

**How is living a holy life a physical commitment?**

This week we are reading Scripture passages that teach us that God's command to "be holy" (Leviticus 19:2) includes both a spiritual and physical commitment. Proverbs 6:27-33 is a warning to avoid the sin of adultery. It seems that simply reading the consequences outlined in Proverbs 6:27-33 would be enough to keep any person from committing adultery! It is compared with being burned with fire (vv. 27-28). The adulterer emerges "wounded and disgraced" and forever shamed (v. 33). Through Christ there is repentance and forgiveness for sin, yet the adulterer may always remember the shame.

The proverb says, "He who commits adultery is senseless. Doing so, he destroys himself" (v. 32). The adulterer, either husband or wife, breaks the marriage vow and destroys the faithful relationship with the spouse. Children are also hurt and families may fall apart. A marriage is an "all-in" commitment. Each spouse promises to be faithful to the other emotionally, spiritually, and physically. God faithfully fulfills God's covenant with us. We are called to be faithful to the covenants we make with others.

Loving God, just as you are faithful and keep
your promises, help me remain faithful and
live a holy life before you. Amen.

## Thursday, March 18

# About Sexual Immorality

### *1 Corinthians 5:1-5*

**How do you respond to sexual immorality in the church?**

Paul packed a lot into these five verses to the church in Corinth. He was upset about a scandal that "Everyone has heard" about a man's sexual relations with his stepmother (v. 1). But it seems that Paul was even more distressed by the reaction of the church. They should be "upset" and expel the guilty party (v. 2). Instead, he accused them of pride.

What is your response when you discover that a member of your faith community is guilty of sexual immorality? Sometimes it is just easier to turn a blind eye, not make waves, and let someone else deal with it. Yet Paul calls the church to intervene not for the sake of punishment but for the sake of the sinner's salvation.

When we commit to living a holy life after the example of Jesus, it is likely that we will not do this perfectly. We will make mistakes along the way. The church is called to be a supportive and redemptive community. We are not helping each other when we turn a blind eye to destructive behaviors. We extend the love of Christ when we call each other to confession and repentance so that everyone "might be saved" (v. 5).

Redeeming God, give me wisdom to invite others to repentance, as I, too, confess my sin before you. Amen.

## Friday, March 19

# Paul's Warning

### *2 Corinthians 12:14-21*

**How do you need to change your heart and life for Christ?**

Paul was planning his third visit to Corinth. He was the founding father of this church and he illustrated his relationship as that of a parent to his children. Paul voiced concern that he would be disappointed in the behavior of the people in the Corinthian church. He would like to find that the Corinthians were treating each other with Christlike love and respect, but as verse 20 indicates, he feared he would find the opposite to be true. He was also concerned that some believers were continuing "what they used to practice: moral corruption, sexual immorality, and doing whatever feels good" (v. 21). He risked being embarrassed before God if he found his evangelistic work in Corinth has been in vain (v. 21).

Always in the gospel there is hope! Paul wrote about "all the people who have sinned before and haven't changed their hearts and lives" (v. 21). No one except Jesus is perfect. We have all sinned before. Through Christ we have the opportunity to confess and repent of our sin. The question is, will we? Will we change our "hearts and lives" and embrace the life of holiness to which God calls us?

God of new beginnings, accept my prayer of confession and repentance. Help me live a holy life before you. Amen.

## Saturday, March 20

# The Message to Pergamum

*Revelation 2:12-17*

**What helps you remain devoted to God?**

Here it is again, the call to "change your hearts and lives" (v. 16). How do you interpret this call—as a welcomed invitation or an unwanted command?

Pergamum was the capital city of the province of Asia Minor. It was a center of imperial government and worship. We can imagine how challenging it must have been to live as faithful believers in this pagan climate. The Book of Revelation describes John's vision of the end times. The unfaithful ones need to beware, for Jesus will return and "make war on them with the sword that comes from [his] mouth" (v. 16). In contrast, faithful believers will receive "manna to eat" (v. 17). This promise reminds us of God's continuing faithfulness. God provided for the needs of the Israelites during their journey through the wilderness. God will reward faithful believers with "manna" in the last day.

As believers and followers of Christ, we take seriously the call to "change your hearts and lives" (v. 16). We worship God and God alone. We engage in actions and behaviors that reflect our faithful love for God.

Ever-faithful God, strengthen me that I may
turn away from false teaching and remain
faithful to you in all circumstances. Amen.

## Palm Sunday, March 21

# Other Sheep Will Listen to Me

### *John 10:11-18*

**How do you listen for Christ's voice in your daily life?**

Who is this Jesus? That was the question on everyone's mind throughout his ministry on earth and even as he triumphantly entered Jerusalem at the start of what we now call Holy Week. In the Gospel of John, Jesus' identity and character are revealed in part by the seven "I am" sayings. In the text for today, Jesus twice said, "I am the good shepherd" (vv. 11, 14). He is "good" because he "lays down his life for the sheep" (v. 11). He said, "I know my own sheep and they know me, just as the Father knows me and I know the Father" (vv. 14-15).

Jesus spoke of "one flock, with one shepherd" after saying that the sheep "will listen to my voice" (v. 16). When we are one with Christ, we recognize his voice just as sheep recognize the voice of their shepherd. We know who this Jesus is, and should strive to make him known. We are called not only to listen but also to follow and obey. How has Christ spoken to you? What will help you remain attentive and listen with an open heart?

Loving God, thank you for caring for me as a loving and faithful shepherd. Open my ears that I may always listen and hear your voice. Amen.

## Monday, March 22

# Scripture Equips Disciples

### *2 Timothy 3:14-17*

**How has Scripture equipped you to do good?**

The statement that "Every scripture is inspired by God and is useful" (v. 16) was referring to the Old Testament since the early church did not yet have what we know as the New Testament. We have the advantage of both and the assurance that everything we need "for teaching, for showing mistakes, for correcting, and for training character" (v. 16) is included within the pages of the Bible. Thus we may have faith in Christ "that leads to salvation" (v. 15).

One of our desires as a "person who belongs to God" is to share the good news of salvation with others (v. 17). When we encounter challenges and resistance in this work, we may lose heart or question our ability. During those times we can remember what we "have learned and found convincing" (v. 14). We can remember the faith of the ones who taught us, as Timothy could remember the faith of his mother and grandmother. God has given us God's holy word to equip us. We can grasp the Bible in our hand. We can read the timeless words and listen to them being read to us. We can bind these words in our hearts and go forth each day convinced that God has provided all that we need "to do everything that is good" (v. 17).

Thank you, God, for the Scriptures that teach us about you and equip us to do good things in your name. Amen.

## Tuesday, March 23

# Do This in Remembrance of Me

### *1 Corinthians 11:23-26*

**Who has handed on the tradition of Communion to you?**

Jesus gave us a way to remember him in the form of broken bread and a cup. The sacrament of Holy Communion is a "tradition from the Lord" (v. 23) that has been given to all of us. Jesus' closest disciples were the first to experience this holy meal just prior to Jesus' death and resurrection. Scholars believe that Paul learned of the tradition from these disciples, and then "handed on" (v. 23) the tradition to the church in Corinth.

The broken bread represents Jesus' body and reminds us of his sacrifice on the cross for our salvation. The cup represents Jesus' blood that was shed during his crucifixion, again for our salvation. God kept the promise of a new covenant and sealed the covenant with the blood of Christ.

Paul wrote to the church in Corinth, "Every time you eat this bread and drink this cup, you broadcast the death of the Lord until he comes" (v. 26). Thus, when we participate in this "tradition from the Lord" we are also asking the Holy Spirit to enable us to "broadcast" the good news of salvation and hand the tradition on to others.

Gracious God, show me how to "broadcast" the
good news of salvation through Christ. Amen.

## Wednesday, March 24

# First Examine Yourselves, Then Eat

*1 Corinthians 11:27-34*

**With what attitude do you approach the Lord's Table?**

Paul instructed believers in Corinth to examine themselves before partaking of the Lord's bread and cup. He warned, "Those who eat and drink without correctly understanding the body are eating and drinking their own judgment" (v. 29). The reference to "the body" has two meanings. First, the bread and cup represent Jesus' physical body and blood that were given up for our salvation. Second, Paul understood that believers "were all baptized by one Spirit into one body" (1 Corinthians 12:13). The Corinthians were eating around the Lord's Table "inappropriately" because they were not honoring Christ's sacrifice and their call to be one body in Christ (v. 27). Paul does not say that believers are required to gather at the table perfectly, just appropriately.

How do you approach the Lord's Table? Do you feel as if you are part of one body in Christ, or do you sense divisions among the people gathered with you? Does everyone feel welcome, or do "outsiders" remain in their seats while others go forward? As you leave and go about your tasks, do you remain mindful of the call to love, repentance, and peaceful living included in the invitation?

Holy God, thank you for the invitation to the Lord's Table. May I come with love, repentance, and peace. Amen.

## Maundy Thursday, March 25

# Wash One Another's Feet

### *John 13:1-5, 12-17*

**How does Jesus' example of washing his disciples' feet influence the way you serve Christ?**

The task of washing the feet of guests was a slave's job. We understand this final meal to have been an intimate gathering and there is no mention of slaves being present. None of the disciples lowered themselves to do this servant's work. The fact that Jesus himself willingly washed their feet was a powerful illustration of what it means to be a disciple and servant of Christ. Jesus asked, "Do you know what I've done for you?" (v. 12). At that point in time, their answer would have been, "No."

The act of foot washing does not have the same meaning in our culture as it did in Jesus' day. Yet Jesus' act of taking on the role of a slave continues to offer us a powerful example of what it means to serve in the name of Christ. There is no act of kindness or generosity that is beneath us. We are called to love God's children. Sometimes this requires that we go to places that make us feel uncomfortable and engage in work we would rather not do. Jesus acted out of love. When we step out in faith to love and serve, we know that we, too, are surrounded by Christ's love and presence.

Loving God, let me follow your example and
serve you with faithfulness and love. Amen.

## Good Friday, March 26

# Jesus Foretells His Suffering and Death

*Mark 8:31–9:1*

**How do you respond to Jesus' suffering and death?**

It is hard to understand, when we are in the moment, that sometimes what appears to be "bad news" can, in the end, be "good news." In this text, Jesus foretold his suffering, death, and resurrection. Peter did not understand the meaning of Jesus' words and scolded him for making such a dire prediction. But salvation through Jesus came about according to "God's thoughts," which we know are not always in accordance with our human way of thinking (v. 33).

We face temptations that have the power to distract us from living according to "God's thoughts" for our lives. Jesus said that his followers "must say no to themselves . . . and follow" him (v. 34). It can sometimes require great strength to deny ourselves the assets and affirmation the world has to offer. It sometimes requires great strength and courage to love and serve our neighbor and live lives of generosity.

Peter was distressed when Jesus declared that "The Human One must suffer many things . . . and be killed" (v. 31). Yet, after the Resurrection Peter and the other disciples willingly said "no to themselves" and accepted the call to follow Christ.

Loving God, grant me courage and strength as I say no to myself, take up my cross, and follow you. Amen.

## Saturday, March 27

# Jesus Meets Disciples on Emmaus Road

### *Luke 24:13-21*

**Have you placed your hope in Christ? Why or why not?**

Have you ever placed your hope in something or someone, only to have that hope crushed? On the day of his resurrection, Jesus joined two disciples who were leaving Jerusalem and walking along the road to Emmaus. When Jesus joined the disciples, "They were prevented from recognizing him" (v. 16), so in response to Jesus' question they freely shared information concerning his death and crucifixion. They admitted, "We had hoped he was the one who would redeem Israel" (v. 21). Specifically, the disciples had hoped Jesus would free Israel from Roman authority.

On the day after the Crucifixion the disciples believed Jesus was dead. They "had hoped" Jesus was the promised Messiah, the long-awaited redeemer. Yet Jesus had died a disgraceful death, hanging on a cross between two criminals. The disciples were not only mourning the death of their friend, they were mourning the loss of hope.

The disciples on the road to Emmaus did not immediately recognize Jesus, yet Jesus was present with them. The good news of the gospel is that Jesus is alive. He is the promised redeemer. Are you open to Christ's presence in your life? Do you believe that your hope in Christ is sure?

God of resurrection and hope, thank you for Jesus Christ and your continuing presence in our lives. Amen.

## Easter Sunday, March 28

# Stunning News

### *Luke 24:22-24*

**How do you respond to the news of the empty tomb?**

Have you ever been "stunned" by good news? Have you ever been "astounded" by something wonderful that has happened? On the day of the Resurrection, two disciples were leaving Jerusalem and walking along the road to Emmaus. Jesus joined them but they did not recognize him. When Jesus asked them what they were discussing, the two disciples proceeded to tell him about the trial and crucifixion of Jesus of Nazareth. Then they declared, "Some women from our group have left us stunned" (v. 22). The women were the first to go to the tomb that morning because they wanted to prepare Jesus' body. They were the first of Jesus' followers to learn that the tomb was empty, the first to hear the news "he is alive" (v. 23), news that stunned all whom they told.

How do you respond to the news of the empty tomb and the fact that Christ is alive? Do you feel stunned, amazed, or astounded? Does the depth of Christ's love seem unbelievable? Do you approach the events of Holy Week and Easter with a sense of wonder?

Loving God, thank you for the Resurrection. Thank you for the promise of new life. I stand before you with wonder and thankfulness. Amen.

## Monday, March 29

# Jesus Lives Again

### *Luke 24:1-12, 30-35*

**What evidence convinces you that Jesus lives again?**

The women went to the tomb to follow custom and embalm Jesus' body. They expected to find Jesus' lifeless body, but instead found an empty tomb. Imagine their surprise when they saw "two men . . . in gleaming bright clothing" (v. 4) and their amazement when the men proclaimed that Jesus was alive! The two men reminded the women of Jesus' words, "the Human One must be handed over to sinners, be crucified, and on the third day rise again" (v. 7). They had not remembered. The other apostles had not remembered either and did not believe the women's report.

It was only as the day progressed that the truth of the Resurrection began to sink in. The two who walked with Jesus on the road to Emmaus recognized Jesus when "he took the bread, blessed and broke it, and gave it to them" (v. 30). Back in Jerusalem Jesus had also "appeared to Simon," and now Jesus' followers were proclaiming the good news with confidence: "The Lord really has risen!" (v. 34).

At first glance, the news of Christ's resurrection may seem like "nonsense." Yet when Christ makes himself known to us through the breaking of bread, forgiveness of sins, and reconciliation with God, we know it to be true.

God of resurrection and new life, open my eyes to the reality of your presence with me every day. Amen.

## Tuesday, March 30

# The Reasons for the Resurrection

### *Luke 24:36-49*

**How has the risen Lord changed your heart and life?**

When "Jesus himself stood among" the gathered disciples, they reacted with terror and fear (v. 36). After Jesus assured them, "It's really me!" their fear turned to "happiness" yet still "they were wondering and questioning" (vv. 39, 41).

The disciples' minds were opened as they listened to Jesus and saw that he was the fulfillment of the promises in Scripture. Jesus called them "witnesses" (v. 48) and charged them with the work of preaching "a change of heart and life for the forgiveness of sins . . . to all nations" (v. 47). Jesus promised not to leave them alone in this task, but to send "heavenly power" as he had previously promised (v. 49).

We, like the disciples, may find ourselves "wondering and questioning" even as we experience the joy of a changed "heart and life." God accepts our wondering and questioning even while offering us the gift of salvation through grace. It really is a simple story, isn't it? God loves. Christ has risen. We believe and inherit eternal life.

Loving God, thank you for the joy of a changed heart and life and the gift of salvation. Amen.

## Wednesday, March 31

# Paul and the Resurrected Christ

### *1 Corinthians 15:1-8*

**How do we share the message of salvation?**

Paul's words in 1 Corinthians 15 provide the earliest written testimony we have of the Resurrection. Paul called "attention to the good news" and reminded his audience of the "most important" aspect of the Christian faith: Christ's death and resurrection (vv. 1, 3).

Paul had lived according to the tradition he had received as a Pharisee under the law and had persecuted the very church he was now helping to build. Through his conversion on the road to Damascus he received a new tradition and he added his voice to those of other apostles who were preaching the good news of salvation through Christ. Paul was a witness to the Resurrection and his life a testimony to salvation.

We can discern a three-step process in these verses from Paul. We hear the good news preached to us. We receive and believe what we hear. We "hold on to the message," for our salvation depends on it (v. 2). We are not called to only "hold on to the message," however. We are called to follow Paul's example and witness to Christ's presence in our own lives so that others may hear, receive, and hold on to the good news of salvation for themselves.

> Holy God, show me how to be a witness for you and share the good news of salvation with others. Amen.

# APRIL

## Contributors:

*Susan Groseclose*
*April 1–25*

*Randy Cross*
*April 26–30*

## Thursday, April 1

# Peace Be with You

### *Luke 24:36-43*

**When have you experienced Christ's peace?**

The two disciples had returned from Emmaus and were telling the others that they had recognized Jesus. While they were talking, Jesus appeared among them saying, "Peace be with you!" (v. 36). While this was a traditional greeting used throughout Scriptures and in Israel as a common greeting of "hello" or "goodbye," this phrase takes on a new meaning with the Resurrection. Jesus' greeting wasn't just a simple hello, but a greeting of assurance and calm. After Jesus' crucifixion and death, the disciples remained hidden away out of fear. Jesus' resurrection appearance gave the disciples the assurance that they could live in peace because Jesus was with them.

Because Jesus lives, we do not have to live in fear, and we can face whatever tomorrow holds. We have the peace and assurance that Christ is always with us and holds us. Through Christ's resurrection, we can live each day as Easter people trusting that we will join Christ in final victory.

What is troubling you? Are you or someone you know afraid? What do you long for in your own life or in a loved one's life? Sit with whatever thoughts and feelings bubble up. Lift up your arms and hold the situation in Christ's light. Feel the weight of your arms. See if you can release all your thoughts, trusting that Christ is holding whatever you are facing. Rest in Christ's peace.

Abiding Christ, surround me with your peace. Grant me assurance that you always walk with me. Amen.

## FRIDAY, APRIL 2

# Go into the World

### *Mark 16:9b-15*

**What do you tell others about Christ's resurrection?**

Today's Scripture passage reminds us that Christ commands us to go into the world and to tell others about the saving grace he offers. Bible scholars tell us that early manuscripts do not include the verses we find in Mark 16:9b-15 and that the vocabulary, style, and theological content of these verses is not similar to other passages in Mark. Yet these verses provide a summary of Jesus' resurrection appearances, ending with Jesus' command to go throughout the world telling others.

As you think about your daily tasks and responsibilities, how do you share the good news of Christ with others? With whom in your family do you share your faith? In your social circle? In your community?

As you live into today's command to tell others about Jesus Christ, think about the ways you serve in your community. What simple statement of faith can you share with others? Where do you practice sharing your faith? With your family? A small group at church? Are there places you visit or could visit on a regular, frequent basis? How might you begin to develop a relationship with another person in that place? How might you be ready to share your faith story and the love of Jesus Christ with another?

Living Christ, you command me to share your
love with others. Put me in situations and with
persons today where I can share your love through
my thoughts, words, and actions. Amen.

## Saturday, April 3

# About Resurrection

### *1 Corinthians 15:12-22*

**What does resurrection mean to you?**

The Christians at Corinth were asking questions and trying to understand the Resurrection. Paul wrote to instruct them and answer their questions. He reminded them of the eyewitness accounts of the early apostles (1 Corinthians 15:1-8), and in today's text, he talked specifically about Christ's resurrection and what it means for his followers.

Paul built up an argument concerning resurrection. If we do not believe in the resurrection of the dead, we cannot say that Christ was indeed resurrected (vv. 12-13). Our preaching and our faith are useless if we don't believe in Christ's resurrection (v. 14), and we become false witnesses of God's power (v. 15). If Christ was not raised from the dead, then our faith is futile, and we are still in sin (vv. 16-17); without Christ's resurrection, when we die we are "gone forever" (v. 18). Our source of hope is in the power of everlasting life in the resurrected Christ (v. 19). It is only through Christ's resurrection that we are alive (v. 22).

What do you say to others who might be trying to understand Jesus' resurrection? How has this belief in Jesus Christ's resurrection made a difference in your life, especially when life is difficult?

Victorious Jesus, you are my Savior. All my love is yours. I put my total trust and belief in your resurrection power that cleanses me from my sins and gives me everlasting life. Amen.

## SUNDAY, APRIL 4

# Resurrection Is New Life

### *1 Corinthians 15:35-44a*

**How have you experienced new life?**

I love the spring! It is a season full of new life! The pink and white dogwoods blossom from the barren branches. Flowering daffodil and jonquil buds emerge from the frozen ground. Butterflies and bees frolic among the shrubs and flowers. The earth awakens with earthy smells from the cool, misty mornings and warm sunny days.

Paul used the analogy of new life to describe the nature of the Resurrection. Just as trees and flowers bloom forth from the barrenness of the winter season, so resurrection doesn't happen without death. He went on to explain that just as God created all manner of plants, animals, fish, and birds as well as celestial and earthly bodies, God's power also raises us into new beings, new life. While we might not know the specifics or what our new life will be, we live in the assurance that we are a new creation. We are given new life that is even more glorious than what has been!

As part of your Sabbath practice, take a walk outside. Pay attention to the signs of new life. What do you discover? Breathe deeply, inhaling the new life surrounding you and exhaling a word of praise to God.

Everlasting Christ, through your resurrection, I experience new life. Open my heart to see and experience all that is blooming and budding forth in my life. I lift up my praises to your resurrected presence. Amen.

## Monday, April 5

# In Relationship with Others

### *Romans 14:7-9*

**How do you honor those with whom you disagree?**

The church in Rome was a mixture of Jewish and Gentile believers. Tensions arose between these two groups as to who was right with God. Paul admonished the Jews and Gentiles not to disagree with one another over differences in opinion or judge one another's actions. No one group is right with God based on whether they eat certain foods or not or how they practice the Sabbath. Rather, we are right with God through our faith in Jesus Christ, who died for our sins. Paul went on to affirm to those in the church at Rome that in life or death, they all belonged to God.

What do members of your church disagree about? Would you consider these as differences in opinions or essential matters of our faith in Jesus Christ? What does it mean that we do not live only to ourselves but rather we live in relationship with others?

We are to act out of love for one another by being peacemakers and building up the body of Christ. As you reflect on the disagreements in your church, list some ways that you and others can act out of love for another. What are ways that you can be sensitive to the opinions and consciousness of another? What have you done that affirms and builds up the church rather than creates division?

Forgiving, reconciling God, open my spirit to welcome those with whom I disagree. Give me a spirit of love and peace. Amen.

## TUESDAY, APRIL 6

# Easter People Are Gentle and Kind

### *2 Corinthians 10:1-6*

**How are you gentle and kind?**

Paul made "a personal request" to the Christians at Corinth "with the gentleness and kindness of Christ" (v. 1). He did not want to be "bossy" with them, but acknowledged that he might have to engage in that kind of behavior when dealing with people "who think we live by human standards" (v. 2), those who "oppose the knowledge of God" (v. 5). Paul said, "we don't fight our battles with human methods" (v. 3). Instead, the "gentleness and kindness of Christ" should characterize our relationships.

Think about the people in your life who are gentle and kind. What can you learn from them? When have you wanted to react to other's opposition of you? What did you think, say, and do? What would it mean for you to live by God's standards rather than human standards?

*Lectio Divina* is a spiritual practice of prayerfully reading Scripture. One way to practice it is to focus on a particular word or phrase from a Scripture passage. Consider from this text the phrase "the gentleness and kindness of Christ" (v. 1). Prayerfully reflect on it and allow God to speak to you through that phrase. Repeat the phrase again and again, and meditate on what you are feeling, what you are thinking, what action God is calling you to.

O God, open my heart to listen deeply as to how
I should respond to others, especially those who
oppose me. Guide my thoughts and actions so
that I reveal your love and grace. Amen.

## Wednesday, April 7

# Living Out God's Blessings

### *2 Corinthians 11:16-31*

**How have difficult times in your life shaped you?**

I dare say that none of us has been shipwrecked, tortured, or imprisoned to the extent that Paul experienced. However, we have each experienced suffering on occasion or have been through times when we have felt defenseless or vulnerable. Recall a significant dark time in your life. Sit for a moment allowing all the negative thoughts and feelings of that situation to arise to the surface of your mind.

Whether our experience is the painful reality and suffering of an illness, an injustice, financial ruin and poverty, or something else, we also live in the hope and assurance that God is with us and that through God's grace we will be healed, comforted, and given new life.

Reflect on your earlier experience. How did you experience God's blessings despite the pain and suffering? How did God shape your life into a new creation? Prayerfully reflect on the lessons you have learned about who God is through that experience, who you are as God's son or daughter, and who you are in relationship with others. Silently express your gratitude for God's grace and blessings.

Gracious God, thank you for always walking with me
no matter what happens in life. In times of difficulty,
remind me not to hide from the pain and suffering
but to also trust in your abiding presence. Continue
to teach and guide me to be transformed through
life's experiences into your new creation. Amen.

## Thursday, April 8

# Easter People Reveal Christ's Love

### *2 Corinthians 5:11-17*

**How have you experienced transformation in Christ?**

The transformation of a caterpillar into a butterfly symbolizes our transformation into a new creation. As we wrap and immerse ourselves in Christ's loving presence, we are transformed into new creatures who emerge compelled to share that love with others. Paul reminded the Corinthians that it was Jesus Christ who died for our sins and was raised; through his resurrection we are restored and created anew. We turn from our old sinful ways to live as faithful followers and servants of Christ. Through Christ's love, we are compelled to be a reflection of Jesus Christ in the world.

One way we wrap ourselves in Christ's love is through our Sabbath practices. These enable us to emerge as new creations and demonstrate our new nature in Christ in our relationships and actions. We follow the practice of Jesus to break away from the crowds for a time of prayer and rest and create space to encounter Christ, who longs to meet with us. Sabbath offers us opportunities to be in Christ's presence and to be renewed through his creative, loving grace.

How can you practice Sabbath this week? What do you need to let go of? How do you need to prepare yourself for Sabbath?

Ever-patient God, you long to be with me. Lead me to be in your sacred presence and to relish in your love. Open my heart to receive your blessings and to be transformed in your new creation. Amen.

## Friday, April 9

# Easter People Are Reconcilers

### *2 Corinthians 5:18-21*

**With whom do you need to reconcile?**

Paul explained to the church at Corinth that Christ, through his death and resurrection, is the initiator who reconciles us to God. As recipients of this divine reconciliation, we have the privilege and responsibility to be ministers of reconciliation to the world. We are called to be bridge builders. "We are ambassadors who represent Christ," Paul said (v. 20). God has given us "the ministry of reconciliation" (v. 18).

Whom have you had a difficult time forgiving? Perhaps it was a loved one, someone you trusted but who betrayed that trust. Perhaps someone failed to live up to his or her promises. Or maybe someone acted unjustly toward you or others.

Place an empty chair across from you. Imagine that Jesus Christ is sitting in that chair. Pour out your heart to him, telling him all about the situation. Release your feelings of hurt, pain, fear, and anger. Thank God that Jesus reconciled you to God. Allow yourself to listen deeply to ways that you might join Christ in the ministry of reconciliation.

Christ the carpenter, teach me to work alongside
you to build bridges in my relationships. Amen.

## Saturday, April 10

# Easter People Are God's Servants

### *2 Corinthians 6:1-10*

**How are you sharing Christ's love?**

Paul calls for us to live an exemplary life so that we are not a stumbling block to others nor is our service discredited. As he reflected on his life, being Christ's servant in the world wasn't necessarily an easy task. In fact, Paul reminded the Corinthians of the numerous troubles, hardships, and imprisonments he experienced. Despite his hardships, he affirms that our true wealth in life doesn't come from monetary gain but rather being one with Christ.

It is through our loving actions that others will know we are believers and followers of Christ. It is as we work with one another and do no harm that we exemplify Christ's love. It is as we walk hand in hand with one another that we reveal Christ's compassion. It is as we love one another that we become unified. We become one in Christ.

We are God's servants both during difficult times and in times of abundance. How would you describe your experience as Christ's servant? What hardships or afflictions have you endured? What blessings and abundance have you received?

God of love, you call me to share your love with others. I promise to be your servant. Amen.

## Sunday, April 11

# Easter People Are God's People

### *2 Corinthians 6:11–7:1*

**How do you breathe in God's living presence?**

The Corinthian Christians failed to live fully in God's presence. They were following false prophets, and their thoughts and lives were being contaminated by these deceptive teachings. Paul instructed them to cleanse themselves of these wrong teachings so that they could be God's people. He reminded them that they were temples of the living God and were called to live as God's people (v. 16).

What contaminates your soul? What prevents you from freely breathing in God's living presence? It might be media or technology that distracts you from God. It might be negative thoughts that prevent you from hearing affirmations of God's love. It might be your bitterness about a situation that blocks you from experiencing God's grace. It might be that you are consumed with destructive rage that blocks you from discerning constructive ways to express your anger. It might be a fear that is holding you from trusting in God's abiding presence and assurance. It might be a toxic relationship or situation that hides God's promise of goodness in your life. It might be that you are envious of what others have so that you fail to recognize the ways God is blessing your life. Prayerfully ask God to show you ways to cleanse yourself from the contamination. Who can you talk with to guide you in ways that foster healing and wholeness?

Living God, I belong to you. Let me freely breathe in your love that rids me of any contamination and prevents me from fully living in your gracious, loving presence. Amen.

## Monday, April 12

# Truth in Love

### *Zechariah 8:14-23*

**How do you reflect God's truth to others?**

Zechariah listed blessings, each beginning with "The Lord of heavenly forces proclaims." He visualized and foresaw the countless blessings God would bestow on the people if they restored their relationship with God. In verses 14-23, he tells the people that in order to be restored to God's favor, they need to speak the truth to and live in peace with one another. Not only will God's people be blessed and restored, but persons from other nations will also seek the Lord.

Those who are in a restored covenant relationship with God care for others and live in community with one another. They make just and faithful decisions through their kindness and compassion to one another. They do not "plan evil for each other," and they "love truth and peace" (vv. 17, 19).

Use your prayer practice to reflect on your actions each day. Review your day with gratitude, paying attention to your emotions. How did your actions reflect God's truth and love? What just and faithful decisions did you make? Were you kind and compassionate? How do your actions bear witness to who you are as God's new creation?

Gracious God, hold me in your love, restoring
me as your new creation. Amen.

## Tuesday, April 13

# People of the Spirit

### *Ezekiel 11:13-21*

**How has God put a new spirit in your life?**

During the first seven years of Babylonian exile, Ezekiel preached a heart-rending, hope-crushing message of divine judgment. It was only after the fall of Jerusalem that Ezekiel's message became a word of hope for revival, restoration, and redemption.

Today's Scripture records Ezekiel speaking of God's promise that the exiles, the remnant of Israel, would return to Jerusalem. He told them that even though they could no longer worship in the Temple in Jerusalem while in exile, God had been their temple. He assured them that they would return and remove the "disgusting and detestable" idols and images in the temple (v. 18). He reminded the people that God had always been with them and God's new spirit would once again affirm an ancient covenant promise God had made to the desert wanderers: "They will be my people, and I will be their God" (v. 20). God promised to "give them a single heart, and . . . a new spirit" (v. 19). As people of the new spirit, they, too, would rid themselves of those "disgusting and detestable" things in their lives that prevented them from fully embracing God and others. God would "hold them accountable for their ways" (v. 21).

What changes has God made in you to better reflect God's love to the world? How does your life need to be changed?

Everlasting One, you are my God and I am
your child. Pour your new spirit upon me. Teach
me to faithfully live with you. Amen.

## Wednesday, April 14

# Newness in Christ

### *Romans 6:1-8*

**What do you need to bury so that you are alive in Christ?**

Paul wrote to the Romans telling them that through Jesus Christ's death and resurrection, they were dead from sin but were alive in Christ. At our natural birth, we are linked to Adam and Eve and fall to sin; however, our baptism signifies that we become dead to our sin and are raised with Christ to new life. Our understanding of sin isn't just a list of wrongful actions. In our sinful nature, we turn our backs on God. We are all sinners and neglect to live fully, wholly in Christ. We fail to love Christ with our entire being and fail to love one another completely. However, Jesus bore our sins on the cross so that we might have new life in him. Therefore, each day we turn around aligning our lives to Christ, striving to be Christlike in our relationships and actions.

Reflect on your relationships with family and friends this past week. When have your thoughts or actions not been Christlike? When have they been Christlike? Thank God for the ways you have been able to experience and be alive in Christ. When you haven't been Christlike, do you find any patterns you need to change? Is there a specific person toward whom you find it difficult to be Christlike? In what situation or with whom do you need God's forgiving spirit to work? How might you allow God to breathe new life into your spirit?

Living Christ, breathe your spirit of love into my heart. Gently guide me to be like Christ in all my thoughts, words, and actions. Amen.

## Thursday, April 15

# New Life

### *Romans 7:1-6*

**How do you live in the Spirit?**

Paul used three images to illustrate our relationship with Christ, thus influencing our relationships with others. First, we are dead to sin but alive in Christ (Romans 6:1-14). Secondly, we are enslaved to sin but in Christ set free to be righteous and holy (Romans 6:15-23). Thirdly, we are bound by our sinful nature, but through Jesus' death and resurrection, we are given new life in the Spirit (Romans 7:1-6).

Paul further explained that we serve in the way of the Spirit. The result of our serving in the Spirit is that we bear fruit. New life in the Spirit isn't just faithfully showing up at church for worship, Bible studies, or times of fellowship. Rather, we are to be fruitful, which means that we are continuously growing in Christ and that we are loving and serving others.

How do you bear fruit for God? How do you live out being faithful and being fruitful? What are the ways you grow in your relationship with Christ and others? Who coaches or holds you accountable? How does your service within your church and in your community enable you to grow in your faith?

Living Spirit, dwell within my soul and continue to call and enable me to live as your faithful and fruitful disciple. Amen.

## Friday, April 16

# Pure Hearts

### *Ephesians 4:17-20*

**What thoughts or actions darken your heart?**

Paul urged those in the church at Ephesus to shine the light of Christ rather than to hide in self-imposed darkness. Paul said that the non-believers were pointless in their thinking and "dark in their reasoning" (vv. 17-18). Those who live in this way are separated from the life found in the Spirit; thus, they live in sinful ways.

Although Paul in his letter was talking about nonbelievers, even as believers we can be tempted by things that would bring darkness into our souls. There are places in the depths of our hearts that we may try to keep hidden. These may be actions we regret, thoughts of revenge, hurt, and pain from a particular situation, or a difficult experience that we relive over and over in our minds. We may try to hide our failure to believe the truth and instead hold on to a lie. We might reason that these thoughts and feelings are manageable but often they cause us to act in selfish, hurtful ways.

Paul reminds us that we are new persons God created. We are not to stay hidden in our dark thoughts and feelings. Rather, we are to stay connected to Christ, opening our hearts to Christ's forgiving and loving presence. We are not to keep Christ's light in the hidden, dark recesses of our hearts, but rather to shine Christ's light for all to see.

Gracious God, I admit that there are parts of my life that I am ashamed of and that prevent me from experiencing your love. Soften my heart and fill me with your grace so that I might shine your light to others. Amen.

## Saturday, April 17

# New Self

### *Ephesians 4:21-28*

**How can you be just and holy?**

Paul reminds us that we are to stay connected to Christ and open our hearts to the truth. Instead of focusing on our own pleasures and greed, we are to change our ways and renew our thinking by being clothed as the new person the Spirit created. We are to be like Christ, living a life of justice and holiness. We are to speak truthfully, not allow our anger to be harmful, not be evil, not steal, and work to help others.

Part of our Sabbath practice calls us to confession. It is an opportunity to name those times that we have not fully lived in the spirit of Christ, asked for forgiveness, and committed to live as Christ's new creation.

Reflect on your thoughts and actions this past week. Write your own prayer of confession using any of these questions: When did I speak untruthfully to another person or about another person? When was I angry? How did I respond? When was I hateful or hurtful to another? When did negative thoughts steal my ability to be kind? When did my words create division? When did I fail to work and share God's love or to speak or act in a just manner?

As you write your prayer and ask for forgiveness, listen for God to reveal thoughts and insights on ways to clothe yourself as a new person.

Forgiving Christ, I have hurt others with my thoughts and actions. Forgive me. Show me how to live as your new creation. Amen.

## Sunday, April 18

# New Creation

### *Ephesians 4:29-32*

**How can you build up the body of Christ?**

In Paul's letter to the Ephesians, he reminds us that Jesus Christ died for each one of us; thus, we are claimed by God. We are sealed through Christ "for the day of redemption" (v. 30). Through Christ's salvation, we are created and called to live like Christ. This means that we are to build up one another, to be kind and compassionate, and to forgive one another. Paul built upon his earlier command to stop unwholesome thoughts and added the instruction that our words are to build up one another. We are to be kind and compassionate rather than attacking another with bitterness, rage, slander, or malice. We are to forgive others just as Christ forgives us. As we live like Christ, we become God's new creation.

As God's new creation, we live and become co-creators with Christ. Reflect on these questions: What unwholesome thoughts or words did I say this week? Where did I experience bitterness, rage, slander, or malice? Who hurt me this week? Who built me up, or who did I build up this week? How? How was I kind and compassionate? Who did I forgive this week? Why?

Is it easy or hard for you to live as Christ's new creation? It goes against our selfish nature. But thanks to God's grace, we are made anew, and can live in joyful obedience.

Creating God, create me anew. Show me how to build up others not only through my words but through my kindness, compassion, and forgiveness. Amen.

## Monday, April 19

# Glory in God's Strength

### *Psalm 29:1-11*

**How do you find peace in God's strength?**

Psalm 29 proclaims the thunderous voice of God with escalating intensity. The majestic voice of God commands the waters, the trees, and the animals. God's voice shakes and unleashes fury as the storm rises. Our response to God's majesty and strength is "Glory!" God's power and might rule, but God blesses us with peace. In a world of uncertainty, we are blessed with the assurance of God's crowning comfort and complete salvation.

What storms are you experiencing, or have you experienced in life? You might have experienced a loss of income or unemployment. Maybe you have experienced the storm of you or a loved one receiving a terminal diagnosis. Perhaps you've ridden the waves of grief, or maybe you've known the inner turmoil and emptiness that come with the loss of a home, loss of independence, or a loss of purpose in life, or the deep hollowness in times of isolation.

God often meets us in the hallway between the closed door and the window yet to be open. Celtic Christians call this liminal space, that sacred space between what is no longer and what is yet to be revealed. How do you give God glory in the storms of your life? How do you find peace in recognizing that God is in the storm?

God of comfort and assurance, when the storms of life ravage in my soul, let me feel your abiding presence and peace. Let my response be "Glory!" Amen.

### Tuesday, April 20

## God's Abounding Love

### *Psalm 103:6-14*

**How do you experience God's abounding love?**

Psalm 103 tells of God's compassion on God's people as sinners and proclaims God's vast forgiving love. It sings of God's compassion on the people as frail humans, ending with God's unending perseverance. We are created out of love. Throughout our lives we grow deeper in our love of God and one another. Then in death, we are welcomed into everlasting love.

How have you experienced God's compassion and justice? How have you experienced God's vast forgiving love? How does the psalmist's comparison of God's love to a parent's love for a child deepen your understanding of God's abounding love?

A spiritual director once told me to "listen with the ear of my heart." She illustrated this by asking me to hold the palm of my hand in front of my face. When you do that, you can see each wrinkle, each smudge, and any other aspect of your palm. Then, she told me, soften your gaze, letting your hand fall to your lap. You no longer see your palm critically or judgmentally. As part of your Sabbath practice, look at your reflection in the mirror. Soften your gaze. You are God's marvelous, glorious, new creation! Give God thanks and praise for God's abounding love. Consider the ways that your life reflects God's abounding love.

God of amazing love! I lift up my praises for the many ways you love me. Let my life be a reflection of your love to the world. Amen.

## Wednesday, April 21

# Power Belongs to God

### *Judges 7:1-22*

**How does your weakness demonstrate God's strength?**

God, seeking to reveal divine power rather than the Israelites' human power, told Gideon that he had too many men to fight the Midianites. With God's ingenuity, Gideon reduced his army from 22,000 to 300 men. Even though the Midianites' camp was like a "swarm of locusts" and the number of camels were like "grains of sand on the seashore" (v. 12), Gideon put his trust in God. With the assurance that God was going to hand over the Midianites to Israel, Gideon courageously led the 300 men into battle. With the sound of 300 trumpets and fire, the Midianites scattered, the Israelites trapping them in the Jordan valley and winning the battle.

Paul in his letter to the Corinthians said that God's strength is made perfect in human weakness (2 Corinthians 12:9-10). Similarly, Gideon's reduction in the number of men fighting in the battle reveals God's power. It was only through God's power that 300 people could win a battle against the throng of Midianites. When has God used one of your weaknesses or failures to help another? How does your weakness demonstrate God's strength? We are a new creation through Christ. How does this story prompt you to see a weakness differently?

Amazing God, all power belongs to you. Use my weaknesses, use my failures to make your strength and power known. Amen.

## Thursday, April 22

# Our Strength Is in God

### *Daniel 10:8-18*

**How have you found strength in God?**

What happens if we are not touched? In the COVID-19 world of social distancing, to slow the spread of the virus, we began touching less. Prior to the global pandemic, researchers named the importance and significance of touch, noting the impact of little or no touch on our mental, emotional, and physical health. Being touched has a communicative and healing effect.

In Daniel's vision recorded in Daniel 10, he had no strength and fell into a deep sleep. While in this deep sleep, he experienced three touch moments. At the first touch moment, Daniel stood up, though shaking, to hear that he was greatly treasured and that the future of his people would be revealed (vv. 10-11). The second time, God touched his lips, giving Daniel a voice to speak (v. 16). The third time, God touched him and gave him strength (v. 18). Progressively, God's touches strengthened Daniel so that he could live with the peace of God's presence, a voice to speak to God and his people, and the strength to lead his people into the future.

When have you longed to be touched? What ways has God touched your life? What new strength can you embrace from God's touch? Who will you reach out to this week to offer God's touch?

God of love and strength, touch me. Give me the ability to stand and be your servant within my circle of influence, the voice to speak your compassion and justice for others, and your strength to face the future. Amen.

## Friday, April 23

# God Renews our Strength

### *Isaiah 40:28-31*

**How does God renew your strength?**

These verses in Isaiah have always been a favorite Scripture passage and one I recite from memory when I need to be reminded of God's strength. Isaiah was speaking to the weary Israelites who were still in exile. They were complaining that God was ignoring them and no longer with them. Isaiah brought a message of hope that our God does not grow tired or weary. God will renew our strength if we wait in faith. Those who wait and trust in God will soar like an eagle. "They will run and not be tired; / they will walk and not be weary" (v. 31). Isaiah reminds us that God's strength is stronger than human understanding and that God has always and will continue to renew and give us power in any situation.

Notice the requirement, though; it is "those who hope in the Lord" who will be renewed (v. 31). Other translations say those who "wait" for the Lord. The implication is that this renewing is not something we do for ourselves, nor is it done in our timing; we trust in God's timing even as we trust in God's strength.

When have you felt that God was silent? What did you learn about God while you waited? What did you learn about yourself? How did God renew your strength? How can you share the message of God's renewing strength with others?

Renewing God, in my weariness you raise me up. Your breath strengthens me. In your faithfulness, you hold me in the palm of your hand and make me to shine. Amen.

## Saturday, April 24

# God, the Potter, Creates Us

### *Jeremiah 18:1-6*

**How is God creating you?**

Have you ever tried to throw a clay pot on a potter's wheel? The potter takes a lump of wet clay and throws it on the wheel head. The potter controls the wheel with his feet and uses his hands to shape and mold the clay. Working from the bottom up, the potter first cones the clay, pressing it down and bringing it up till it is centered into a perfect symmetry. At that point, the clay is ready to respond to the directives of the potter. The potter opens the clay into the desired shape and pulls up the sides, shaping it from the inside until it is finally ready to be cleaned and trimmed. The clay undergoes a long, painstaking process before a newly created piece of pottery is ready.

The prophet Jeremiah followed God's instructions to go to the potter's house. As he watched the potter, he came to the realization that God, like the potter, holds us in God's hands and creates us into a perfect creation.

How would you describe the skill of God, the potter? Clay comes in different types and colors. How would you describe your nature? Potters follow several steps in making the clay pliable and responsive to their directives. What does that mean for you? How does God mold and reshape you, including your flaws, into a new creation? A potter must focus on shaping the inside rather than the outside. What does it mean for you that God creates you from the inside?

God the potter, I place my soul and life into your hands.
Mold me, shape me into your new creation. Amen.

## Sunday, April 25

# God Is Our Treasure

### *2 Corinthians 4:7-18*

**How do you experience God's treasure?**

Paul in his letter to the Corinthians described "this treasure" we have "in clay pots" (v. 7). It was customary in his day to hide one's treasure in clay jars that had little value or beauty, thus not attracting attention to their precious contents. Paul likened our human frailty, hardships, and sufferings to the clay pots. He explained that our daily dying magnifies the wonder of our daily resurrection life that is hidden away inside our bodies, our clay pots. He went on to say that what others see on the outside doesn't last; however, the treasure inside cannot be seen, but is daily being renewed and producing "an eternal stockpile of glory" (v. 17).

What hardships or difficulties do you struggle with? What does Paul's message reveal to you about God's power and life that is found in Jesus? How do you experience renewal and life in the midst of your struggles?

On this Sabbath day, affirm your faith as you say: "We are experiencing all kinds of trouble, but we aren't crushed. We are confused, but we aren't depressed. We are harassed, but we aren't abandoned. We are knocked down, but we aren't knocked out" (vv. 8-9). Praise be to God.

Healing God, renew me with your life-giving power.
Let me embrace your eternal glory. Amen.

## Monday, April 26

# Psalm 18:1-6

### *Like a Rock*

**Where do you feel most safe?**

The psalmist carries us into an image of a "rock" saving us, something so strong, so immovable, so substantial that it truly is a shield, a strength, a "place of safety" (v. 2). The psalmist recounts a horrible time when his enemies were taking him close to death. In that terrifying moment, he called to the Lord, and "God heard my voice" (v. 6).

How about those times when it felt as though your own enemies were surrounding you, binding you with the cords of the grave? Perhaps the danger was a physical ailment or injury when you realized you indeed could die. Or maybe it was simply an uneasy, unsettled sense of dread or concern or uneasiness because of what was happening around you. Whatever the setting, did you or have you ever cried out to God? Were your prayers nothing more or less than "Save me!"? I can recall that happening a couple of times in my life, and what hope I had that I, too, would be able to take refuge in God who is my rock as well.

For our lives to have meaning, we need Someone we can always count on, who will always bring us to safety, who hears our cries and will bring us life itself when it seems to be slipping away. This is the God we worship and in whom our trust makes sense. This is the firm foundation that is carefully set for our lives by the God who loves us. How have you recently experienced God as the Rock in your life?

God of power and love, I thank you for your care for me and the way you bring me to safety. Amen.

## Tuesday, April 27

# God's Merciful Choice

### *Romans 9:6-16*

**What seems fair when it comes to salvation?**

We don't earn or merit or deserve to be the chosen or preferred children of God. Instead, it is always God's choice. That's actually great news for those of us who are not direct descendants of Isaac or Jacob! For us as Christians, it means that through the grace of Jesus, without our work or preferential treatment, we are offered the gift of salvation. Our only "work" is to trust in what God has done for us and for this world. We may not all be biologically descended from Abraham, but we are "children from the promise," thus we have hope of salvation (v. 8).

God's concern truly is for the entire world, but salvation isn't an automatic token given to everyone born of Abraham's stock. Instead, salvation is a gift of God's mercy, given to all who call on the name of Jesus. We can't assume that because someone has the right last name they are assured of something that they own.

The difference it makes for you and me is to know that our eternal life is based on our relationship with Jesus and not simply the luck of a genetic draw. You see, if it were only a matter of Abraham's children, then many of us would never know the joy of eternal life with God. Thanks be to God for the better path!

Can you celebrate today as a gift instead of an earned or "deserved" place in eternal life?

God of grace, I thank you for the blessing of
offering me eternal life this day! Amen.

## Wednesday, April 28

# What's in a Name?

### *Exodus 3:13-20*

**How does knowing God's name make a difference in life?**

When Moses was negotiating with God about going to Pharaoh and to the children of Israel, one point was to take along the answer of what God's name would actually be. You see, people living in that time believed that when you discovered the name of someone, especially a god, you had certain power over him or her. When Moses sought to gain that kind of advantage over God, God's answer was wonderfully stated, "I Am Who I Am" (v. 14). A name, a title, yet still fundamentally unknown and unknowable in the way Moses assumed he could know.

Like Moses, you and I only know one part of God's self-revelation to us. Instead of having power because we know a name, what we have is further mystery and the sense that we are coming before One who is far greater than we will ever be. God is known by how God acts, and God was preparing to free the children of Israel and restart the road to freedom and salvation. So it is for you and me, as we decide in our lives to trust and no longer negotiate with the One who will not be known in terms of our having power over God. When we give up that aim of having to have power over God, we allow God's love and grace to have power over us instead, which grants us a place in this world and the assurance that we are always cared for and chosen.

Oh Great I Am, let me follow you with my
heart and my actions this day. Amen.

## Thursday, April 29

# A Change of Plans

### *Exodus 33:1-6*

**What it would feel like to have to go through life alone?**

While Moses was receiving the Ten Commandments on Mount Sinai, the Hebrews convinced the high priest Aaron to build a golden calf so they could worship it instead of God (Exodus 32). It was a terrible sin. When Moses finally got up the courage to talk with God about the sin of the people, God's reaction was that Moses should take the people and go to the Promised Land! However, God said, "I won't go up with you because I would end up destroying you along the way since you are a stubborn people" (v. 3).

What a heartbreaking story, with no easy answer. Even God had to figure out what to do (v. 5). Imagine God saying to you, "I can't go with you in your life, because you have disappointed me so badly, I would destroy you." I can't imagine having to go through my life completely alone with God nowhere to be found.

God was not being petty in saying this to Moses. God was being righteous. God could not bear to be with such a stubborn and disobedient people. This tells us not that God has limits, but that it is the nature of God to dwell in holiness, and God will not tolerate such blatant sin.

Thanks be to God for Jesus Christ, who has taken our sin and brought us into relationship with God. Will you choose to walk with God? How will you live today in God's presence?

O Holy God, help me find my way on
the journey with you. Amen.

## Friday, April 30

# Working It Out

### *Exodus 33:12-16*

**When have you tried to strike a deal with God?**

I think some people just like to argue. In today's Scripture, Moses banters with the God of the Universe to get God to go with the people to the Promised Land, with God's approval and presence! Even after it appears that God agreed to go with Moses and the people (v. 14), Moses wasn't quite done with the argument. He told God that only if God would go with them would they be seen to the world to have God's special approval (v. 16)!

It's a very interesting story, because it flies in the face of all the things we have been taught about prayer. Is Moses giving us a different example of how to get God to act the way we want? I think there are two very drastic differences happening in this story. First, Moses had a special relationship with God, and in that context, he had been given the liberty and access to speak to God nearly face-to-face. Moses used that access to try to change God's mind. The other difference is that it's not at all about Moses. Moses was interceding on behalf of Israel, hoping God would see that this other path would be better for all.

Let me suggest that we not try to act like Moses! Instead, let's tell God humbly and honestly what we hope for the future and then receive the gift of future as God brings it to pass. I think we are better off to leave the negotiations to Moses!

Hear my prayer, O Lord, and accept the
truth of my heart this day. Amen.

# MAY

## Contributor:

*Randy Cross*
*May 1–31*

## Saturday, May 1

# Catching a Glimpse

### *Exodus 33:17-23*

**What do you imagine God looks like?**

Moses made an odd request of God: "Please show me your glorious presence" (v. 18). Apparently, Moses wanted to see the holiness of the One he had been talking to. God agreed, but said Moses would die if he saw God's face. Instead, God told Moses, "As my glorious presence passes by, I'll set you in a gap in the rock, and I'll cover you with my hand until I've passed by" (v. 22).

It seems like that was enough and it worked for Moses, and it is more than we have ever experienced. I suppose the story goes to show how special Moses was, and how close—but not too close—he got to God. It, of course, also tells us about God, that God allowed Moses (and us) to get close, but not so close that it would become casual or something we take for granted. It tells me that through it all, God is still God and remains that way for Moses, and for us.

When we "see" God in the world, what we actually see is the product, the reflection, the almost managed glorious part of God as Creator. And that seems to be enough, most of the time. Still, we wait for that day when we shall see face-to-face and experience the eternal and wonderful presence of God with us.

What is the best "view" you have ever had of God? What is the most memorable moment of encountering God in your life?

Dear God, thank you for your presence, and
help me see you in all things. Amen.

## Sunday, May 2

# The Real Thing

### *Exodus 34:5-8*

**What words would you use to describe yourself?**

Context is important. During biblical times, as each subculture worshipped its own small gods and idols, the normal behavior of the gods was much like the Greek gods. They were petulant, greedy, egotistical, preferential, manipulative, and often held a grudge. In contrast, the children of Israel came to hear that the God who had chosen them is a God who is far different than the imagined gods of the surrounding peoples. God was not boasting at this point. God was self-revealing, as a matter of grace and hope for God's people. God is forgiving and just, will punish sin, but also be compassionate to those who suffer. It should have been powerfully good news to Israel as it is to us, as we strive to live out our days under God's care and guidance.

When we think about our faith and the important things we trust to be true, we find words like *grace*, *faith*, *hope*, and especially *love*. No, God does not want us living self-centered, do-what-we-want lives. God wants us to be holy, loving, honest, and pure in our own lives so that we might reflect who God is to this world.

What joy to know that God—our God—is truly an awesome God who cares for us, blesses us, and calls us to be blessings to this world.

Which quality of God have you experienced lately? What qualities of God do you hope to express to others today?

Wonderful God, I thank you that you are
my Lord and I am your child. Amen.

## Monday, May 3

# An Amazing Sight

### *Ezekiel 1:1-6, 22-28*

**How does God appear to you?**

With Ezekiel feeling as though he was looking at "the form of the LORD's glory" (v. 28), he could do nothing but fall on his face before it all. It was too much! It would be too much for any of us. It is an opening of our lives and souls to God's intention and unfettered presence.

The entire Book of Ezekiel was written to help Israel as it went through a terrible time in its history. Of course, that is when we would all hope for a vision to give us insight and courage! It is gift of God for those who are willing to be open to receiving it, as strange and unworldly as it appears. The final sentence of today's text holds such power in its simplicity. As Ezekiel fell on his face, he then "heard the sound of someone speaking" (v. 28). He heard the voice of God, directing him to call Israel to a new way of living and renewed faithfulness. After all of the incredible images and actions, which brought Ezekiel to his knees, it was the voice of God that changed everything.

So it should be with you and me. Beyond miraculous things we might see that amaze us and perhaps terrify us by their presence, it is when we hear the voice of God, speaking clearly and surely, that our lives might change and find a direction and purpose different than what we had before.

As you go to that place where you might listen to God's voice, what do you imagine God has to say to you today?

God beyond imagination, I pray that you would
speak your will to me today. Amen.

## Tuesday, May 4

# Don't Answer the Phone!

*Isaiah 6:1-13*

**Have you ever wished you hadn't answered a call?**

Normally when we read Isaiah 6, we focus on the prophet's response to God's questions, "Whom should I send, and who will go for us?" and Isaiah's response, "I'm here; send me" (v. 8). We sometimes overlook what God was sending Isaiah to do. He was to preach and prophesy to the people, but they would not be able to hear, see, or understand what he was saying and not know what God wanted them to do (vv. 9-10). Isaiah was to be God's voice, prophesying of ruin and desolation, of exile and complete loss, save for a stump that would be the seed for the future.

Can you imagine God commanding you to take that word to God's people today? I can't imagine any one of us being excited about telling our own community that they should ignore God and so bring the ruin of all they know.

I'm not saying that those words are what God is saying to you today. We live in a different time. But we do need to ask whether we are prepared to hear God's voice at all. Are we willing to open our eyes and our hearts to see beyond the normal to the holy? Or are we also dull and blind to what God is calling us to do and be? I believe it is only through the power of constant and quiet prayer that we might begin to see and hear and to witness God's work around us today. How might you form your life so that you can hear God's voice calling you to serve where God needs you right now?

Holy One, help me to say, "I'm here;
send me," and mean it. Amen.

## Wednesday, May 5

# A Difficult Road Ahead

### *1 Kings 19:1-8*

**When have you feared the future?**

Elijah was in trouble. Queen Jezebel sent a message threatening Elijah's life, and Elijah believed her! The Scripture says that he was "terrified" (v. 3). He ran for his life and went out into the desert, where he "longed for his own death" and prayed for God to take his life (v. 4). Elijah was in a horrible way and saw the future as a bleak and terrifying spectacle. But that's not how God allows things to remain! God sent a messenger to give the prophet food and water for the journey ahead, and Elijah then went on the long journey to Mount Horeb, where he would find God's answer to his fear (vv. 5-8).

Isn't that what we all want when we are faced with a huge desert of fear before us? God didn't say, "Oh, everything's all right. You're fine." No. Like Elijah, we may have a difficult road ahead before we are able to answer the fear, but God promises to sustain us for the journey, to give us rest, and to help us to finally arrive at God's mountain in our own lives, where we, too, can listen to what God has to say to us.

What are you struggling with? What brings you a sense of unease or even fear? What is the name of the "enemy" who seeks to do you harm? As followers of Jesus Christ, we are offered the confidence to move forward, even when those things loom at us and threaten to make us want to give up. The Christian life is a life of victory and hope and of trusting in God's grace and care, especially when it's rough.

O God, give me the strength for the
journey I must take. Amen.

## Thursday, May 6

# God's Faithful Reply

### *Romans 11:1-5*

**Have you felt like the "only one" in a struggle for faith?**

When Paul wrote to the Romans, he used part of the story of Elijah that we read yesterday and that we will consider the rest of the week. Elijah was feeling sorry for himself, as though he was the only Israelite left who was faithful. Elijah thought God had given up or rejected God's people. Not to tell the end of the story, but it becomes very clear that just because Elijah hadn't seen anyone stand in line with him against evil, it doesn't mean they weren't there. God had not thrown Israel away, with Elijah the only one. Elijah's faithfulness needed to imitate God's faithfulness, and Elijah needed to trust that God was in charge.

Sometimes it indeed does feel as though we are fighting a lonely fight for something we feel strongly about. Standing on principle or for what we believe to be the true and right path is always important. Sometimes, in going along to get along, we end up losing a vital part of our own lives and character.

The only way through all of that is to remain focused and connected to God's will and intention. When it is no longer what we alone believe to be true but what we discern God is showing us, then we can have the confidence to stand, even when it feels as though we are alone. When we stand with God, we stand with the right choice.

My God, lead me to make the decision
you desire in my life today. Amen.

## Friday, May 7

# The Quiet Sound

### *1 Kings 19:9-13*

**Where do you best hear the voice of God in your life?**

As Elijah huddled in a cave on Mount Horeb, he in succession experienced a strong wind, an earthquake, and a fire. All of those were loud, ear-shattering events, but the writer of Kings states that "the LORD wasn't in [them]" (v. 11). With all the deafening, crashing, and earth-splitting sounds, what was significant was the absence of God. And then . . . "there was a sound. Thin. Quiet" (v. 12). Some Scripture translations have interpreted it as "sheer silence." At that moment, in the silence, Elijah covered his face and went to meet God.

The question Elijah was asked was important: "Why are you here, Elijah?" (vv. 9, 13). Elijah explained about Israel's abandonment of the covenant, the destruction of holy things, the murder of prophets, and fear for his own life. After God heard Elijah's answer the first time, God invited Elijah to listen to God in the framework of a thin, quiet sound—not trumpets, cymbals, earthquakes, wind, or fire. No, instead it was in the simple quiet that God responded, a setting that seems to have no strength at all, no power, and yet it was perhaps the most powerful experience. God and God's power do not require a contest of strength or might. Instead, in the thin, quiet sound we can receive the word of God.

Perhaps the best way for us to listen for God's word in our lives is in the silence, the quiet, the thin places, as we cover our own faces and wait for God's word.

O God of power and silence, please speak
your word to me this day. Amen.

## Saturday, May 8

# Make It So

### *1 Kings 19:14-18*

**When in your life when you were given a direct order?**

After the Lord asked what Elijah was doing on the mountain and Elijah took a moment to offer some self-pity, it seems that God practically ignored what he said and directed Elijah to get to work. God seems to have said, "OK. Now it's time to reclaim my people!" No questions asked. God even named Jehu to replace Ahab, which meant a war was set to begin.

What is interesting in this story is how Elijah was transformed. We began with a scared, fleeing, hiding, self-pitying fellow, and with God's words we will not see that person again. He was instead replaced with a confident, powerful prophet. We have to marvel at how clear and compelling God's Word was to Elijah that made him respond with such compelling actions himself.

What does God sound like to you? How have you heard the Word of God for your life? Imagine what our lives and our faith would be like if we were to truly listen to God and then use all that we could muster to follow those instructions for our lives. Instead of finding excuses and reasons why right now is not a good time, or why we're not quite ready, willing, or able, imagine hearing God say, "Make it so," and then responding in obedience to indeed make it happen.

How willing are you to listen to God's Word to you and then expend your life living out that will in all its ways?

Give me the word today, dear God, and
direct my path, I pray. Amen.

## Sunday, May 9

# Goodbye, Mom and Dad

### *1 Kings 19:19-21*

**What is the most urgent command you have been given?**

Elisha's first comment and reaction upon receiving Elijah's coat is very typical: I'll follow you, just let me kiss Dad and Mom goodbye and let them know I'm going! That's reasonable, even respectful. So, it is hard to read of Elijah's reaction: "Go! I'm not holding you back!" (1 Kings 19:20). In other words, who's stopping you? Don't ask for my permission! This natural gesture of respect and love had no place in the urgency of Elijah's calling of Elisha.

It's sometimes hard to know the right thing to do, isn't it? I am more than willing to answer the call to a life of ministry or service. But does that mean I have to give up everything I know? Do I have to turn away my lifelong relationships, my family, my love? It seems odd that God, who created humans to be together and to create families, would then demand such a harsh and near brutal cutting off.

I believe the lesson for us is that nothing is more important than following Jesus. Nothing is more important than letting God use your life. In this case, Elisha did care for the people before he followed Elijah, but the call was still there, and the need to follow was still as strong as ever. God needs for us to do God's will now. How are you answering the call when the mantle is placed on you?

My God, give me the strength to follow you
when you call me in my life. Amen.

## Monday, May 10

# Magnify the Lord!

### *Psalm 99:1-9*

**How do you "magnify" the Lord?**

I have always loved magnifying glasses. I love to zoom in, focus on an object, and be able to see intricate detail. The idea of being able to view something at a different level than "normal" has always been a fascination. So, I found it odd in today's Scripture to hear the command of "Magnify the Lord" (vv. 99:5, 9). It sounds like the psalmist is asking us to make God bigger than God is! Or perhaps the writer is suggesting that we have trouble seeing God, so we should pull out our reading glasses or our magnifying glasses and look more closely, so that we don't miss God!

In the Bible, to "magnify" God means to exalt, to lift high, or to hold in deep respect. More powerful even than the word "praise," magnify means to approach God with worship at all times because of who God is apart from anything God does. But of course, God's actions only deepen our "magnifying." As we "magnify" God, we view God at a different level. We are able to see God more clearly and to understand the incredible deeds God performs. We should exalt God above all else because God "loves justice" (v. 4), forgives, blesses, loves, and brings hope and life.

What difference does "magnifying" God make? It reminds us of our own place in the world, and of our own reliance on the God who loves us. How do you see God today in your life? In what ways can you magnify that understanding?

God who rules, help me to magnify and
worship you each day. Amen.

## Tuesday, May 11

# What Do You Have to Lose?

### *Luke 9:18-27*

**What does "following Jesus" mean to you?**

After Jesus had prayed and asked the disciples about who they thought he really was, he laid out a difficult and challenging future. If you want to follow me, he might say to us today, it's far more than being a nice person, going to church, or saying that you love others. The path to following Jesus means that you must take up the most difficult part of living every day, and frankly it means you must lose your life, die to the idea of earning this world and its benefits. That's hard, Jesus! Shouldn't I be saving for my retirement? And can't I just enjoy my life when it's going well since I know at some point I will have to deal with the hard parts of it? Is my entire life meant to be only a matter of giving my life away?

Difficult questions, aren't they? They tear a bit at our life of ease and comfort, of doing some nice things and being kind to people. Jesus was speaking to his disciples who had already professed a loyalty to Christ, and he asked them and asks us to completely change and even deny ourselves.

Today's Scripture, unfortunately, doesn't give us clean and simple answers to Jesus' challenge. Instead, we are given that challenge to conform to Christ and to follow not only when it is convenient and we know the path, but also when it means carrying a cross, bearing a burden as we follow, not in order to gain eternal life, but because that is what Jesus asks of his disciples.

Jesus, your path is difficult! Grant me the
grace to follow you today. Amen.

## Wednesday, May 12

# What Did I See?

### *Luke 9:28-36*

**When have you seen Jesus most clearly in your life?**

It's important for us to realize that Jesus didn't change or become something *other* than who he was and is. Instead, the disciples with Jesus that day saw him as he truly was and is: the Son of God. It was a mysterious and beyond-our-imagination event. Jesus appeared unfettered and in all his glory and the disciples had the opportunity to realize even more fully his identity. Jesus was far more than a rabbi, or teacher, or even a prophet or healer. In this account, we find Jesus described in a way that should do more than catch our attention. It should fill us with awe and make us nearly speechless as we encounter the Son of God, glorified.

In the normal days of our lives, it is perhaps easy to shrink our image of Jesus down to human size, as we think that our faith is only a matter of following Jesus' teachings or learning how to be loving and caring people. Of course, the Christian faith is much, much more. We are invited to place the trust of our very lives in the hands of the Son of God who lived on earth and now reigns with God! We are called to live a big faith that can't be carefully managed and must sometimes only be experienced as something we can't fully explain. It is then that we begin to understand a bit more of our relationship with God and who God is. In that understanding, we are invited to follow Jesus in a much more profound way.

What image of Jesus will you follow in your life of faith?

Glorious God, bring me to awe as I find
myself before you today. Amen.

## Thursday, May 13

# A Fuller Explanation

### *Matthew 17:9-13*

**What makes you sure that Jesus is the Messiah?**

As Jesus and his disciples were coming down the mountain after the Transfiguration, he told them, "Don't tell anybody . . . until the Human One is raised from the dead" (v. 9). Apparently, it wasn't the right time for the world to know. Jesus' words are often somewhat shrouded. He didn't say "this is the truth," but instead gave hints as to the truth. That's a hard part about some of Jesus' sayings.

We have the benefit of reading Scripture in our time instead of trying to figure out a mystery of Jesus' time. Still, many persons refuse or simply cannot accept Jesus' Messiahship. What is critical not only for our faith but for our role in the Christian faith is that we not be shy or hesitant about sharing what we know of who Jesus is. Do you believe Jesus is the Son of God, the Messiah? Are you willing to announce that to those you know? Have you taken on the task of how to share a full explanation of who Jesus is and what he means to our world? As a follower of Jesus, that information is critical to have in our hearts and in our heads as we share the good news!

Part of following Jesus is giving up our own preference about how we will live our lives and instead take on the cross. Another part, however, is that we combine our feelings and our belief with a willingness to share the truth of Jesus with our world.

Dear God, let me tell the story today
of Jesus and his love. Amen.

## Friday, May 14

# The One Who Came Before

### *Luke 1:12-17*

**How do you think it would feel to be John the Baptist?**

John's life mission was to bring God's people back to God and prepare them to meet the Christ. An important distinction must be made between John and Jesus: Jesus was the Messiah, and would be responsible for bringing salvation to the world through God's grace and his sacrifice. John would also experience sacrifice, but not for salvation's sake. His death was the result of his preaching that called to Israel to return to God, repent, and live a new life and proclaimed the coming of the Messiah.

There is no record of John growing tired or disgruntled or even questioning what God had called him to do. He may have felt this way, but our Gospel account records nothing of that. Instead, we find a strong, passionate preacher who called people to prepare for the Messiah, who was at hand.

Wouldn't it be nice if we had that consistent and strong faith and call to ministry? In my lifelong ministry, I have grown weary, disappointed, or have wished for another path. Most all of us do. I think what God calls each of us to do is simply what God called John to do, to be a voice calling this world to faith. Be a word of hope sounding a different way of living, using the strength we have and the strength that God gives us for that task. Our job is to be faithful and give our love and our energy toward turning the face of the world to the face of God through our words, actions, and hearts.

God, call me today and prepare me to do what
I can to bring this world to Christ. Amen.

## Saturday, May 15

# Hide It Under a Bushel?

### *Exodus 34:29-35*

**When have you felt the need to hide your faith?**

Today's Scripture records what happened after Moses came down from Mount Sinai having received the Ten Commandments. His face "shone brightly because he had been talking with God" (v. 29). When Aaron and the other leaders and the rest of the Israelites saw Moses' face, "they were afraid to come near him" (v. 30). So, after Moses shared God's Word with them, he covered his face with a veil. Moses was changed by his encounter with God. He shone brightly in a way that was inexplicable. He represented the powerful Word of God. It was too much for the people, so it was contained with a veil and only seen from time to time.

What about us? What's the reason for us "putting on a veil" as it were when we meet the world? Is it true that we also hide that light, hide that experience of God from the world that needs to see it more clearly? Or perhaps that light is something that scares us too. Is it too great of a reminder of God's claim on us that we want others also to hide that light under a bushel? Imagine what might happen if we would be bold and open about our faith and about God's place in our lives and share that with others, without a veil?

Who do you know today who needs to see God's love shining through you, unfettered, so that their lives might be touched and changed and they might receive the good news of salvation?

God of glory, fill my life today with the power
and grace of your presence. Amen.

## Sunday, May 16

# From Glory to Glory

*2 Corinthians 3:12–4:2*

**How have you been transformed through Christ?**

I love today's Scripture, where Paul rejoices that we have hope and great confidence and that we are looking at the glory of God, like we are looking in a mirror! What a joyful image! He said that we are being transformed into the same image of God's glory, "from one degree of glory to the next degree of glory" (v. 18).

On this Sabbath day, it is our invitation to claim the same relationship and the same experience that Paul named in this Scripture. We who follow Jesus Christ have the right and the access to look unveiled at the glory of God. What a magnificent thing to ponder, don't you think? We are invited to be transformed in our lives and then to share God's word with the world around us, having received this opportunity for ministry (4:1) the same way we have received God's mercy for our lives.

What a great day for us, to know of our place with God and our call by God to offer the good news and unbounded love of Christ to a hurting world or to one person who needs to know that he or she is a cherished and beloved child of God too.

Can you accept and live with the glorious love of God for you today? Who in your family or among your relationships needs to know their veil can be removed and they can receive the glory of God for their own lives?

Thank you, God, for all your love, and for the
blessings of sharing your glory with others. Amen.

## Monday, May 17

# God's Strong Hand

### *Psalm 48:1-14*

**Where and with whom do you feel safe?**

This psalm praises God's strength and care and the righteousness and justice God brings to the land and to the people as they are protected at all turns from those who would attack or beset the place God has created, including the Temple. To be in Zion is to be held on the lap of God, as it were—a place of peace and safety. I don't know anyone who lives in the safety of Jerusalem/Zion itself, although it's a large city. Instead, we spend our lives finding those safe places ourselves, where we believe God has encircled us and protects us. I know that our home is a place of blessing for many reasons, and when we "dwell" there, it is well. You certainly can identify those places in your own life where you may have experienced the presence of God in the same way the psalmist did and are able to declare praise to God for how you, too, are protected and well cared for.

This is a critical part of our faith as Christians. Who and where do we trust? How can we place our very lives in the care of God and know that it won't be in vain? What do we claim as a promise from God in terms of how we can live our lives? No matter what comes to pass that seeks to tear down the walls of our sanctuary, we know that we are held on the lap of God and there, we are safe.

In what ways can you affirm God's saving grace for your own life? How has God protected you?

O God, I stay within your protecting arms.
Grant me abundant life. Amen.

## Tuesday, May 18

# God Is Not Us!

### *Ezekiel 10:1-5*

**How might you act when faced with the image of God?**

I have never preached from Ezekiel 10. It is indeed a wild, truly inexplicable vision, as is much of the Book of Ezekiel itself. When we are able to set aside the sense of confusion and can stop shaking our heads, what we are faced with is the vision of what it means to stand in the presence of God. No, we don't understand it. This is not meant for us. All these things are beyond our ability to calculate or explain. Instead, we are invited in these words to stand in awe of something that is so other-than-human-limitations and to believe that even this vision is possible because God wills it to be so.

When I read such an account, instead of trying to figure it out, I like to go to a different part of my brain that doesn't have to analyze and make sense out of things. Instead, I like to read these words and just say, "Wow." God truly is not One who can be contained or tamed or made to be our servant. To read these words should change our prayers from "Give me what I want, O God," to "Have mercy on me, O God."

I think that's what it means to approach the throne of God. Our prayer is not intended to be a coffee break with the Lord of the Universe. Our prayer is having the awareness that God is powerful enough to know the deepest part of who we are, even more than we know ourselves. Our prayer is to come to understand that we are God's children, a sacred and holy relationship, but we sure aren't in charge!

What should be the substance of your prayer today?

God above all, may all praise you this day! Amen.

## Wednesday, May 19

# God's Harvest

### *Revelation 14:14-20*

**How do you figure into God's harvest of this earth?**

Harvest should be a joyful, happy time with a field ready for a bountiful crop. In today's Scripture from Revelation, we hear of two different harvests, both fairly baffling. The "Human One" who sits on the cloud is invited to reap the harvest of the earth and does so with a sickle (vv. 14-16). This is followed by another harvest of the "vineyard of the earth," putting the grapes into "the great winepress of God's passionate anger," and blood pours out (vv. 18-20).

It's messy devotional reading, I must say. Revelation was first written to give hope to those who were being persecuted, so we have the vision of some being gathered in by Jesus' hand and others crushed beneath God's anger. Where do we fit in all of this? Well, certainly, I've always felt that I am with the "wheat." After all, I've been a nice guy, good family man. I'm even a pastor, for crying out loud! Yet the harvest to eternal life or the harvest to destruction are never based on our actions or even our pedigree, are they?

It seems that today's Scripture asks us repeatedly, "Who will you be?" How will we live our lives so that God knows us and claims us as God's children? It's a good caution for us, since our story is not yet complete. How we live today in God's covenant through Jesus makes all the difference in the world.

What will you do today to show your faith in Jesus Christ?

Prepare me for the harvest, dear God,
as I seek to serve you. Amen.

## Thursday, May 20

# The Nightmare Vision

### *Daniel 7:1-8*

**How do you handle disturbing visions in your life?**

Daniel had a vision. This vision is perhaps the strangest one we could read. We will spend the next four days dealing with Daniel 7, so I don't want to jump to the end, but the vision that came to Daniel certainly is compelling and demands attention. At this point in the chapter, Daniel simply reported what he dreamed. He had no real understanding of what it was all about or what those terrifying beasts were presenting to him.

Have you ever been caught up in a disease of your spirit as profoundly as Daniel was? Whether you are awake or asleep, a sense of calm and serenity is hidden from you, and you are only left with an edgy, uncomfortable perspective about the world, or at least about your own life. Again, we will learn more about the dream over the next couple of days, but for now, perhaps the most important thing is to discover or reclaim an understanding of what we can do when we have those types of feelings, those images invading our lives.

I believe that when we are feeling set upon, it's critical to speak to our own hearts and to remind ourselves that the last words have not yet been spoken, and that God is ultimately in charge of our lives. Can we truly trust in the Lord and lean not on our own understanding? Can we reaffirm that our lives are blessed, no matter what the circumstances may be right now, and that God is with us, and we are not alone?

God, I know you care for me. Help me each day
to know your blessed assurance. Amen.

## Friday, May 21

# The Story Changes

### *Daniel 7:9-14*

**What do you hope for in your life?**

In today's portion of Daniel 7, the horrible images of yesterday's Scripture are resolved by the intercession of powerful good that destroys the beasts and brings the everlasting rule of glory and indestructible kingship. I wish all of my own dreams ended in such a nice and powerfully strong way. Even though this is an Old Testament text, many Christians throughout the ages have claimed this part of the vision as the coming of Christ as the Messiah and Savior.

What today's reading provides for us is the image and word of hope. Granted, we are all going to encounter horrible "beasts" in our lives. We are going to experience scary and threatening events and situations. We all face the possibility of having everything we know and cherish being broken or stolen or devoured. Today's Scripture leaves us with far more thrilling and eternally more powerful things to keep in mind. Notice that there is no battle in the Scripture between good and evil, or the chance that good might lose. No! As soon as good comes on the scene, evil is destroyed, overcome, or brought to an end. God always wins!

When our lives get full of threatening beasts, we are called to be patient, to trust in the future and not despair, and to know that there is indeed no contest when it comes to God's love and God's powerful presence. It requires us to trust, even when it appears all we see are threats around us.

O God, I await your powerful love in my life this day. Amen.

## Saturday, May 22

# Understanding the Vision

### *Daniel 7:15-22*

**How might this section of Daniel help you in your life?**

Some scholars refer to the four beasts/kingdoms in this passage as Babylon, Midian, Persia, and Greece, but others have different interpretations. The kingdoms are all threatening and attempting to conquer Israel. We know from history that this was a reality for Israel. So maybe that's what the vision means. Or perhaps there is another interpretation. The writer of Daniel isn't around to confirm or deny it, so we can't be sure whether this is prophecy that looks to the future, was meant to speak a word to Daniel's time, or is something else.

One way to look at the interpretation of the images is to consider that the Scripture proclaims that any time of persecution or enslavement will eventually come to an end, with the hoped-for result of good conquering evil. Indeed, one of the important tasks we each have as we study Scripture is to find the truth, however that truth is explained. That is, was Greece the fourth beast? Or is it that whenever a beast like that arises, eventually it will be destroyed and good return and rule in its place? That's a truth we want to hang on to, even if we have a lack of facts to pin it on.

As you read and reread today's words from the Bible, take time to ask the question, "Where is the truth that I can claim for my own faith from God's Word?" What difference might it make for you to approach Bible study this way?

Loving God, open my eyes and heart to see
and know your truth for me. Amen.

## Sunday, May 23

# The Final Explanation

### *Daniel 7:23-28*

**What would you claim as a final word of Daniel's vision?**

One scholar camp says that the Book of Daniel must have been written between 604-532 BC, during the Babylonian exile. Another camp says it was written to help Israel as it went through a horrible time of persecution nearly 400 years later, in 164 BC. One is a historical account, and the other is a story using the imagery of the time Israel spent in Babylon. But which one is right? I guess that is left to the reader. However, please remember the idea of looking for truth instead of uncovering disputable facts in the Scripture. What is the "truth" that we find in this passage?

Even though the writer of Daniel admitted that his own thoughts were disturbed, it still remains that God is in charge, will destroy that which is evil, and will place in the care of all of the kingdoms on earth the One who deserves the everlasting rule. I think that truth is what I need to hold on to. Granted, there will most certainly be evil in this world, and some of us have received a huge portion of that evil upon us, with tragedy and wickedness abounding. Still, the last word? God rules. Evil will not go unchallenged forever, and indeed, its time will soon be over, and God's grace and rule will reign.

In our personal times of pain and struggle, we need to claim this truth for us as well. Can you recall a time when knowing God was in charge was enough to get you through the current struggle?

Dear God, if my life makes no sense today, please give me the love and grace to make it through. Amen.

## MONDAY, MAY 24

# God to the Rescue

### *Psalm 107:17-22*

**When have you been redeemed by God's love?**

Redeem is a powerful word. It means "to buy back," or "to pay the ransom for." Redeem is also a holy word. It's God's work, in which God "buys back" the lives of those like us who have taken a sinful path, so that those who have acted wickedly (a word that means living apart from God) may be brought home. Psalm 107 includes numerous examples of those who have been redeemed. Verses 17-22, today's reading, includes fools who finally cried out to God to save them after living a way of life that brought them close to death. God indeed does save them, the psalm proclaims.

Perhaps we do not fall into the category of "fools," and maybe we are not "wicked," but we are all sinners in need of God's saving love! Each of us at times needs to be brought home to God as we cry in distress because of the mess we have made in trying to go it alone. The good news of today's Scripture is that God indeed is love and will reach out and redeem us. Our work, of course, after that is done, is to offer our thanksgiving and declare God's wonderful work in joy!

Imagine how God might redeem you today. What blotch exists in your life that came because you thought you knew best, better than God, on how to live, or because you just decided you would go it alone? Certainly a primary characteristic of a life of faith is humility, as we without pride call out to God to bring us home.

Hear my prayer, O God, and in your love
redeem my life this day. Amen.

## Tuesday, May 25

# Looking for the Sheep

### *Matthew 18:10-14*

**What effort do you make to find something you have lost?**

Losing, searching, and finding are all part of our human existence. That's probably why Jesus used the parable of a lost sheep to talk about God's children. Sheep are not very intelligent and tend to wander off. The work of the shepherd is to bring wandering sheep back to the fold. We probably have seen all sorts of pictures of the smiling shepherd with the sheep over his shoulders, but the sad fact is, more often than not, the shepherd would find a dead sheep, either killed by predators or from a fall. What a happy situation, though, when the shepherd found the sheep safe and uninjured. It brought a true sense of relief, with everything back to how it should be. Until of course, another sheep wandered off.

Do you see how much work we are for God? Do you see and understand the incredible, careful, and diligent love that God pours out on us when we wander off or forget where we should be? God does not want to lose the one who is least able to care for herself or himself . . . that is, you and me.

As we rely on God for our lives, not living proudly but humbly, we have the assurance that God will take special care of us. Can you accept for yourself the image of being a cherished child of God who needs God's care and careful watch over you in every aspect of your life? What is your role in this world in ensuring that others are protected and receive loving care?

Dear God, please find me and bring me safely
home when I wander away from you. Amen.

## Wednesday, May 26

# Live in Peace

### *2 Corinthians 13:11-13*

**What would you say is the best way to live?**

We are given three short closing verses of Scripture from 2 Corinthians today. They are Paul's farewell. He listed what we would assume to be typical last words of direction; yet as we look more closely, we can indeed find some powerful words of advice for living the good life.

"Put things in order" (v. 11). I read that to mean that Paul wanted the Christians in Corinth to get ready for Jesus' coming, which they believed was right around the corner. Paul also wanted them to do three other important things: "respond to my encouragement, be in harmony with each other, and live in peace" (v. 11). These are all positive, normal things we would wish to do, but in the context of believing that Jesus could come tomorrow, they become urgent patterns of behavior: don't be discouraged, don't bicker with each other, and don't wage a battle to see who will win.

The reason Paul brought these things forward for the Corinthians to claim as their way of living was because he knew that when and if they lived this way, the result will be evident: "the God of love and peace will be with you" (v. 11). That is, as you make room in your life for cherishing each other and allowing love, peace, and harmony to be your intentions, then you will know the very presence of God with you. What do you pray for God to bring as you seek to live this way today?

Come, Lord Jesus. Be my guest. Let me trust in you. Amen.

## Thursday, May 27

# Nothing New

### *2 John 4-6*

**How does God want you to live as part of the church?**

In the short letter that we call 2 John, the elder wrote words of encouragement and reminder to the congregation. "I am requesting that we love each other" (v. 5). Wouldn't that be nice to hear each Sunday as you went to church? When we love each other in all the various wonderful and difficult ways, then we find ourselves following Jesus' commands.

How sad it is that we often choose other paths, even as we work and live together as the followers of Christ. We seek to win, or to lord our power over others, or to ignore the needs of others and instead put ourselves first. May God forgive us when we act that way and give us the strength, insight, and humility to turn and choose love for what we do!

It becomes a unique way of life. We probably all know those who understand that truth and have made the choice to fill their lives with that important act of love. They see and understand that giving their own lives away for the sake of others, as Jesus did for us all, is the finest and purest expression of love we can offer. It becomes the intentional work of living as a Christian.

How might you offer your love to this hurting world today? How will you fulfill God's command in your life?

God of Love, teach me to love with all
I am, for my whole life. Amen.

## Friday, May 28

# Connected by Love

### *1 John 4:7-10*

**How can you know God?**

First John is a letter to encourage believers to hold together in a time of persecution and struggle. The way that John offers for us to hold together? Love. Love as John described it is a determined activity, a perspective of life, and the first choice for any actions we might take. Only when we live with this approach are we able to love in a way revealed to us and respond to God's first love for us that brought us life.

What's interesting in all of this is that our worship of God, our connection with God, in a real way comes to life as we love each other! When we love one another, we know God. When we love one another, we know God's love of us. When we love one another, John says, we are "born from God" (v. 7). The critically necessary part of our entire spiritual and physical life comes as we place love at the core. Only then can we have our eyes opened to what God has done, is doing, and what we are called, invited, and encouraged to do with each thought, word, and action that fills our lives.

We have to wonder why even good Christian folk would at times choose another way of living other than love. When a family, a congregation, or even a denomination finds itself at odds, it happens when we forget or decide that we will just set aside this core command to live only this way. It's then we need to ask forgiveness in love from all we have affected and from God and turn back to what we know we need to do!

Dear God, help me to know you, and help me to love. Amen.

## Saturday, May 29

# No Fear in Love

### *1 John 4:11-21*

**What does it mean to be made perfect in love?**

What does *perfect* even mean? Sinking a 12-foot popcorn kernel in a bottle of pop? The word itself really is translated to mean "to be completely finished." When something is perfect, there is no further work to be done. It has reached the top, and nothing can improve it.

In today's Scripture reading, John offers up the idea of perfection. Notice, however, the way he approaches it: "This is how love has been perfected in us" (v. 17). John considered the real possibility of perfect love but understood that it happens when God acts upon us, not when we do perfect things on our own. As God remains with us in love, that very love of and from God is perfected in our lives. We aren't perfect, but God's perfect love is.

He went on to talk about the opposite of love: fear. When perfect love exists, then fear vanishes. "There is no fear in love, but perfect love drives out fear," John said (v. 18). Those who are afraid have not yet understood perfect love. When love is made perfect, however, those impediments to acting toward our world in the way God would act disappear, and we freely and purely can offer our love. That's the way we can test love's perfect influence on us—when we indeed can love with no hesitation, no condemnation, and no resistance that comes from fear. What steps can you take that will open your life to having God perfect love in you?

God of perfect love, grow that love in
me this day, I pray. Amen.

## Sunday, May 30

# Blessed Assurance

### *1 John 5:6-12*

**How do you know who Jesus is?**

Today's Scripture is John's work at making a testimony about Jesus. He said that three things are witnesses to Jesus as God's Son when our faith is involved and open to seeing it: The water of baptism claims Jesus as God's beloved son; the blood of crucifixion claims Jesus as the only sacrifice that could redeem us from our sin; and the Spirit with us today is assurance for our hearts that we have new eternal life, both on this earth and throughout the future (vv. 6-8).

Can this be denied? Well, it can be rejected by someone who chooses not to believe. However, we Christians are in the business of believing. We are invited to participate in the work of hearing and trusting the testimony that God has brought us to new life, and that life rests in Jesus. It is the cornerstone of who we are and our identity in this world.

So, how do we hold this to be the truth? I believe it is true if it changes who I am. I'm not talking about just a little alteration of my behavior, but instead something that transforms my life from fear, worry, and uncertainty about the past, present, or future to a life of confidence and openness. It transforms me into someone who offers love as the first action and not only a response. The truth of Jesus Christ doesn't have to be proven. It is for us to accept and embrace and celebrate with changed hearts and lives.

O God, thank you for the gift of Jesus.
Let me share that gift today. Amen.

## Monday, May 31

# Joseph Forgives His Brothers

### *Genesis 50:15-21*

**What is the biggest act of forgiveness you have made?**

Joseph was the 11th son out of 12 in Jacob's line. Easily Jacob's favorite, Joseph would share his dreams of how his brothers were subservient to him, and he received a beautiful coat from Dad, which made the brothers hate him. His brothers got revenge by selling him into slavery. It all concluded with the family reuniting in Egypt where Joseph was a leader, and today's Scripture brings us to the point where Jacob had died, and the brothers were certain that Joseph would finally get his revenge for their terrible acts.

However, Joseph didn't destroy his brothers. Instead, he forgave them and offered his love. However, Joseph's forgiveness came after the pleas from the brothers, weeping for what they had done and promising to become Joseph's slaves. At that point, Joseph wiped the slate clean, and for the rest of their lives, they lived in peace and love.

Unfortunately, today most experiences of profound forgiveness are few and far between. Sadly, many of us hold tightly to victim status for what are sometimes the smallest of offenses against us, as though we are somehow more noble for having been hurt by others. But incredible power comes when we can forgive someone, even for a monstrous sin against us. Forgiveness allows us to reclaim love as the guiding force in our lives. Who do you know today who needs to receive the gift of forgiveness from you?

O God of love, give me the chance to forgive with that same love today; in Jesus' name. Amen.

# JUNE

## Contributors:

*Sue Mink*
*June 1–27*

*Stan Purdum*
*June 28–30*

## Tuesday, June 1

# Joseph Dreams of Power

### *Genesis 37:1-11*

**How do people respond to those who seem to get blessings they don't deserve?**

Joseph dreamed two dreams. The first dream foreshadowed Egypt's famine and how he would be put in charge of the food that would save the people, including his family. The second was a vision of his importance in the heavenly realms. He told these dreams to his brothers and his parents. He must have been boastful; even his father reprimanded him for speaking this way. Needless to say, it didn't help his relationship with his brothers at all.

Joseph already threatened his brothers' positions as heirs and beloved sons, but these dreams gave voice to the threats. If the dreams were to be believed, then God would disrupt the entire status quo. Like his father Jacob before him, who stole the blessing from his elder brother Esau, Joseph, the son who society and tradition had relegated to a back burner, was the one God chose.

But that's what God does. God chooses those who seem the least likely and whom society says are the "extras." Younger sons, barren women, and the poor are all heroes in the Scriptures, carrying the hope and promise of a new future. The older brothers, those who thought they were first in line for the blessings, were passed over. Joseph, the dreamer of dreams, was a threat to the order of the world, but would ultimately save many from starvation.

Lord, help me to recognize you working
through unlikely people. Amen.

## Wednesday, June 2

# Plotting to Kill the Dream

### *Genesis 37:12-22*

**What dreams for good are threatened by the status quo?**

Dreams are an important theme throughout Joseph's story, three times telling the future and changing the course of Joseph's life. But when God sent dreams, they could clash with the dreams of others. The brothers wanted what they could expect as the older sons. Joseph told them of a future in which God would choose him as a ruler. The brothers' solution was to kill the dreamer and thus kill the dream.

Throughout the Scriptures and history, people tried to kill the dream by killing the dreamer. The prophets dreamed of righteousness and obedience to God from Israel, yet their lives were in constant danger. Jesus taught about the dream of the kingdom of heaven coming to earth; he was crucified by those in power. In modern history, Martin Luther King, Jr., repeated Scripture's dreams about a just and equitable society where character mattered over race or ethnicity, and he was killed for his vision. God's dreams can be challenging, and following those dreams often means risking rejection and danger from those in power.

Joseph's brothers didn't kill the dream. Throughout Joseph's story, God's way continued to move forward. God's vision for the salvation of humanity always finds a way through our mistakes, errors, and sin. That is the great hope of humanity. We can't destroy God's plan. The empty grave of Jesus Christ is the most profound proof of God's refusal to let the dream killers destroy God's plan of salvation.

Lord, give me the courage to join in your dreams. Amen.

## Thursday, June 3

# Joseph's Brothers Sell Him into Slavery

### *Genesis 37:23-30*

**Is God's will ever thwarted by human action?**

Imagine what it must have been like for Joseph, sitting in the bottom of a dry well, listening to his brothers. He had been stripped of his beautiful coat, the one his father had given him to show his favor. To Jacob, Joseph was more than a favored son. He was the embodiment of a promise from God.

Of course, Joseph would live to fulfill his dreams, but it must have been difficult for him to continue to believe in it as he sat in that well. No doubt he was thinking about what God had meant by those dreams if God had allowed his brothers to capture him. Were his dreams still believable? Would God let them come to pass?

God's plans rarely have easy paths from beginning to end. That's because God works with and depends on capricious human beings to follow the divine word and will. Disobedience may change God's pathway and delay the plans, but it's only the ways to completion that change, not the plans themselves. God's ultimate will and desire is for relationship with all humanity. Joseph was the son of promise, so God would find a way for him to survive and prosper, despite human interference. In the same way, we can live with assurance that God clears the way to our salvation. It's God's desire and will, and even capricious, disobedient human beings can't stop the plans of God.

Lord, praise be to you because I know that no
one can stop your plan for salvation. Amen.

## Friday, June 4

# Crying Out in Faith

### *Psalm 31:9-13*

**Is it okay to be angry or plead with God?**

Psalm 31 alternates between cries of anguish and shouts of praise and gratitude for deliverance. Underlying the entire psalm is a bedrock trust in God and God's steadfast love. God's guidance, even through miserable circumstances, is our salvation if we put our life into God's hands.

The psalmist described especially deep suffering in verses 9-13. There was nothing left and no one to turn to except for God. The psalmist was stricken with grief, weak and stumbling and scorned by others. He or she felt as worthless as a broken piece of pottery. Yet verses 14-15 sing of trust in the Lord. The future rests in God's hands, and the psalmist praises God's goodness. Even cries of distress, sorrow, and uncertainty are cries of faith when directed toward God.

Crying out in pain and sorrow to God means that the relationship we have with God can handle real life. The relationship matters and can deal with honest feelings. The first step in healing pain in our hearts is to know that someone is listening and cares. How wonderful to know that we can go to God with our sorrow, our pain, and even our anger, be heard, and be gathered up in God's arms of love.

O Lord, thank you for listening to my pain,
my sorrow, and even my anger. Amen.

## Saturday, June 5

# Jacob Grieves for Joseph

### *Genesis 37:31-38*

**Why was the loss of Joseph so devastating to Jacob?**

The brothers didn't even have to lie. Jacob immediately assumed that Joseph had been killed by wild animals and went into deep mourning. No other son or daughter could comfort him, and he vowed to mourn Joseph for the rest of his life.

Of course Jacob loved his son, but I suspect his deep mourning was also for the covenant he believed was lost. Perhaps more than any other person in the Book of Genesis, Jacob understood the importance of God's blessing and wanted it for himself and his family. Now he believed the boy he had seen as the carrier of the covenant to the next generation was dead. It was a tragedy that went far beyond the death of a beloved son.

The brothers didn't get what they wanted, either. They had gotten rid of Joseph so that they could be favored in their father's eyes. But Jacob would not be consoled. Instead of gaining Jacob's love, their deceit made him into a broken man. Their hatred poisoned the relationship they had with their father and brought them all into deep despair.

But in the midst of this heartache and tragedy, God was working. Joseph was sold to Potiphar, and God would use this tragic situation to bring about salvation. Despite the sins of human beings, God's plan for salvation would not be stopped.

Lord, thank you that, even in the midst of devastating grief,
you do not abandon the dream of our salvation. Amen.

## Sunday, June 6

# Moses' Blessing for Joseph

### *Deuteronomy 33:13-17*

**What is the purpose of a blessing?**

When the events in this passage took place, Moses had been with the Hebrew people for forty years in the wilderness. He brought them to the edge of the Promised Land, but he wasn't able to continue on into the land with them. Before they entered, he gave each of the twelve tribes of Israel his blessing. There was no tribe of Joseph because his two sons, Ephraim and Manasseh, each had a tribe. But Moses' blessing specifically named Joseph too.

Moses' blessings were a prayer to the Lord asking for all that they needed to succeed in the new land. They were totally dependent on God as they entered a strange land to claim it. Moses' blessings reminded the people of the power of God for their protection and the wisdom of God's commandments for their community's well-being. Their strength was both outward-facing to their enemies and inward-facing to their unity and commitment to the Lord.

The blessings told the people of both their strengths and their weaknesses. They also reminded the people of their dependency on God. God's blessings can inform how we pray for others by asking God to give them resources, strength, and enlightenment. Prayer for others can also ask for them to trust and depend on God, their only true source of strength. Offering blessings is a great gift we can give others as they face the challenges of their lives.

Lord, teach me to be an effective blessing-giver for those in your care. Amen.

## Monday, June 7

# Rooted in the Way of the Righteous

### *Psalm 1:1-6*

**Why is it important to cultivate deep roots in God's word?**

Psalm 1 compares righteous people to a tree that is planted by streams of water. While the tree in the psalm is fruitful, that's really a by-product of its deep roots that gather nourishment for the tree. Those deep roots keep the tree healthy, green, and productive. The psalm says that righteous people are like a tree with deep roots, watered by the Word of God and by their openness to God's instruction.

The wicked, or those who arrogantly reject the teachings of God, have no roots at all. Verse 4 compares them to dust, or in the NIV or NRSVue, to "chaff." Chaff is the worthless light outer coating of grain that is removed before the grain can be eaten. Completely opposite to a well-rooted tree, it can easily be blown away by the lightest breeze.

The roots of righteousness sustain God's followers through any circumstance. The way of the righteous connects us with the very source of life itself, grounding us and keeping us strong. This psalm doesn't promise wealth and ease for those who follow the Lord, but it does promise stability and a source of power. By staying intimately connected to the Lord and living a life centered in God, those who are righteous have a source of unshakable strength. Like tree roots that are hidden, the prosperity given by God may not be apparent to the world, but it will sustain all who have cultivated them.

Lord, strengthen my roots in you, because
you are my source of stability. Amen.

## Tuesday, June 8

# Joseph as a Godly Businessperson

### *Genesis 39:1-6a*

**How can obeying the tenets of God affect one's business?**

Joseph succeeded in everything he did while he ran Potiphar's household. He was sold to Potiphar at a young age and very quickly made a good impression. Joseph was a savvy businessman and a godly man besides. Actually, Joseph was successful because he was godly. The Scripture says that God was with Joseph, but Joseph also was with God. Joseph was obedient to God, and God helped him to prosper. God's care for Joseph enabled him to become so trusted that Potiphar handed all his decisions over to Joseph. The only choices Potiphar made while Joseph was in his employ was what he should have to eat.

God works through all aspects of our lives. A godly person is godly all the time and follows God's precepts in both personal and professional arenas. Potiphar recognized that his household was blessed by God through Joseph, even though Potiphar was not a worshipper of the Lord. Joseph's everyday actions as an ethical and godly person made his business practices honest and ethical too. They were a witness to his devotion to God and not only blessed Joseph but Potiphar as well.

Lord, may my faithfulness to you extend
through all areas of my life. Amen.

## Wednesday, June 9

# Potiphar's Wife Betrays Joseph

### *Genesis 39:6b-20a*

**How does one person's sin impact others?**

In this passage, Joseph suffered for the sin of another for the second time in his story. First his brothers betrayed him, and in this passage, Potiphar's wife struck out viciously and falsely accused him of attempted rape when he turned down her sexual advances. She used his cloak to "prove" his guilt, just as his brothers had used the beautiful coat his father had given him to "prove" that he had been killed by wild beasts. Within moments, Joseph went from his well-earned spot in Potiphar's home to a jail cell.

Because we live in a world where human beings can choose sin, like Joseph we all are vulnerable. The entire world suffers when people sin because the effects of sin can be far-reaching, rippling out to touch multitudes. Pollution, greed, poverty, callousness, and racism are just a few examples. But God continues to remain with God's beloved people, even as we have freedom to make choices that impede God's great plan for salvation. Through miracles both grand and subtle, God works despite human sin and interference to draw us to God's self. The story of Joseph illustrates the tension of a life of righteousness, trying to live in obedience to God, within a world that is constantly impacted by our very human mistakes.

Lord, strengthen my trust in you as I navigate
a world tainted by sin. Amen.

## Thursday, June 10

# The Commandment Is a Lamp

### *Proverbs 6:20-26*

**What are important maxims parents teach their children?**

Proverbs is a collection of wise sayings that, according to tradition, were teachings passed down from parents to children. Based on God's commandments, they center on morality, ethics, and right living. Just as parents today teach their children how to navigate the world ethically, the ancients taught their children the truths in these verses. This passage has a very specific teaching aimed at an adult son, describing the pitfalls and dangers of adultery with a married woman. The passage does not condone prostitution, but the sage clearly felt adultery was an even more serious offense. A prostitute had a set fee, similar to the cost of a loaf of bread, but becoming involved with a married woman could cost a man his very life (v. 26).

Tradition claims that Joseph and Potipher's wife were attractive people who were attracted to each other. Yet Joseph refused her advances out of loyalty both to Potiphar and to God. Because they had shown him mercy, had trusted him, and had both been loyal to him, he would not betray that trust and honored his relationships with them. Though it seems that she destroyed his life for turning down her advances, we see that God remained faithful to Joseph even as Joseph remained faithful to God. May we, like Joseph, remain faithful and true, lest we find our lives destroyed by our own bad decisions.

Lord, help me to stay loyal to your teaching
and loyal to those who trust me. Amen.

## Friday, June 11

# Blessings Amid the Chaos

### *Genesis 39:20b-23*

**Why did God allow Joseph to suffer a false accusation?**

It was unfair. If God was truly with Joseph, why did this bad thing happen to him? Why did God allow him to be sold into slavery in the first place? For that matter, why do people get sick? Why do bad things happen to godly people?

People through the ages have grappled with this question. We know that God has the ability to control every event that happens. We also know that God leaves room for our free will and for chance. Bad things happen because God allows human choice, sin, and chaos to survive in the world. Good things can happen, too, by chance or human choice. But if God stopped all bad things from happening to those God loves, we would have no ability to choose our own paths, and our very lives would be irrelevant.

But read deeper. This does not mean that God is passive and that we don't have hope. God was with Joseph, even in the jail. Blessings continued amid the chaos of the world. Just like in Potiphar's house, God made sure that Joseph prospered. The jailer trusted him and Joseph again worked his way into a position of authority and power. God was with him in the pit.

As Jesus told his followers in the last words he spoke on earth, "Look, I myself will be with you every day until the end of this present age" (Matthew 28:20).

Lord, comfort me and remind me of your love
when I confront the chaos of this world. Amen.

## Saturday, June 12

# God Tells Joseph the Meaning of the Dreams

### *Genesis 40:1-15, 23*

**Why was Joseph sure he could interpret dreams?**

When the cupbearer of the king and the king's baker both dreamed the same night, it seemed to indicate something important. They had already been in prison for a while, awaiting their fate. Both of them dreamt similar dreams, so it seemed to them that a decision had been made about them, and they were troubled that they could not interpret what it was. Joseph heard their concern and he told them to tell him their dreams. He made an audacious claim that dream interpretations belong to God. Joseph's Hebrew God was the only one able to interpret dreams, even Egyptian dreams in Egypt. And as God's emissary in Egypt, God would give Joseph the correct interpretations.

Joseph could interpret the dreams because God was with him and God created the dreams. Joseph suffered because of human mistakes and sin, but he benefited from the love and presence of the Lord.

The interpretation for the cupbearer was good news. In three days, he would be released and once again serve Pharaoh. Joseph took the opportunity to ask the cupbearer to mention him to Pharaoh so that he could get out of prison. For the third time, Joseph was betrayed when the cupbearer forgot him. It would be two more long years for Joseph in the prison. Once again, human mistakes caused this man of God to suffer.

Lord, you are the Creator of all things! Gift me
with insight into your creation. Amen.

## Sunday, June 13

# Joseph Interprets the Baker's Dream

### *Genesis 40:16-22*

**What was the significance of the baker's dream?**

The interpretation of the baker's dream was not positive. Ironically, he only asked Joseph to interpret his dream when he saw that the cupbearer's dream was good news. He began his description of his dream by hopefully saying, "It was the same for me" (v. 16). But instead of dreaming of serving Pharaoh again, he dreamed that birds would eat his baked goods from three baskets that he was carrying on his head. Joseph told him the horrible news that his dream foretold his death in three days.

Joseph was confident of his interpretations and asked the cupbearer to remember him when he was released from jail and request that he also be released. He didn't make the same request of the baker, for obvious reasons. He delivered the bad news to the baker in the same matter-of-fact way that he told the cupbearer about his upcoming release. But while it was a harsh message for the baker to hear, it clearly was a message from God.

One correct dream interpretation could have been attributed to chance, but both dreams taken together were stronger proof that God indeed was with Joseph, giving him insight and guidance. That proof would come into play when the cupbearer, two years later, finally remembered Joseph and brought him before Pharaoh to interpret his dreams.

Lord, may my words be compassionate,
no matter the situation. Amen.

## Monday, June 14

# Joseph Credits God with Interpretations

### *Genesis 41:1-16*

**What does it mean to glorify God in one's daily life?**

Two years after the cupbearer was released from prison, Pharaoh had two disturbing dreams. Both had the same theme. In the first one, seven fat cows were eaten up by seven ugly, skinny cows. In the second dream, seven healthy heads of grain were swallowed up by seven scorched, diseased heads of grain. None of the dream interpreters could tell him what the dreams meant.

Finally the cupbearer remembered Joseph, now that it was advantageous for him to do so. He recounted to Pharaoh how Joseph had accurately interpreted not only his dream but the dream of the unfortunate baker. Joseph was brought from the prison and prepared to meet Pharaoh.

Remarkably, the very first thing that Joseph said when he met Pharaoh was to give God glory. Joseph knew that God was the giver of dreams, and he knew that God would interpret the dreams. Joseph's entire future was at stake, but his response was to give the glory to God. He knew that without the Lord, the interpretations would be impossible. But he also knew that God had placed him in a critical position and that God would not abandon him there. Joseph's trust and confidence in God enabled him to boldly stand before powerful Pharaoh and promise that because God was with Joseph, Pharaoh would get the answers he needed.

Lord, may I be humble before you and bold
before others in your name. Amen.

## Tuesday, June 15

# Joseph Interprets Pharaoh's Dreams

### *Genesis 41:17-32*

**What happens if you try to control the uncontrollable?**

Every June the Nile River flooded its banks, bringing rich minerals from the mountains and watering the desert fields. If the floods were too big, towns were destroyed. If the floods were too early, crops were ruined. If the water didn't come at all, people starved. Pharaoh was worshipped as a deity who controlled the waters of the Nile. Imagine how that must have felt! He truly could not influence his own success. No wonder Pharaoh was so concerned about his dreams!

Have you ever been in a situation like Pharaoh where you've felt responsible for something you couldn't control? There's probably nothing more stressful or damaging to inner peace. But Joseph demonstrated two important lessons to Pharaoh. The first was to recognize there are many things we just cannot influence. Pharaoh had no power over the Nile River waters, and he had to stop trying. But the second thing he learned is that we can hand those things over to God. God can guide us through the outcomes of uncontrollable things, helping us to manage them with divine knowledge and direction. Because of God, Joseph could counsel Pharaoh on how to manage the upcoming famine. Joseph taught Pharaoh how to accept the limits of his power as well as how to depend on the power of God to deal with life's difficulties.

Lord, teach me how to relinquish control to you,
and then to listen for your guidance. Amen.

## Wednesday, June 16

# The Spirit of God Rests on Joseph

### *Genesis 41:33-45*

**What does it mean to have the Spirit of God rest on you?**

When Joseph heard and interpreted Pharaoh's dreams, he realized he was in a moment of opportunity. He outlined a concrete plan to solve the crisis. He didn't offer himself for the job of overseer, but Pharaoh and his servants all realized that they had a man with "God-given gifts" standing right in front of them (v. 38). Joseph got the job.

This was not a reward from God for Joseph because he had been righteous. Joseph was put in a position of responsibility to fulfill the desires of God. Through Pharaoh's dreams, God had made the divine plans clear, but that didn't mean that Joseph wasn't expected to act too. Like many other places in the story of Joseph, God's interaction hinged on human action. The future that God revealed needed human response to complete the story. Without the dream, they wouldn't have known to act, but if they hadn't acted, no one would have been saved. Joseph was the right man to respond to the dream, and Pharaoh was astute enough to recognize it.

Joseph's boyhood dreams had come true. The pathway to his place of honor was convoluted and unpredictable, but God had guided him there even through human sin and misfortune. As Pharaoh realized, the spirit of God rested on Joseph, enabling him to use his gifts and abilities to further the vision of God for him and for his people.

Lord, may your spirit rest on me and empower
me to do your will in the world. Amen.

## Thursday, June 17

# Joseph Names His Sons

### Genesis 41:46-57

**How do God's blessings change our view of the past and outlook for the future?**

Egypt had seven years of bumper crops, just as Joseph had said, and stored the surplus. Then came seven years of drought. Without the grain that Joseph had stored up, the entire area would have been devastated by famine.

The account of the births and naming of Joseph's sons seems to be an intrusion into the story, but it's really the only insight into what Joseph was thinking at the time and tells us a lot about his faith. Joseph named his first-born Manasseh, which is derived from the Hebrew word meaning, "to forget," because "God has helped me forget all of my troubles" (v. 51). The second son he named Ephraim, which means "fruitful," because of the blessings God gave him in Egypt. Both are poignant names for children of an alien making a home in a new country.

The names of Joseph's sons celebrate God's goodness in creating and preserving something good out of suffering. Because of God, the past is not a blueprint for the future. Joseph used the knowledge God gave to him and Pharaoh to build a land of plenty in a time of need. He was able to put the past behind him and look to the future in a new land with thanksgiving and praise. Joseph's future was one of hope, and he thanked God daily for his blessings by calling his sons names of praise.

Lord, may I always be mindful of the ways you've shaped my life with your blessings. Amen.

## FRIDAY, JUNE 18

# Joseph Struggles with Seeing His Brothers Again

*Genesis 42:1-24*

**What groundwork must be laid before true forgiveness?**

Some argue that Joseph set out to test his brothers to see if they were worthy of his forgiveness; I think it's important to understand how difficult it can be to mend broken relationships. Joseph was being tested too. Was he willing to risk being rejected? Was he able to work through the past pain to a new relationship with them? Was he strong enough to forgive? Not at first, at least.

Joseph accused his brothers of spying and threw them in jail, demanding that all but one stay in the pit, as he had been, until Benjamin was brought to him.

After three days, Joseph relented enough to agree that all but one could go home as long as they brought Benjamin back. Simeon was chosen as the hostage. But Joseph overheard them speaking in their native tongue, lamenting their sin against Joseph. This, Reuben said, was the reason that they were being punished. Their horrific action against their brother was haunting them. After all those years they had not forgotten him and were full of regret.

Joseph overheard them and wept. Three times in this story he wept over his brothers, each time coming a little closer to forgiveness. But it's a difficult path to reconciliation, and Joseph's heart was still too wounded to allow a reunion.

Lord, soften my heart toward those who
need my forgiveness. Amen.

## Saturday, June 19

# Joseph Struggles Toward Forgiveness

### *Genesis 43:1-34*

**Why is forgiveness so difficult?**

Joseph's brothers were very concerned about seeing "the man" in Egypt again (v. 3). When they had returned home, they found the silver they had taken to pay for the grain inside their grain sacks and thought that they would be accused of theft. Jacob told them to take twice the silver they needed to pay the man back. They would do whatever they could do to soften up that strange man in Egypt.

Scripture doesn't tell us who put the silver in the sacks, but we could easily suspect that it was Joseph. If so, the guidance of God was softening his heart. Joseph was working toward forgiveness. He saw how his brothers had regretted what they had done to him, and he was beginning to respond with kindness. He still had a way to go to forgive.

Forgiveness is difficult. It is often not fair. It means letting go of the wrongs that were done to us and living with an eye to the future instead of dwelling in the past. Joseph had a lot to forgive, and it's no wonder he struggled. But God was working, not *through* Joseph but *in* Joseph by changing his heart. It was God's prompting that led him or someone he directed to put the silver back in the bags. It was God's prompting that made him weep at the sight of Benjamin. It was God's prompting that told him to give his brothers a feast. But he still sat on the other side of the room, his heart not yet open to complete forgiveness and grace.

Lord, open my heart so that I can forgive
others as you forgive me. Amen.

### Sunday, June 20

## Joseph Manipulates to Keep Benjamin

### *Genesis 44:1-17*

**What are examples of manipulative behavior?**

Joseph orchestrated a plan to keep Benjamin in Egypt. He let the brothers leave with their grain, again putting the silver they used as payment in their sacks. But he put his silver divination cup in Benjamin's sack. Soon after they left, Joseph sent his steward after them to look for the cup. When the cup was found on Benjamin, the brothers turned around and followed behind, offering themselves as slaves as well. Joseph rejected them and attempted to send them home. It was only Benjamin he wanted. He didn't expect to see the other brothers again.

Joseph tried to manipulate events to get what he wanted. He was sure that the brothers who sold him into slavery would also walk away from Benjamin to save themselves, but he underestimated them. They wouldn't leave a brother behind again.

Throughout the story of Joseph's life, God changed events to move Joseph into greater and greater positions. This was so that Joseph could do the will of God in saving God's people. But in this passage, Joseph was only concerned with saving one person, his brother Benjamin. The rest had hurt him. They could leave. He wasn't interested in their future. But God was. God worked through the repentant hearts of Joseph's other brothers and had them offer themselves, an action that resulted in saving them all.

Lord, remind me of the possibilities for salvation of all people, even those who have wronged me. Amen.

## Monday, June 21

# Judah Pleads for Benjamin

### *Genesis 44:18-34*

**When have you witnessed an act of self-sacrifice?**

When Joseph's brothers left to return to Egypt, Jacob had not wanted Benjamin to go with them. He had lost Joseph, his older son with Rachel, and he couldn't bear the thought of losing the younger as well. Judah pledged himself as the guardian of Benjamin. So when Joseph orchestrated his ruse to keep Benjamin in Egypt with him, Judah had to make a plea. He told Joseph about how his family had lost Joseph, and Benjamin was all his father had left. For the first time, Joseph heard how deeply his father had mourned him. Judah offered himself in place of Benjamin. It would be better for Judah to be imprisoned in a foreign country than to see his father's misery if Benjamin didn't return home.

What a change from the brother who had suggested Joseph be sold into slavery! He had suggested that to save Joseph's life, but he had lacked the courage to stand up to his brothers. But now, he was standing up to the second most powerful man in Egypt for the sake of his father and brother. God had used his regret for his part in Joseph's fate and his sorrow at his father's grief to change his heart.

Imagine how Joseph must have felt, listening to the speech. He heard how much he had been grieved. He saw what the brothers' betrayal had done to his family and how it had changed them. And he saw the willingness to change and live a new life of self-sacrifice and love for one another.

Lord, may I respond to others with a
spirit of sacrifice and love. Amen.

## Tuesday, June 22

# Joseph Comes to a Place of Forgiveness

### *Genesis 45:1-15*

**How could forgiveness change the world?**

After Joseph listened to Judah's plea, his heart finally broke. He wept so loudly that the entire household could hear him. It was the final breakthrough to forgiveness. Joseph now understood his new place in their lives as a preserver of the family. They had all suffered because of their past, but now they were in a better place because of it. This family had grown past jealousy and bitterness into people who would even sacrifice themselves for each other.

It was not because Joseph was gracious that the family reconciled. It was because God was gracious. God's healing and loving activity amid human sin brought them restoration. People can do horrible things, and God allows us that choice. But even within all that sin, pain, and confusion, God is there. God guides us and allows our very human hearts to see glimpses of how we could live if we chose to try to become God's heavenly creatures. God lifts the veil to let us see a new way of living past the pain, grief, and sin.

And so, we can live in hope. God's work can be mighty and inescapable, or as subtle as a changed perspective. But it's there in everyday rebirths of the human spirit, in flashes of hope or in moments of grace and forgiveness. When we stand at a life-affirming place of reconciliation, we can all state with confidence that God has brought us to this place to save lives. It's the very work of God.

Lord, may I live a hopeful, forgiving life
in this sinful world. Amen.

## Wednesday, June 23

# Jacob Learns That Joseph Is Alive

### *Genesis 45:16-28*

**How does God show us that we can trust the future?**

When his sons returned from Egypt, Jacob heard the wonderful news that Joseph was still alive and was in fact the "ruler of all the land of Egypt," v. 26)! It must have sounded unbelievable to him.

When Jacob wrestled with God on the banks of the Jabbok as a young man, he told God, "I will not let you go unless you bless me" (Genesis 32:26 NIV). His entire life he struggled with God, reflected in his new name "Israel" which means, "you have struggled with God and with humans and have overcome" (Genesis 32:28 NIV). He struggled with the relationships with his parents, his wives, and his brother. In his old age, he struggled with crushing grief after he believed Joseph had died. But now, God would give him this final, wonderful blessing before Jacob let go of his life on earth.

As he prepared to leave for Egypt, God visited Jacob again (Genesis 46:2-4). God promised to be with him in Egypt and make him a great nation. The promises of God still remained. The covenant was still intact. After all his grief, Jacob could still trust in the future and in what God had in store for him and his family. Joseph was alive and so were the promises of the Lord.

O Lord, I give you praise for the joyful news
that your promises never die and that I can
trust you with the future! Amen.

## Thursday, June 24

# God's Great Care for Joseph

*Psalm 105:16-23*

**How is Joseph's story our legacy?**

Psalm 105 recounts how God lifted Joseph from slavery and set him in a place where he could rescue his people. It tells of Joseph's suffering, but then celebrates Joseph's power to save, given to him through the grace of God for the care of God's people. It's a wonderful and important story. But the truly wonderful thing is that it is only one story in the long history of Israel. The history of God's people is one of grace after grace, intercession after intercession, and a constant demonstration of God's great and never-ending love. Joseph's story is remarkable, but it is only one remarkable story. Israel's legacy is of constant remarkable works of God.

That's our legacy, too, as people of faith. The historical psalms tell of how God was active in the world from the dawn of history, protecting and sustaining God's people. And we can join in because we are among the multitudes of descendants promised to Abraham! Our faith story winds back through the centuries, always telling of God's provision and grace. Historical psalms remind us of the work of the Lord in the entire history of humankind, and in so doing teach us that this work is continuing on today and into the future. Although Joseph's story happened a very long time ago, the power, grace, and care of God that is evident in his life is present in our own. God continues to craft events and send God's people ahead to preserve life. Praise be to the Lord!

Lord, thank you for the legacy of care and
provision for your people. Amen.

## Friday, June 25

# Jacob Asks to Be Buried in Canaan

### *Genesis 47:27-31*

**Why did Jacob ask to be buried in Canaan?**

Joseph swore to Jacob, also named Israel, that he would take his body back to the land of promise. Jacob had dreamed of a ladder to heaven and had received God's promise of covenant and land as a young man; now nearing the end of his life, Jacob wanted his son's reassurance that his body would be returned to the land the Lord had promised him.

Verse 31 is difficult to interpret, and different translations render it different ways. The CEB says that after Joseph gave his word, "Israel slumped down at the head of the bed." The NIV says, "Israel worshiped as he leaned on the top of his staff." Some of the translations suggest that Jacob died at that moment, but it is most likely that he bowed his head in worship to God, grateful for his son's assurance.

Jacob may have lived in Egypt at the end of his life, but his heart was in Bethel. God told him not to be afraid to leave the land because God would also be with him in Egypt, and he would bring Jacob back again (Genesis 46:3-4). Even though the land was integral to the covenant, God was not tied to the land. God assured Jacob that he would travel with him and never leave him. His ancestors would become a great nation in Egypt too. Jacob longed to be buried in the sacred place he first met God, but God was not confined to any place and would travel everywhere with him.

Lord, may I feel your presence everywhere I go. Amen.

## Saturday, June 26

# Jacob Blesses Joseph

### *Genesis 49:22-26, 28*

**What would you say to your family on your deathbed?**

Genesis 49:22, which describes Joseph, is very difficult to interpret. Depending on your translation, you may have read that Joseph is a vine, a branch, a donkey, or a young bull! The overall image, however, is that Joseph is strong and fruitful with an ever-widening influence. The underlying idea that God was his protector is a strong theme all throughout his story.

Just in case there was any doubt as to why Joseph had prospered, Jacob named the Lord God five different ways as the one who watched over Joseph. The CEB translates these names as "the strong one of Jacob," "the shepherd," "the rock of Israel," "God, your father," and "the Almighty" (vv. 24-25). These names reflect the history of the covenant, God's strength and power, and God's great care for Joseph.

Joseph was the keeper of the covenant who, with the help of God, provided food for Egypt and all the region during the devastating famine. He remained faithful and loyal to God, even in the midst of difficulties. It was because of God working through Joseph that the story of God's relationship with God's people could continue. The Lord God of his fathers, the rock, the shepherd, the strong and the almighty one, remained with Joseph and blessed both him and his descendants.

Lord, help me to have a legacy as faithful
and obedient as Joseph. Amen.

## Sunday, June 27

# Stephen Tells Joseph's Story

### *Acts 7:9-16*

**How does Joseph's story fit into the history of God's love and care for humanity?**

Stephen's retelling of the story of Joseph made three points. First, God was with Joseph. God worked through Joseph to change evil into good, to reveal God's promises, and to protect God's people. Joseph's story demonstrates that God is intimately involved in the world and human lives.

Secondly, God gifts those whom God chooses. Joseph dreamed and knew how to interpret dreams. He also had the wisdom to manage Potiphar's household, the jail, and the kingdom of Egypt itself. When God calls a person, God also equips that person with the resources he or she will need.

Finally, Stephen used the Joseph story to tell the Pharisees that God's work with humanity is not bound by any particular place or time. God went to Egypt with Joseph and promised Jacob to go there with him too. The Pharisees got their power by running the temple system, but Stephen told them that God does not dwell in houses made by men.

The way that God dealt with Joseph was the same way that God dealt with God's people throughout time. The *hesed* or steadfast love that God showed Joseph started with Abraham, continued to Moses, and then was made incarnate with the birth of Jesus Christ. God's love has been a continuing theme throughout the history of humankind.

Lord, thank you for your *hesed* through the ages, calling all to salvation. Amen.

## Monday, June 28

# The Righteous Enter the Lord's Gate

### *Psalm 118:19-29*

**Why aren't the world's markers of greatness and power what really matter in life?**

The rejected stone in today's reading is a symbol for Israel itself, thought of by other nations to be of no account, but which in God's plan "has become the cornerstone" (v. 22 NIV). In the New Testament, Peter quoted Psalm 118:22 and used it to say that Jesus was the stone the builders had rejected, the stone that would now become God's cornerstone (Acts 4:11).

This verse about a rejected stone becoming the cornerstone is about reversal, which is itself a significant theme in Scripture. Jesus' whole life and ministry is an extension of this great reversal theme. Christ wins our salvation through losing his life and achieves power through service. Those who receive his salvation are those who admit they are weak and lost. Or, as the apostle Paul put it, "God chose what the world considers low-class and low-life—what is considered to be nothing—to reduce what is considered to be something to nothing" (1 Corinthians 1:28).

We followers of Jesus should pay attention to this great reversal theme and not count on the trappings of power, prestige, wealth, and fame. Our real contribution to the world cannot be measured by the standards of success and achievement or the money in our accounts. It is measured by how well we have loved God and our neighbor.

Thank you, Lord, for modeling for us in Christ
what really matters in this life. Amen.

## Tuesday, June 29

# Be a Righteous Neighbor

### *Exodus 20:13-17*

**What is the fruit of good desiring? of desiring gone bad?**

Do not kill, commit adultery, steal, or testify falsely against your neighbor are all basics for a peaceful existence, the boundaries of decent conduct. The last commandment goes beyond specific actions and warns against desiring what belongs to one's neighbor. Of course, wanting is a necessary part of being human. At its best, it's a form of energy and motivation that drives invention, discovery, mastery, improvement, and accomplishment.

But like any appetite, desire needs to function with some restraint, because when it goes too far, when it becomes our primary motivation, it becomes destructive, both to us and to others. The fruit of desire gone bad is injury and discontent. Thus, the tenth commandment warns about letting desire—coveting, to use the older word—run rampant. Desire gone bad works against being the sort of neighbor Jesus told us to be.

Well, how do we avoid covetousness? For one thing, we can engage in practices that lead to better thoughts. Instead of resenting someone because they have more than we do, we can do something helpful for someone who has less. We should remember that life is more than arriving at goals. We can focus on the example of Jesus. I may resent that I am feeling left out or shortchanged by something, but I must do my best to act as Jesus would in my situation.

O Lord, help me to be a good neighbor,
desiring only to do your will. Amen.

## Wednesday, June 30

# Rules for Living Side-by-Side

### *Exodus 22:5-15*

**When have you been a true neighbor to someone nearby?**

Several years ago, I was the pastor in a rural community. One summer day, I received a phone call from one of my farmer parishioners asking if I was free to help in a situation. His neighbor, another of my parishioners, had misjudged the wind on a day he needed to burn some stumps, and now there was a danger of the flying embers spreading the fire to others' property. Thankfully, it all ended well, but it could have gone otherwise.

The same was true in ancient Israel, where people lived in such proximity that carelessness or bad behavior by one person could cause loss for another. Thus, it was necessary to have rules to guard against unfair loss of property, which would disrupt the stability of the community. Today's verses include six possible neighbor interactions where loss was possible, and rules for determining who was responsible for the restitution. In cases when it's not clear who is the offending party, those involved are "brought before God," likely meaning a local tribunal that administered covenantal law made the decision (vv. 8-9).

The rules and rulings were to protect individual property owners for sure, but more than that, they were to declare that the neighbors had a responsibility for one another. The idea was that the individual prospers only by maintaining a stable and fair community for all.

Help me, O Lord, to be a good neighbor not only to those who live near me and those who live far away. Amen.

# JULY

## Contributor:

*Stan Purdum*
*July 1–31*

## Thursday, July 1

# Treat Your Neighbor Right

### *Proverbs 3:27-30*

**When have you found it difficult to be neighborly?**

In ancient Israel, people seldom lived in isolation, but rather in villages and towns. Even farmers, who may have commuted to their fields during the day, had their homes in villages. Bandits and marauders made it too risky live without neighbors nearby. In addition to providing safety in numbers, neighbors also became part of one's social circle. Recall how, in Jesus' parables of the lost sheep (Luke 15:4-6) and the lost coin (Luke 15:8-9) when the sheep/coin was found, the finder called neighbors together to help with the celebration. That's not something one would do with someone who wasn't his or her neighbor.

Neighbors were so important that Proverbs 27:10 advises, "don't go to your relative's house when disaster strikes. / Better a neighbor nearby than a relative far away." Having good relations with one's neighbors was not merely a nice thing to do, but a necessity. And the proverbs in today's reading were, if not actual laws, wise practices to maintain harmony in the neighborhood. Note that all four verses start with "Don't." Whereas verse 27 and 28 advise against the withholding of "good," verse 29 tells not to plot evil against one's neighbor. Verse 30 tells not to stir up trouble, not just with a neighbor, but with anyone. Wisdom is as much a matter of knowing what not to do as knowing what to do.

Thank you, Lord, for those who are neighborly to me. Amen.

## Friday, July 2

# Maintain Proper Neighbor Relations

*Proverbs 6:1-5*

**When should you treat neighbors and strangers alike?**

These verses start off advising against guaranteeing a loan (cosigning, in today's financial lingo) for a *neighbor*, but the verses quickly give the same advice against "shaking hands" (entering in contract) with a *stranger*. Do you find it odd that the same advice would apply to both? Proverbs 6:2 indicates that in both cases, one can be "trapped" by one's words of agreement. In the case of guaranteeing a loan for a neighbor, you could lose money if the neighbor fails to repay the loan, or you may end up becoming resentful of the neighbor. In the case of the stranger, someone you do not know could be seeking to take advantage of you.

With all these as potential problems, the advice is given to do what is necessary to avoid being the guarantor of the neighbor's loan and avoid the contract with the stranger. The takeaway from the verse is not that we should never lend to a neighbor or enter a contract with a someone not previously known, but that we need to have experience and mature judgment to assess the character and reliability of the neighbor and to do due diligence before signing a contract. It also helps to know our ability to sustain the loss should our assessment or due diligence prove wrong.

The other takeaway is not stated in the verses, but in the case of a neighbor in financial distress, the better action may be to give what is needed as a gift, with no strings dangling to ensnare either the giver or the recipient.

O Lord, help me to be wise, but also generous. Amen.

## Saturday, July 3

# Love Your Neighbors, Near and Far

### *Proverbs 14:20-22*

**Is it easier to love to people you do or don't know?**

Today's verses call us to think about our attitude toward neighbors, whether they are people who live next door or on the other side of the world. Verse 20 suggests that knowing a person can affect whether we love them, saying that those who live near the poor (neighbors in the narrow sense) "hate" (disparage) them, but they "love" (idealize) the wealthy who don't live nearby (neighbors in the broad sense).

While the verse focuses on the difference in economic status between the poor and the rich, it also implies a difference in proximity and in the definition of neighbor. In all likelihood, you live near others of a similar economic level as yourself. It becomes easy to disparage those you know who have less than you, while idealizing those who are more distant from you and appear to have more wealth.

Some years ago, I took a church team to another state to do some volunteer work with an organization that repairs and rebuilds homes for low-income families. One day while we were working on a home, a local pastor stopped by. He said when he organized such service trips, they had to go to areas far away; it seems church members would look at the people we had traveled to help and claim, "They don't need it." He said that some people find it easier to extend Christian love to people they don't know than those they do.

Lord, help me to look beyond my feelings
to love as Jesus taught. Amen.

## Sunday, July 4

# Treat Enemies Like Neighbors

### *Proverbs 25:20-23*

**When have you seen someone overcome evil with good?**

The upshot of these verses is the one stated in the title of today's reading: Treat enemies like neighbors. We get that memo plainly from verse 21, but other verses in the passage may obscure that message for modern readers.

For one thing, we simply are not certain what verse 22 means when it says that by feeding hungry enemies, we in effect "heap burning coals on their heads." Presumably this expression had meaning for the original audience of Proverbs that is not obvious to us. We get a clue of what might be the intended meaning when we look at Romans 12:20, where the apostle Paul cites Proverbs 25:21, but he does so in the context of advising his readers to try to live peaceably with others and leave matters such as revenge to the Lord. Paul concludes by saying, "Don't be defeated by evil, but defeat evil with good," which communicates that rather than letting evil done to us provoke us to respond in kind, we should do our best to overcome evil with goodness (Romans 12:21). So piling fiery coals on someone's head cannot be meant to be done literally, since that cannot be something good.

It is tempting, when seeing someone we dislike suffering, to laugh at their misery. Instead, godly wisdom tells us to do good even to those we consider enemies, and allow God to be at work in their lives as well as our own.

O God, help me to treat my enemies as neighbors
and leave their response to you. Amen.

## Monday, July 5

# Make Your Hope Sure

### *Hebrews 6:9-12*

**How do you treat others because of Christ?**

In our assigned passage, the writer of Hebrews begins by saying, "But we are convinced of better things in your case . . . things that go together with salvation" (v. 9). He says that God knows of the "efforts and the love" they "have shown for [Christ's] name's sake when you served and continue to serve God's holy people" (v. 10). The writer urges readers "to show the same effort to make your hope sure until the end" (v. 11).

The theme of our readings this week focuses on neighborly treatment of immigrants. While today's passage isn't about immigrants per se, it is about serving "God's holy people." Those who don't want to help immigrants might read verse 10 as an escape clause. If immigrants are of a different faith or have no obvious religion, one might say, "Well, since they aren't Christians, they aren't God's holy people and therefore I have no obligation to them." But shame on us if we think that way.

All people are created by God and thus are God's people by birthright. But even if the Hebrews writer meant "God's holy people" in a more selective way, we're still not excused, for it's not our prerogative to decide who is, and who is not, among God's people. That's God's prerogative. Our role, as today's passage says, is to continue love toward others and efforts on their behalf for Christ's name's sake.

Lord, help me to be generous with my love and efforts for Christ's name's sake. Amen.

## Tuesday, July 6

# Leave the Gleanings for the Needy

*Deuteronomy 24:17-22*

**What feelings does news about immigration raise in you?**

The reason the Bible frequently mentions immigrants, orphans, and widows together is because they comprise a group of people who were vulnerable financially and politically and often lacked a surrounding circle of kin for support. Israel's law called for extending help to them. The law included first, a provision that the legal rights of this vulnerable group should not be obstructed (v. 17). Second, the law appealed to the Israelites to remember *their* history: what it was like to be enslaved in Egypt, and how the Lord rescued them (v. 18). Third, the law called for leaving the gleanings of the harvests for widows, orphans, and immigrants, which would have cost the farmers some potential revenue (vv. 19-21).

The difficulty for us may come at the point today where, simply because of their large numbers, widows, orphans, and immigrants place strain on the programs intended to help. Some of us may even worry about whether the resources of this country are enough for all who want to live here. It's easy to feel that what's here is for "us" and not for "them." And yet, that doesn't feel like a "love your neighbor" response.

There are no simple answers, but Bible verses such as these we read today suggest that keeping everything just for "us" is not what God wants us to do.

O Lord, help my first impulse to be openhanded
and reflective of your love for me. Amen.

## Wednesday, July 7

# Job Helped the Needy

### *Job 29:11-17*

**Do you consider good deeds as essential to your identity?**

Job's list of good deeds should not be heard as though Job were scorekeeping. Rather, he was reflecting on actions that gave his life meaning and value before troubles turned his world upside down. Job's view of God was shaped strongly by his understanding of his own place in this moral scheme, and his naming of his social deeds of mercy reflects that understanding. In verse 11, Job indicates that he has been judged by the ear and eye of the community, and the implication is that because he has been gracious and generous to the needy, he has been respected and appreciated.

But when Job's world was suddenly upended, he was adrift, no longer certain how God interacts with human life. He felt cast out from God's moral realm. Whereas he had previously received respect from his peers for his help to the needy, he now received from them an assumption that he had sinned. Job was working here to hold on to his identity—in relation to God, to his peers, to those who need his protection, and to those who need his leadership. He awaited God's confirmation of who he (Job) was.

It's worth thinking about what defines our identity in relation to God and others, and what gives our lives meaning and value. For Job, what he did for the needy was part of who he was. It should be part of our identity as well.

O Lord, may both my personal and relationship
metrics be pleasing to you. Amen.

## Thursday, July 8

# Appointing Elders

### *Titus 1:5-9*

**What religious leaders have helped you grow in faith?**

Titus was a Gentile (Galatians 2:3) follower of Jesus and worked with Paul in the latter's missionary efforts. He had the maturity and stability of character to be Paul's representative in Corinth during a difficult time in that church (2 Corinthians 7:6-7, 13-16; 8:6-7, 16-21; 12:17-18), and now Paul left him in Crete to oversee the development of the churches there.

Among his tasks, Titus was to appoint "elders in each city" (Titus 1:5). In the passage for today, Paul outlines some points of character, personality, and righteousness to be used in selecting these leaders.

If we read verses 10-16, immediately following today's passage, we see why leaders with maturity and strength of character were needed. Those verses describe people—members of the church, no less—who "upset entire households" (v. 11). Titus was to appoint leaders who can "correct them firmly, so that they can be healthy in their faith" (v. 13).

The connection of today's passage with this week's theme of neighborly treatment of an immigrant may not be immediately obvious. But, as other readings this week make clear, caring for those in need is a religious obligation and having leaders who help us to be healthy in our faith is an aid to seeing our obligations to others clearly.

Lord, thank you for leaders who help
us stay healthy in faith. Amen.

## Friday, July 9

# Love Your Neighbor as Yourself

### *Leviticus 19:18; Matthew 19:16-22*

**When has someone loved you as Christ commands?**

The account in Matthew 19:16-22 is of the wealthy young man who approached Jesus and asked what he needed to do to have eternal life. Jesus told him to keep the commandments, but the man asked, "Which ones?" (v. 18). In response, Jesus stated several, including "love your neighbor as you love yourself" (v. 19). When the man then said he was already keeping those and asked, "What am I still missing?" (v. 20), Jesus told him to sell what he owned and give the money to the poor, adding that doing so would give him treasure in heaven. There it was: a specific way to apply that command, but it was not what the rich young man wanted to hear.

The upshot of this story is not that every follower of Jesus needs to sell all possessions and give the money to the poor, but that loving our neighbors needs to be expressed in tangible ways rather than merely in good wishes.

One thing loving our neighbors means is making the kinds of allowances for them that we want made for us. We live in an age when taking offense is common and criticizing others is standard fare. But everyone, including us, does dumb things. We're all works in progress. We all have bad days. So maybe, when we see someone acting badly, praying for them rather than ridiculing them is one way to love them as we love ourselves.

Help me, O Lord, to be gracious, slow to
criticize and quick to help. Amen.

## Saturday, July 10

# Gleaning in Bethlehem

### *Ruth 1:14–2:3*

**When has someone blessed you by being with you?**

In the patriarchal culture of Ruth's day, a woman without either husband or sons was in real difficulty. There were few options for single or widowed women and no way to make a living. They had to rely on the charity of family members or the community at large. Following the death of her husband and two sons, Naomi had little left. Living in a foreign land, a widow with two daughters-in-law, Naomi saw no better option than to journey back to her homeland alone

Ruth, however, would not leave, saying to Naomi, "Don't urge me to abandon you, to turn back from following after you. Wherever you go, I will go; and wherever you stay, I will stay. Your people will be my people, and your God will be my God" (Ruth 1:16). So Naomi relented, and Ruth went with her.

Ruth's refusal to leave her mother-in-law turned out to be a blessing beyond their reckoning. Not only was Ruth able to walk alongside Naomi in their shared grief, but she was able to assist Naomi in finding food and, eventually, provide Naomi with a new family, a family that would give birth to David, Solomon, and eventually Jesus.

We never know how God will use us to bless others. Even as God has been faithful toward us, let us be faithful to one another.

Thank you, Lord, for those who have helped
me at sacrifice to themselves. Amen.

## Sunday, July 11

# Boaz's Kindness

*Ruth 2:4-16*

**When have you wished God's blessing on someone and then been the channel for that blessing to come?**

When Boaz arrived and saw Ruth gleaning, he was impressed by how hard she worked on behalf of his relative, Naomi. He called Ruth to him and welcomed her to glean in his fields. Boaz was, in effect, offering her his protection. Boaz also instructed his reapers to leave extra grain behind for her. Before parting, Boaz, impressed with Ruth's loyalty to Naomi, spoke a blessing upon her.

Boaz eventually realized that the fulfillment of his wish for good fortune for Ruth could come through him, but he was a little dense and practically had to be hit over the head with the idea. It finally dawned on him that merely expressing the hope that God would reward Ruth wasn't going to do it. He realized that he had to act himself to make that expressed hope come true, and then God followed that with blessing. Boaz married Ruth and provided for her as well as Naomi.

We need to make Boaz's discovery, but even better, we need to make Ruth's discovery. She wanted to see fullness return to Naomi, but instead of just wishing her mother-in-law good luck, she stuck with her and helped out. She took the initiative.

O Lord, as I wish others well, help me to
consider whether I may be a channel for that
well-being to come to them. Amen.

## MONDAY, JULY 12

# About the Wicked

### *Psalm 94*

**Are you troubled when wrongdoers go unpunished?**

The first seven verses of Psalm 94 are a prayer of complaint. Addressing the Lord as "avenging God" (v. 1), the prayer goes on to describe the abusive acts and boasting of "evildoers" (v. 4) whose deeds seem to go unpunished. Thus, the psalmist urged the Lord, in God's role as "judge of the earth" to "Rise up . . . [and] Pay back the arrogant exactly what they deserve!" (v. 2). We have that complaint too. Perhaps we've even prayed, as the psalmist did, saying, "Lord, don't let them get away with this. Pay them back what they deserve."

Though he doesn't appear to have yet received any answer to his prayer, the psalmist speaks a warning to the wicked, telling them that they'll get what they deserve eventually. We've probably had thoughts like that as well, and they likely come not only out of our wish for wrongdoers to get their comeuppance, but also out of our confidence that our Lord is indeed a God of justice.

The psalm starts with appearances. It does not appear that God reigns, for the wicked prosper and crime pays. The psalmist does not deny appearances, but neither does he or she waver from the conviction that God rules and that God is the help and hope of God's people. We are called to either believe the appearance of prosperity of the wicked or to find happiness and inner peace in God, our Lord forever.

Let me have that peace, O Lord, that does not rely
upon appearances but on your character. Amen.

## Tuesday, July 13

# Learn to Do Good

### *Isaiah 1:10-18*

**When have you given yourself permission to do wrong?**

In today's passage, God tells the people of Judah that because of their sins, "When you extend your hands, / I'll hide my eyes from you. / Even when you pray for a long time, / I won't listen. / Your hands are stained with blood" (v. 15). The sins to which God referred include that people were carefully observing religious festivals, but also running corrupt court systems, oppressing the poor, and leaving orphans and widows to fend for themselves. So God said, "learn to do good. / Seek justice: / help the oppressed; / defend the orphan; / plead for the widow" (v. 17).

The overall lesson of this passage is "don't do the wrong thing; do the right thing," but that leaves us wondering why the people of Judah needed to be told that. They surely already knew what God wanted of them, so why weren't they doing it?

We could ask the same question about ourselves. When we deliberately do the wrong thing and nothing bad happens to us, it becomes easier the next time to do it again. The people Isaiah addressed were a lot like us. They wanted to stay in God's good graces, but by coming up with their own rules for their behavior, they justified mistreating others while piously observing the religious rituals their religion required. But God does not value ritual without right treatment of others.

Let me, O Lord, live out the spirit of love
for you and for my neighbors. Amen.

### Wednesday, July 14

## The Early Church

### *Acts 2:36-42*

**How did a congregation contribute to your faith in Christ?**

Today's passage tells of the response to Peter's sermon on the Day of Pentecost. A notable part of the response was that about 3,000 people accepted Peter's message and the church was born. That's an impressive number of converts, but how many active followers of Jesus were there before that? According to Acts 1:15, at the time of Jesus' ascension, the entire band of believers numbered about 120. About 120 people—not exactly a megachurch!

Yet look what that small group, empowered by the Holy Spirit, accomplished. Look how they spread the word. Look how they took what they had learned about Jesus and blessed the world with it. Acts largely tells the story of the growing church in terms of individuals, but every time it returns to the larger narrative, we find that the church has grown in ways that are not explained by the actions of those individuals alone.

Case in point: On Pentecost, Peter and others of that 120 rushed out to testify in the streets and some 3,000 people were converted on the spot. Keep reading, and you'll see that God keeps adding to their numbers. Their energy as believers, their praise of God, their glad and generous hearts, drew people to embrace the Lord's call.

Now consider what we, in conjunction with fellow believers, can do to demonstrate God's goodness to all.

Lord, help me contribute to the power of my congregation to demonstrate your love. Amen.

## Thursday, July 15

# The Church Grows

### *Acts 9:26-31*

**What led you to follow Jesus?**

Our reading today tells of Saul's early efforts following his conversion to join with other followers of Jesus but being turned away because "they were all afraid of him" (v. 26). His reputation as a vicious persecutor of Jesus' followers preceded him. But even if that wasn't the case, they likely wondered if Saul's conversion would last. Some people, caught up in the emotions or impulses of a moment, may pledge to repent and follow Jesus, but then, in the cold light of day, backpedal. Not every conversion results in radical personal transformation.

While some evangelistic programs and revivalist preaching often display an orientation toward dramatic transformation, many Christian groups teach that it's equally possible for a child of faith to gradually grow into Christian maturity, not through the giant leaps of conversion but through the small steps fostered by a nurturing congregation. Many Christians cannot remember a time when they were not believers. Conversion and nurture are both routes to faith in Christ. In this passage, Saul the convert is placed within a faith community that confirms his salvation and directs him to Tarsus for his own safety. The reception of Saul by the church leaders made possible his subsequent missionary activity. While Saul's young faith was being nurtured in church community, the church continued to grow in numbers.

Lord, thank you for leading me to follow Jesus. Amen.

## Friday, July 16

# Harvest Workers Needed

### *Luke 10:1-12*

**In what evangelistic sense might you work for the Lord?**

Although the Bible sometimes uses "harvest" to refer to the final judgment or for the gathering of Israel in the last times, here Jesus was referring to those ready to receive the gospel, and thus he spoke with evangelistic fervor. They were ready to be "harvested" for the Lord. Obviously, Jesus was speaking in metaphor, but it fits. Harvesting is a positive activity. The harvested crop is that part that is kept. What's left in the field afterward is chaff, which is plowed under, gathered for animal bedding, or left to blow away. But the harvested part is the fruit, the joy, the gift of the land.

During harvests, farmers need all the help they can get. Thus, Jesus said to the 72, "Therefore, plead with the Lord of the harvest to send out workers for his harvest" (v. 2b). But, what do you suppose happened when the 72 did ask God to send out workers? They likely heard that *they* were to be those harvesters. It wasn't to be left up to Jesus to do all the reaping.

With Jesus sending out the 72 and speaking about harvesting, we can hear the beginnings of both ordained and un-ordained ministry. God needs people, professionals and laity, who are willing to labor for the Lord, since reaping is hard work. Being willing to serve in the places that the circumstances of our lives and the invitation of God put us is what allows the harvest to be brought in.

Lord, when I meet someone ready for harvest,
make me willing to do the work for you. Amen.

## Saturday, July 17

# True Devotion

### *James 1:21-27*

**Why are widows and orphans singled out for special care?**

After my grandfather died, my grandmother was surprised at how drastically their shared pension was cut. She was even more surprised to learn that her contemporary widowers did not lose nearly as much pension after the loss of their wives. She organized her fellow widows into a letter-writing campaign until the widows' pensions were brought up to par with widowers'. This was hardly the first time that a widow has had to deal with a system that seemed weighted against her

That's why, in today's passage, James mentions caring for "orphans and widows in their difficulties" as examples of how true devotion to God ought to express itself (v. 27). In this way, believers could be "doers of the word and not only hearers who mislead themselves" (v. 22). James rightly believed that one way we learn what God wants from us is through what we hear from the word of God. And so he said that those who are devoted to God, "don't listen and then forget, but they put [what they have heard] into practice in their lives" (v. 25).

We might think about the care of widows and orphans—and the other modern equivalents—as matters of social or political concern. James did not see it that way. He said it was a matter of religion. In fact, James said it was part of what makes our religion "pure and faultless" (v. 27).

Lord, help me put into practice what I
have heard from your word. Amen.

## Sunday, July 18

# The Selection of the Seven

## *Acts 6:1-7*

**How should a church take care of its members?**

The church was growing rapidly, and the converts were living communally, sharing goods so that "There were no needy persons among them" (Acts 4:34). With so many joining, their numbers included not only Jews from Jerusalem and the surrounding region who spoke Aramaic, but also many from the larger Mediterranean world, who spoke Greek. The language differences naturally led to some separation into culture groups within the church. Eventually, some of the Greek-speakers complained that "their widows were being overlooked in the daily food service" (Acts 6:1). There's no suggestion that this was deliberate; it's possible the language barrier was the impediment causing some to be overlooked.

The church leaders agreed the problem needed to be corrected. So, they instructed the whole body to choose seven well-respected men from among them to oversee the food service for the community, and these men became the first deacons of the church ("deacon" is derived from the Greek word for "serve," used in verse 2, *diakoneō*).

With this matter cared for, the church continued to increase and "Even a large group of priests embraced the faith" (v. 7b). When the church cares for one another, God does amazing things.

Lord, thank you that you have called us to different roles in the church. Help me to know what mine should be and make me willing to do it. Amen.

## Monday, July 19

# The Apostles Witness to the Council

### *Acts 5:27-42*

**When have you seen partisanship work for the good of all?**

Partisanships has likely been around as long as human have, and it runs in the background of today's passage. In the Sanhedrin, both major groups of Jewish leaders were represented: the Pharisees and the Sadducees. The two groups were as different as chalk and cheese, but both had seats in the Sanhedrin.

In the council, the high priest, who was a Sadducee, demanded that the apostles stop teaching in Jesus' name and stop holding the high priest and his cohorts responsible for Jesus' death. But the apostles responded that they must obey God, not humans, and added a testimony about Jesus as the Savior.

Hearing those words, many on the council wanted to have the apostles killed, but one council member, a respected Pharisee named Gamaliel, urged his colleagues to adopt a wait-and-see approach to the Jesus movement, leaving the final judgment about the movement to God. The council members agreed and released the apostles, after having them flogged. Despite the suffering, the apostles once more returned to the work of proclaiming the good news of Jesus.

Partisanship often works against the common good, but here, God used it as a force to free the apostles and keep the church growing.

Lord, when I choose to be partisan,
let me also be loving. Amen.

## Tuesday, July 20

# Clean Hands

### *Luke 7:36-50*

**How do you weigh your sins against those of others?**

Jesus accepted an invitation to eat at the house of a Pharisee. A woman of the town slipped into the house to see Jesus. She cried on his feet, then dried his feet with her hair and anointed his feet with oil. The Pharisee thought, "If this man were a prophet, he would know what kind of woman is touching him" (v. 39). In other words, he was saying, "She's sinner; I'm not."

I'm reminded of an event that happened at a church I pastored. One Saturday I decided to harvest some of the walnuts that had come from the tree in the parsonage yard. I tried for an hour to shuck the thick outer husks, only to end up with two walnuts for all my effort. When I washed up, I found that the husk juice had left dark stains on my hands that would not come off, not even with undiluted bleach. That's when I remembered that I was to serve Communion the next day, stained hands notwithstanding. So in church the next morning, before starting the ritual, I told the congregation of my walnut fiasco and that despite appearances, my hands had been washed.

Only later did I realize I had missed an opportunity for a theological lesson before the ritual: Nobody comes to the Lord's Supper with clean hands.

Not the woman who cried on Jesus' feet, not the Pharisee, and not the rest of us. But Christ can cleanse them.

Thank you, Lord, for the washing of
righteousness you offer me. Amen.

## Wednesday, July 21

# The Longsuffering God

### *Romans 2:1-16*

**What challenge do you hear in the final judgment?**

Romans 2:1-16 is about the final judgment, the time when God will put all the world to right and judge all people according to their deeds. The first part of verse 4 reads, "Or do you have contempt for the riches of God's generosity, tolerance, and patience?" Paul's point is that God withholds the payback for our unrighteous deeds until the end out of "generosity, tolerance, and patience," not to let things slide, but to give us time to repent. Then Paul continues: "Don't you realize that God's kindness is supposed to lead you to change your heart and life?" He describes God as holding back from summary judgment to give people a chance to repent—but, as verse 8 indicates, the holding back stores up wrath for the hard-hearted, who refuse to repent.

The Greek word translated as "patience" is *makrothymia*, which in the old King James Version was translated as "longsuffering." God's longsuffering means we can never say there's no hope for any one of us while there is still life in us. God is not eager to unleash wrath on us. God loves us, disciplines us, teaches us, and enables us to see object lessons in what happens around us. How we respond remains our decision, but God gives us some time.

In Christ's light, our sins are increasingly revealed so we can deal with them. Only then will we be able gently and firmly to articulate a standard and denounce evil in others without also condemning ourselves.

Make me open to the Spirit's searchlight, O Lord. Amen.

### Thursday, July 22

## Don't Get Discouraged Doing What's Right

*2 Thessalonians 3:6-15*

**How do you deal with calls to do more or better when no supporting helps are offered?**

Rather than rely on financial support from the Thessalonian church, Paul and his fellow missionaries "didn't eat anyone's food without paying for it" and "worked night and day . . . so that we would not impose on you" (v. 8). At the same time, Paul and his colleagues were also teaching that, "If anyone doesn't want to work, they shouldn't eat" (v. 10). The emphasis wasn't on refusing to help those who couldn't work, but on encouraging those who could to do their part.

In short, Paul was calling for a disciplined life, one where the believers "don't get discouraged in doing what is right" (v. 13). His words suggest that the problem for some was not laziness or disinterest, but burnout, where even those who otherwise wanted to do right could face fatigue if not disillusionment in their efforts to follow Jesus consistently and faithfully.

Admittedly, it's hard not to get discouraged in doing what is right when there is little to no support, and often even few visible successes and no expressions of gratitude. But the call to do what is right is clear throughout Scripture. This is why encouragement is so important. I am sure that you have needed encouragement to do what is right; where and how can you offer similar encouragement to others?

O God, keep me from giving up when doing what
is right seems thankless and hard. Amen.

## Friday, July 23

# In Him It Is Always Yes

### *2 Corinthians 1:15-22*

**In what ways has Jesus said "Yes" to you?**

In today's passage, Paul is saying, in effect, that if Jesus had never come, there would be room to doubt the promises God made, promises including forgiveness, peace, healing, deliverance, blessing, fellowship with God, and so on. But, because Jesus came, we have every reason to count on those promises. Jesus is the personal guarantee of God that all the divine promises are true.

Paul next said that because Jesus is the divine Yes, "we say Amen through him to the glory of God" (v. 20b). "Amen" means "so be it." That implies that when we pray, we can do so in confidence that the promises of God are true and we can rely on them. God has given the Spirit as "a down payment" on those promises (v. 22). The Spirit of God in our hearts can be thought of as the first installment on the kingdom of God to come. Or, to say it another way, the kind of life we live with the help of God's Spirit is a foretaste of eternity.

Saying that Jesus is God's Yes means that those who think of Christianity in terms of being a No to life have misunderstood the faith. Following Christ is not about having to say no to all the things you might enjoy; rather, it is about saying yes to a life beyond what you could conceive of on your own.

Thank you, Lord, for saying Yes to me through Jesus. Amen.

## Saturday, July 24

# Jesus and His Family

*Matthew 13:53-58*

**What part of your testimony might it be good to share with a family member who is not a follower of Jesus?**

This passage is one of the few places in the New Testament where Jesus' siblings are mentioned: four brothers by name—James, Joseph, Simon, and Judas (v. 55)—and "sisters" (v. 56), not named. There is mention in several places of the New Testament of some of these brothers being leaders in the church following Jesus' resurrection, and even that the resurrected Jesus appeared to at least James and Jude. It appears that most if not all of Jesus' direct family members came to believe in him as the Messiah. But today's passage gives us an opportunity to think about our family members who may not share our faith.

Matthew 12, Mark 3, and Luke 8 all mention Jesus' family coming to speak with him while he was preaching, with Mark indicating this was out of concern for his sanity and well-being. We are never told of any sort of fighting between Jesus and his family. Given that they came to accept Jesus as Messiah, we can surmise that their acceptance of him as Messiah was because of what they saw him do, not because of belligerent arguments about faith and religion. May the way we live our lives and the good we do for the Lord speak Christ into the lives of our own families and loved ones.

Lord, may my faith be a witness to my loved ones, but not a barrier to their knowing my love for them. Amen.

## SUNDAY, JULY 25

# Neighbors Enable Healing and Forgiveness

### *Mark 2:1-12*

**When have others helped you reach out to Christ?**

Given Jesus' growing reputation as a healer, it was obvious that the man being lowered through a hole in the roof had been brought to Jesus for healing, not forgiveness. Somehow, Jesus realized that while the man needed to be healed of his paralysis, he had a greater need, which, if not taken care of, would leave him crippled in his mind even after his body was made whole.

In any case, Jesus' response to the man on the mat immediately sparked controversy. Some of those in the crowd were professional teachers of the Scriptures. At once, they accused Jesus of blasphemy, saying that only God can forgive sins. And they were right, given that they knew nothing of Jesus' divinity. But Jesus said to them, "Which is easier—to say to a paralyzed person, 'Your sins are forgiven,' or to say, 'Get up, take up your bed, and walk'?" (v. 9). Without waiting for an answer, Jesus said, "But so you will know that the Human One has authority on the earth to forgive sins," he turned to the paralytic and told him to stand up, pick up his mat, and go home (v. 10). Immediately the man was healed and did as instructed. In other words, the man's sudden ability to walk was proof that his sins had been forgiven.

This story shows us that Jesus possesses the ability to heal the *whole* person. He puts people back together again.

Thank you for forgiveness, O Lord.

## Monday, July 26

# Our Lives and God's Purposes

### *Ecclesiastes 3:9-17*

**How do you deal with the good and bad news of life?**

You've no doubt heard someone begin a statement by saying, "We've got good news and bad news." The author of Ecclesiastes was doing something like that in this passage, only in reverse. He started with the bad news but then gave the good.

He gives the bad news first by asking a rhetorical question: "What do workers gain from all their hard work?" (v. 9). The implied answer is "Not much." And he's not just talking about the workplace.

But now for the author's good news: "I know that there's nothing better for [us] but to enjoy [ourselves] and do what's good while [we] live" (v. 12). In fact, in verse 13, the author concludes that God intends for us to enjoy the results of our labors.

From the perspective of the whole Bible, this "good" news may seem meager; it falls short of the complete joy Jesus spoke about in John 15:11. Nonetheless, even if we have a stark outlook on life, as the author of Ecclesiastes did, and knowing that we mortals cannot fully perceive God's purposes, declaring enjoyment of our labors a good thing is a statement of faith, if only a partial one. And these verses convey that God wants us to be occupied with *something* productive and not devalue the life our Creator has given us.

Thank you, O Lord, for the gifts of time and of eternity. Help us to live according to your purposes insofar as you want us to know them. Amen.

## Tuesday, July 27

# The Shepherd Lays Down His Life

### *John 10:11-18*

**How valuable do you think you are in God's estimation?**

Jesus said, "I am the good shepherd" (vv. 11, 14). In so doing, he identified himself with Old Testament imagery of a good shepherd found in such passages as Psalm 23 and Ezekiel 34. And to elucidate for his listeners what he meant by "good," Jesus contrasted the actions of the good shepherd with those of a hired hand who did not have the well-being of the flock as a primary concern.

The hired help may take care of the sheep well enough when there's no threat, but he's not about to risk his life to protect them when he "sees the wolf coming" (v. 12). In contrast, "the good shepherd lays down his life for the sheep" (v. 11).

In actual sheep-tending, this expression might mean that while the shepherd risks his life for the sheep, he doesn't necessarily lose it. But in context of Jesus' mission, this becomes a literal act. Thus, in verse 15, Jesus says it even more directly: "I give up my life for the sheep."

One response to that statement might be "Wow! Those must be some valuable sheep!" But, of course, that was Jesus' point, and we realize that he wasn't talking about the wooly animals but was using sheep as a metaphor for humankind. He was saying that every human life is of immense value.

Thank you, Lord, for the immense value
you assign to me and to all. Amen.

## Wednesday, July 28

# The Value of the Law

### *Romans 7:7-12*

**When has a thing intended for good become a channel for you to sin?**

Paul here wrote about the Law and sin. He said that if the Law labels some action as sin, then when one commits that act, one knows one is acting against God's will. As an example, Paul used the tenth commandment, the one about not coveting what a neighbor has. Once the commandment was given, people desiring their neighbor's wife knew that God considered that sin.

But Paul was not talking only about the Law's ability to define sin. Rather, he was saying that the Law, through no fault of its own, became a channel through which sin operated. When God's law forbids something, our sinful nature makes us desire that thing all the more. Thus, Paul's leading question in this passage: "So what are we going to say? That the Law is sin? Absolutely not!" (v. 7).

One way to make sense of this is to think of a strong-willed, impulsive child who, when he knows where his parents have set the boundaries of behavior, purposely steps over those lines just to assert himself and see what will happen. The boundaries remain good things, but they also become channels for the child to challenge his parents and violate their will.

So the Law is good, but people still need Christ, as the Law makes them aware of sin in their lives.

Let me be to you, O Lord, not a strong-willed, disobedient child, but a willing child, doing your will. Amen.

## Thursday, July 29

# The Purpose of the Law

### *Galatians 3:19-29*

**Who were your most effective mentors while you were growing in faith in Christ?**

To illustrate that God never intended the Law as a permanent measure, Paul introduced the metaphor of "our custodian until Christ" (v. 24). "Custodian" translates a Greek word that in Paul's day referred to a trusted household slave who was responsible to watch over his master's son, accompany the boy to school, make sure he attended to his studies, and keep him out of trouble. The time would come, of course, when that son reached adulthood; and from that time forward, he no longer needed the protective and corrective care of the slave. In the same way, Paul implied, the Law protected and corrected Israel until faith in Christ came and "we are no longer under a custodian" (v. 25).

This has important implications for us today. Paul explains in this passage that everyone who unites with Jesus Christ through faith is a child of Abraham. And collectively these persons, gathered in the church, become inheritors of the promise to Abraham. Thus, while the Law was for Israel, the promise of God is for Israel and for the church, and membership in the church is open to all, regardless of any other factor, through faith.

Holy God, thank you for all the ways you have taught me right from wrong and for the gospel today. Amen.

## Friday, July 30

# God Is Faithful and Fair

### *Romans 3:1-8*

**What events have caused you to think that God isn't always fair?**

Today's reading picks up after Paul has made an argument to the Romans that Jewish identity as one of God's chosen people is not enough for salvation. Paul anticipates some questions his audience might have, and so addresses those questions. The first three questions are: "So what's the advantage of being a Jew?" (v. 1) "What does it matter, then, if some weren't faithful?" (v. 3) "But if our lack of righteousness confirms God's justice, what will we say? That God, who brings wrath upon us, isn't just . . . ?" (v. 5).

While Paul addresses a couple more questions in this passage, those three, when aimed at our circumstances, are sufficient for us. We might reword them as follows:

What's the advantage of being a Christian?

If we fail to be faithful to God, does that cancel God's faithfulness to us?

If God expects righteousness from us who have human failings, does that mean God isn't fair?

I think the answers to those questions are:

God entrusted us with the gospel message.

God is faithful, no matter what.

God knows our failings. That's why the gospel is based not on our obedience but on God's grace.

Thank you, O Lord, for your faithfulness and grace. Amen.

## Saturday, July 31

# All Are Under the Power of Sin

### *Romans 3:9-20*

**When have you been acutely aware of your own sinfulness?**

Paul was right. All have sinned. And so in the church, we still talk about sin *and* salvation. We don't say people are sinners just so they'll see the need for Christ. Rather, we recognize a deadening glitch in our own relationship with God and others. We have called it sin, but we have learned that Christ brings reconciliation and overcomes the glitch.

We also talk about sin because sin is parasitic. When sin is given free rein in our lives, it destroys not only what it touches but the one who hosts it.

I heard the story of a pastor who preached about sin. Afterward, one of his church officers said, "We don't want you to talk so plainly about sin because if our boys and girls hear you, they will more easily become sinners."

So, the minister led the church officer to the janitorial supply closet where he took a bottle off the shelf. It was clearly marked "Poison." The minister said, "You want me to change the label to something like 'Essence of Peppermint.' But don't you see? The milder you make the label, the more dangerous you make the poison."

Along with proclaiming the gospel, the church needs to label that which pushes us away from God and distorts our lives for what it is: sin. No matter how else we try to dress it up, it can never be essence of peppermint.

Help me, O Lord, to recognize sin in my life and
to turn from it by the power of Jesus. Amen.

# AUGUST

## Contributor:

*Randy Cross*
*August 1–31*

## SUNDAY, AUGUST 1

# Keep Insisting until Justice Comes

### *Luke 18:1-8*

**How well do you trust God with your life?**

A widow decided that enough was enough. She appealed to a judge for justice. The judge was corrupt and couldn't have cared less, yet he was worn down by the persistent woman. He answered her need for justice not because he cared so much about her plight but because, frankly, he was just tired.

Jesus reminds us that when things are rough and it doesn't feel fair or right that the entire world seems lined up against us, we, too, need to know what our Savior once told a worrying world: "Won't God provide justice to his . . . people who cry out to him?" (v. 7) God asks, "Do you trust me?"

I'm not sure why humans are often wired with the tendency to take all of the blessings we receive in the course of a day, wad them up, and stick them in our back pocket without much thought. But when something bad happens, we frame it, put a spotlight on it, and focus all our attention on it. We seem to forget that, good or bad, we can trust God to be with us, no matter what. Jesus' lament is pretty powerful in verse 8: "When the Human One [the Son of Man] comes, will he find faithfulness on earth?" That's the very question that we certainly can personalize. When Jesus comes, will he be able to recognize my faithfulness, or will it be so weary that it looks just like the rest of a worrisome world? What will be your choice in how you live your life?

O God, fill me with your love, and teach me
to trust you; in Jesus' name. Amen.

## Monday, August 2

# The Power of the Gospel

### *Romans 1:16-17*

**Where do you find your power?**

Do you consider the gift of salvation to be a gift of power? Sure, we think of it as good news, as a wonderful and loving act of God, or as an outpouring of grace for our lives, but when we begin to think of salvation as power, it ought to create within our minds the understanding of the strength and fortitude given to us through the power of God that flows through our lives. Here in our Scripture, Paul is clear to affirm that we live—we exist—through faith in the power of Christ. It can and should give us the ability to move in our lives with assurance and with confidence that God is for us, and will guide us in ways that bring joy and hope.

God's power brings us new life and the ability to stand and work for holy and just purposes in our world. Sure, the gift of salvation changes us and restores us to the loving and wonderful relationship with God, but it also brings us the power to make a difference, to save other lives as we have been saved and to become the very hands and voice of Christ where we live. The most powerful chapters of the Christian faith have been written by those persons who saw their own salvation as the doorway to love others and to bring justice to our world. When you think about the grace of God, how will you live today to express that faith to others?

Dear God, empower me today to live for you and to find the means to serve you for all eternity; in Jesus' name. Amen.

## Tuesday, August 3

# Luke 3:7-14

### *Bear Fruits of Repentance*

**How do you show your repentance as a follower of Jesus?**

I can't imagine having John as my pastor! When was the last time you heard a sermon begin with "You children of snakes!" (v. 7)? Yet, I am sure John was able to get the attention of those who were coming to be baptized by this wild prophet in the wilderness. John brought a huge challenge to the way in which persons were to live their lives. John was almost brutal in his demand that those listening to him utterly change the way in which they lived and acted in the world. "Repentance" meant far more than just feeling sorry for something that you might have done. It meant to turn around and away from anything that was not holy or did not reflect God's presence.

It's important for us to realize that repentance does not mean refraining from doing wrong; repentance means to return to where we should have been all along. It means living and acting in full accordance with our place and relationship as a child of God.

Our "fruit" of repentance is not simply refraining from doing wrong—it is to live holy and wholly in Christ. What is part of your life now that you would be better off losing or getting rid of? What does God want you to do that you can take up in its place? How do you show Christ that you are following him? What are you willing to change to truly become his disciple?

O God, direct my path, and lead me in your righteousness this day; in Jesus' name. Amen.

## Wednesday, August 4

# Genuine Christian Behavior

*Romans 12:14-21*

**What is the most important action for a follower of Jesus?**

What would be the most important actions you and I might take on as followers of Jesus? Our Scripture for today, and especially the larger section out of which our Scripture comes, might give us some good clues. Paul invites the Romans to become "living sacrifices," or holy offerings to God (Romans 12:1). This happens as we let go of the way the world forms us and live as very different kind of people.

You see, it's not so much the actions or even the behavior that matters—it's why we act in a certain way. When our behavior is based on our belief, our faith, then the actions we take on will be far more genuine than simply going through the motions of living as good people. Today's eight verses simply highlight ways in which we can live out our faith, in holy and often surprising ways. Those instructions become far more powerful and compelling when we realize they are far more than moral behavior or manners. They arise out of our core belief and trust in Jesus as the compass and motivation for all our actions toward others.

It, of course, boils down to love. God's love for us is the reason that Christ came to earth, and our love as a grateful response for that powerful gift then moves us to act in ways that might seem countercultural (like caring for your enemy—verse 20), but in fact are ways of acting that express and reveal God's love in Christ to this world—through us.

Loving God, move in my heart to love and serve
others in all that I do; in Jesus' name. Amen.

## Thursday, August 5

# Gentiles Experience Repentance

### *Acts 11:15-18*

**How has God surprised you in your life?**

Acts 10 and11 are perhaps two of the key chapters in the New Testament after the Gospels. As the church came into being, and multitudes came to know Jesus as Savior, they were still limited to those of the Jewish faith. Peter was a faithful Jew and a great disciple. But he had received a vision to preach to a group of Gentiles, and he recounts in verse 15 how the Holy Spirit fell on them while he was preaching. His huge surprise was in realizing that if the Holy Spirit can come to them, as the Spirit came to the disciples on Pentecost, then God truly offers salvation to all (v. 17). This utterly changed the focus and direction of the church!

I would never say that we should just simply throw out all rules and limitations that we find in our lives. The Christian faith is not an excuse for any kind of living we want to pick up. However, it could be that sometimes in our passionate and strong desire to "keep the faith," we may need to be careful that we are not trying to limit where God's love may grow or build a barrier between our own acts of love and the world that needs it.

Maybe God has some surprises in store for us as well! Where might you imagine God's wonderful surprise not yet opened in your own life?

Open my eyes, Lord—I want to see and experience
your entire love for this world; in Jesus' name. Amen.

## Friday, August 6

# Paul's Joy at Corinthians' Repentance

### *2 Corinthians 7:9-11*

**Where have you experienced godly sadness?**

Paul writes of the Corinthians experiencing "godly sadness" (v. 9). Godly sadness is different from the normal type of sadness we experience when something bad happens in our lives. Godly sadness comes as we realize that we have acted in a way that breaks God's heart. Godly sadness is linked to penitence and to repentance because it produces the desire deep in our hearts to no longer sin. It's far more than being sorry for something. It arises out of the core desire to be one with God, to resolve never to do what we did again, and to take up the holy and eternal life of love.

Does your repentance before God look like this? Is there within you the pure and strong desire to no longer live a life of sin? Have you experienced a changed heart yourself and a sensitivity to what sin (that broken relationship with God) does to destroy your own life?

When we take our faith as the most serious thing we can claim, it also becomes the most freeing and joyful thing in our lives. Imagine living a day before God with no regrets—not because you didn't care, but because you experienced oneness with Christ! What will you do to move toward that experience? How will you work so that your heart's desire and your actions reflect the same? Where can you begin to feel godly sadness that inspires you to change your life?

Make me a captive, Lord, and then I shall be free. Let me give myself to you today; in Jesus' name. Amen.

## Saturday, August 7

# Doers of the Law are Justified

### *Romans 2:12-16*

**How do you know that you are a righteous person?**

Paul spends a little time in Romans 2 talking about how laws and the Law will become an issue for righteousness. Of course, it's easy to see how the Jews would need to obey the Jewish Law, since that was the pathway to their relationship with God and proved their faithfulness. However, the early Christians found themselves in a different world, since Gentiles, who never had to obey the Jewish Law, were also required to show their righteousness. Paul explains in verse 14 that "when they instinctively do what the Law requires," even though they have no Law, they fulfill the law written on their own hearts and are righteous. Of course, the opposite is also true, and not having the Law didn't mean that the Gentiles could act any way they wished! No—they still were expected to live holy.

We are still expected to live holy and just and to seek to be righteous in whatever way we can. In fact, you could almost say that The law is like the riverbank—we know when we have left the river! But where we are called to be is deep within the life-giving current in the center of the river, where we know and can trust that God will judge us and find us truly righteous in our relationship with Jesus.

As you listen to your own conscience, and spend time in prayer, can you become more aware of God's call and claim on you, and God's invitation to live the "lawful" life?

Most holy God, grant me the ability to see and to live where you call me to be; in Jesus' name. Amen.

## Sunday, August 8

# God's Righteous, Impartial Judgment

### *Romans 2:1-12*

**Why is it so easy to judge others?**

Judging others isn't just bad manners. Our judgment of others is bad, for one reason, because it's rarely true. We expand and overblow the speck in the other person's eye. Judging others also calls into question our viewing of the judged person's holy place as a child of God. We lessen their value in our own eyes, sometimes in the eyes of others, and sometimes in their own opinion of themselves. When we judge others, we do exactly what Paul writes about in verse 4: we have contempt for the riches of God's generosity. God's kindness is supposed to lead us to change our hearts and lives! Although God had the right to utterly toss us away, God chose instead to cherish us and to reclaim eternal life for us. When we judge, we throw all of that away for the sake of feeling self-righteous or better than others.

How can we possibly accept God's grace and then carelessly go on living as though Jesus doesn't matter and the entire work of salvation is just for my benefit, not for my transformation? In that, we will certainly know God's judgment, not as doing bad things, but living without God's love in our hearts. The word "wicked" doesn't mean doing bad things; it means attempting to live as though God doesn't exist or matter at all. When we judge others, we attempt to place ourselves on God's throne.

O God, bring me humility and the desire to live in
true love before you; in Jesus' name. Amen.

## Monday August 9

# God Provides Food to the People

### *Exodus 16:13-17*

**How do you know God will take care of your needs?**

God providing manna in the wilderness is a powerful image of how God cared for the nation of Israel. Peering back into the early part of the chapter, we read that the people whined and complained like a nation of toddlers, because they were hungry, and just wished that God had killed them all in Egypt! At least there, they had food to eat (Exodus 16:3).

We humans certainly do know how to whine and complain when we feel the slightest needs in our lives. Our prayers can become accusations that God has not cared for us as we thought God should. We grumble over the amount or the timing, as though we think we are the ones who have the power and authority to manage both.

The stories of Scripture sometimes show us not how we are supposed to act, but examples of how poorly we could behave. Today's Scripture tells us a powerful truth: God will take care of you. God will even perform miracles if necessary, because there is nothing God cannot do. God's love and grace flood our world with amazing and wonderful results—like manna in the wilderness—and it is our responsibility to pay attention to what God is doing even as we wait, and then to offer our praise and thanks for the blessings that come with every new morning.

What can you offer to God to show your faith in the waiting and your gratitude for such abundant care?

God of power and love, lead me to trust in your desire to care for me both today and always; in Jesus' name. Amen.

## Tuesday, August 10

# The Widow's Generosity

*Mark 12:38-44*

**How generous are you?**

In our Gospel reading today, Jesus observes the giving patterns of folks as they make their offering to the temple. He saw many rich people making their offering, and it was for a lot of money. Shouldn't there be praise for that? I mean, they did give, and the Bible says "lots" of money. But a "lot" apparently wasn't that much to them, and Jesus was aware of it.

Then we get to the core of the story. A poor widow gives two copper coins, hardly worth anything at all. It was all she had.

Suddenly, we are clear as to what generosity means. She didn't give from her loose change—it was the heart of her "fortune." Nothing now stands between her and absolute destitution. She has nothing and will earn nothing. Why do that? She must have known that those coins would not save her, but her trust in God would. Her gift has become the gold standard for a generous heart, and something we might aspire to, but rarely match.

When we give whatever we give with generous hearts, our perspective is always changed. When we give in love and trust in God for all else that may come, it truly becomes a life of faith and generosity.

Accept our gifts each day, loving God, and help us to offer our hearts wherever we can; in Jesus' name. Amen.

## Wednesday, August 11

# Generous Self-Giving of Jesus

### *Philippians 2:5-11*

**How might you live out the attitude of Jesus?**

Philippi may have been Paul's favorite church. At least, the letter he sends is full of love, hope, joy, and encouragement to the Philippians to grow in love and peace with one another. Verse 5 in our reading is a powerful hope: "Adopt the attitude that was in Christ Jesus." What follows is a magnificent song of praise about the life and person of Jesus, which ends in a fantastic doxology in glory to God.

However, it's the attitude of Jesus that is so compelling and powerful for us to imagine for our own lives. Jesus was equal with God, yet he emptied himself of all the glory, all the power, and all the might, so that what was left was simply and purely love to share with the world. He shared it in humility to the point that he offered his very life for us. Out of that, and through resurrection, Jesus was raised, not only to life again, but to glory itself, and to honor in heaven and on earth, where he is declared Lord of all.

How do we possibly "get" that attitude? How could we, as distracted and self-interested humans, possibly approach that way of thinking and being? Please understand—it's not what we do. After we claim the gift of eternal life given to us as new life in Christ, then the Holy Spirit begins the wonderful work within us. Then with that same holy power, we offer our lives in love however we can be used to serve others in Christ's name.

God of power and love, fill my heart to love this
world as I love you; in Jesus' name. Amen.

## Thursday, August 12

# Excel in Generosity

### *2 Corinthians 8:1-6*

**To whom would you be an example of giving generously?**

Judea was in the midst of a horrible famine, and the church, already persecuted in Jerusalem, begged for resources to survive. Paul put the message out and the church in Macedonia, which itself was caught up in extreme poverty, still offered a "surplus of rich generosity" (v. 2).

When the power of the Holy Spirit is at work in our lives, and we understand that we are all connected to each other, the offering of my resources becomes far less a burden. As the Macedonians recognized, it becomes a privilege to share from our own depth of wealth and generosity.

The key to it all, of course, is not to wait until a dire emergency before you and I give of ourselves. As we cultivate the habit of giving generously and living for others, our gifts become more profound, and our love makes it even easier to share what we have in a joyful spirit. We excel in generosity ourselves as we realize that all that has been entrusted to us is an opportunity for offering ourselves to God through our gifts and resources.

What is your experience of generous giving? In what ways can you cultivate that ability in your life?

O Giver of all good things, help us to imitate you in our own lives this day; in Jesus' name. Amen.

## Friday, August 13

# Generosity Results in Mutual Thanksgiving

### *2 Corinthians 9:11-15*

**In what ways have you offered generous thanksgiving?**

As Paul writes to the Corinthians, he moves beyond a plea for them to give to a prediction of what they themselves could expect as they begin to give from their hearts. The church will become "rich in every way so that you can become generous in every way" (v. 11). What a glorious prophecy! The people of Corinth will learn what it means to give, not as a burden, but as an offering of worship and thanksgiving to God. In addition, those who receive their blessing will also learn and find evidence of the church's generous and loving heart. The result is not just that money gets shared—it is that the bond between the churches grows deeper and richer, and the understanding of God's grace to all becomes more profound.

How will you learn to become even more generous in your life? Some folks are satisfied to give out of their leftovers, saving all they have to care for their own needs. That practice is absent in our Scripture and in our way of life as the redeemed children of God. Instead, we are invited to not be conformed to the world's practice of hoarding, but instead to live with thankful and generous hearts and to prove how God's grace has transformed us into those persons who will offer all that they are so that the powerful presence of God's Spirit may flourish in this world.

God, allow us to give thanks with a grateful heart, and
so love your people daily; in Jesus' name. Amen.

## Saturday, August 14

## 2 Corinthians 8:16-24

### *Support the Ministry of Church Leaders*

**How have you supported your church leaders?**

We certainly are living in challenging times for churches and pastors. So many changes have occurred, making ministry that much more difficult. That's why we all have the opportunity and responsibility to pray for our pastors and their work, that God would guide them and help them to bear fruit in what they do.

In 2 Corinthians, Paul is excited that Titus is coming to visit the church. Paul has such confidence and support for this missionary and wants to make sure that Corinth understands the excellent work Titus has done and the commitment he has to the work of grace. Today's Scripture is a commendation for Titus and others, so that their work is done with the support and love of the people.

How wonderful when we do have excellent leaders and enthusiastic followers, and together, folks are committed to a goal or task that requires God's power and leadership to accomplish. I hope that you, as a student of Scripture, would see this important work as a blessing in your own church and in your own life. As well, how significant it would be if you could serve as a positive and excited leader yourself and encourage others to take on the same ministry. When we do this, we honor Christ ourselves, and we show our love for the One who has first loved us.

I pray this day for my church and those who
lead me that together we might honor you,
gracious God; in Jesus' name. Amen.

## Sunday, August 15

# Balance Need and Abundance Fairly

### *2 Corinthians 8:7-15*

**How much can you afford to give away in your own life?**

There is a type of balance that is required as we attempt to live faithfully, and Paul offered instructions about this balance in today's passage. Paul is careful to help the church members understand that they are to be clear about what indeed they can afford to give for the sake of others. He really does say that there is no expectation for someone to fall into financial difficulty because they have given so much away to care for the financial difficulties of others (v. 13). However, he is also clear that what we can afford will meet the shortcomings of others, and then when the need is reversed, we will also be cared for in the same way by God's people. He uses the quote from Exodus (v. 15) to remind them that the manna was collected by all and divided equally among all as a community.

Am I generous enough? Have I balanced my resources with others' needs? Do I understand the way in which we are all interconnected as children of God? When we learn how to hold on to our resources loosely, as stewards and not owners, we are more capable of caring when need arises in others' lives.

Who stands in need of your riches today? What joy and enthusiasm can you find in sharing in a balanced way with our world?

Reveal to me this day, O God, the way in which I can serve you with all I am and all I have; in Jesus' name. Amen.

## Monday, August 16

# 1 Corinthians 12:12-26

### *Many Members in One Body*

**What part of Christ's "body" do you see yourself as?**

Paul was a genius to write about Christ's body. The analogy moves us beyond thinking we are part of a community, or a town, or even a family, to the point where we are interconnected as spiritual "parts" of the same body of Christ. Such imagery invites us to recognize both how important everyone is and how we need each other as this spiritual being—a living and moving "body."

Why, then, is it so easy for us to consider other members of this holy body as though they don't matter or are not pulling their weight? If our thinking strays that way, we might discount anyone who's not doing what I am doing in the church.

Paul calls us back to a different image. He says that we are all placed here by God (v. 18). There are no members more valuable, no pillars of the church. Instead, we all claim the same precious place, as we fit into God's call on us to live together and be in ministry together no matter what part we may be.

Has there been a time when you didn't feel much like part of the church, or perhaps a time when you wished others would just leave? Prayer, forgiveness, and humility are all part of our life together—even when the "big toe" misbehaves!

Lord, lead me to love and care for all parts of your wonderful creation of the church; in Jesus' name. Amen.

## Tuesday, August 17

# Aim to Live by the Spirit

### *Galatians 5:16-26*

**What challenges do you have in trying to live by the Spirit?**

As we look at today's Scripture, it may at first glance look to be simply a huge list of things a Christian is forbidden to do. Paul writes that, guided by the Spirit, you shouldn't simply do whatever you want to do. However, we need to once again go back to the basics of living the Christlike life and remember that it's not made up of "do this, don't do that" type of rules. Instead, the warnings that Paul offers against certain actions are meant to frame what happens when we live with selfish motives (v. 19). Selfishness creates a mess and is in direct conflict with the Spirit (v. 17). If we give ourselves over to selfish ways, we prove that we have disdain for the Spirit and eternal life.

Instead, verses 22-23 offer the images of what happens when the Spirit is active and leading your life: love, joy, peace, self-control, and the rest are evidence of living a holy and Spirit-filled life. Certainly, we choose the second set of verses when we are thoughtful and open to God's leaning. The challenge, of course, is to remain with that bearing in our lives day-to-day. The way in which we do that is by staying connected with God in prayer and study and seeking God in every part of our lives. Without that connection, we will walk away from God's kingdom, in the greatest tragedy of all. The greatest joy, on the other hand, is life in Christ!

How will you live by the Spirit in your life today?

Holy God, guide me that I would stay on the path
you call me to take; in Jesus' name. Amen.

## Wednesday, August 18

# Respond to Abuse with a Blessing

### *1 Peter 3:8-12*

**How challenging is it for you to live the Way of Christ?**

Anyone who says that living the authentic Christian life is simple is either living blessed in such a way that they have no challenges, or else they are deceiving themselves and not engaging with the simply hard and important work of living holy in a world that at times is just plain unholy. So, we need to be reminded of Peter's words once again. A huge part of living faithfully is also learning how to live humbly with one another. Humility opens the door to sympathy, to compassion, and to truly loving someone even though they treat you cruelly. Peter says that we are called to be "modest in your opinion of yourselves" (v. 8).

As we allow the qualities of humility and peace to be forged in us through our connection with God, we are better equipped to respond in love, and to bless those we encounter, no matter how they treat us. Of course, the most important response is one of love—not a reaction to the "junk" that others toss at us, but instead with a grateful response to what God has blessed us with—a life of meaning, purpose, and peace. We don't allow others to take advantage of us. We don't remain in harmful, abusive situations that could bring injury to ourselves or others. But we respond to the people who might put us in those situations with love and not by returning harm for harm.

Guide me and lead me. Let me turn my eyes upon you, loving God, and respond to others with that same love; in Jesus' name. Amen.

## Thursday, August 19

# Treat Enemies with Love and Mercy

### *Luke 6:27-36*

**Who is your enemy?**

Jesus brings a radical and challenging invitation to his followers: Love that person who may be intent on destroying your life. Your actions are never to be a reaction to their actions. Instead, bless and pray for those who mistreat you (v. 28). It doesn't mean we put ourselves in positions where we could be harmed, emotionally or physically. God doesn't expect us to submit to harm when we have the ability to protect ourselves. But the change comes in our attitude toward those who seek to hurt us. We protect ourselves and others from the damage they can cause, but we still love the one who caused us pain, because of the love Jesus gives us.

How can this be? It can only happen as love dominates and acts sacrificially in our lives. Once we give ourselves over to love, to the point that nothing else matters, then we have the power and the grace to love those who would harm us.

We are called to act "the way children of the Most High act" (v. 35). How do we do that? It comes as we focus on Jesus and the love he had for us, and the sacrifice that he made so that we might live as children of God ourselves. It takes prayer and the transformation of our minds and hearts so that nothing else matters but Christ. Can you begin to claim that kind of life and attitude as you clear your heart of all that would stand in its way?

> O God, help me do the impossible. Help me to love my enemies, as you love me; in Jesus' name. Amen.

## Friday, August 20

# Don't Act by Human Standards

### *2 Corinthians 10:1-5*

**How do you fight your battles?**

In today's Scripture, Paul recounts fighting a battle. Although it's not a physical battle with weapons and marching, Paul does see it as a literal, spiritual conflict. He deploys arguments and the power of God in order to destroy things that "oppose the knowledge of God" (v. 5). Paul is deathly serious about this battle—it's not just a sharing of ideas or debating principles; it is a matter of capturing the thoughts and beliefs of those who would dismiss the truth of Jesus Christ and turn them to a new understanding and a new approach to life.

I'm not saying that we need to go to war over Jesus, but it might be worth considering that we are not on earth to live by human standards but by the grace and power of Christ. Our greatest calling, beyond living lives of love, is to live lives of truth and to find ways to help those around us understand the reality of God's grace in Christ and our response to that grace in all that we do. The "battle" before us each day is to live a life of faith and to share the gospel whenever and wherever we can. To fail in that work is to surrender our world to an existence of not knowing the Lord of the universe, which would be a terrible loss.

Will you use what Christ has given you this day to "win" someone for Jesus?

Give me the strength and courage, loving God, to serve you in all that I do; in Jesus' name. Amen.

## Saturday, August 21

# New Life in Christian Community

### *Romans 12:1-8*

**What gifts do you bring to church?**

In today's reading, the first few verses talk about the way in which we should see ourselves as living sacrifices, or holy offerings. Everything we are and have and do is meant to be offered to God. It fits with what follows: Paul talks about the different "gifts" that each of us has. Prophecy, service, teaching, encouragement, and others are all gifts that reside within us, but when we offer ourselves completely to God as an act of worship, they become the gifts that we are privileged to give away to build up the body of Christ. Any spiritual gift that we "possess" is not ours to hold and keep.

So, of course, you can see that it's critical that we discern what gift we are given to use for the church. If it is silent and hidden away from even our knowledge, it's kind of like loose change under a couch cushion, where it sits unused and uncelebrated. Therefore, one of the finest things we can do is to identify gifts in ourselves and also to point them out in others. This isn't to boast about who we are or what we can do—it's not our gift to boast about. It's only entrusted to our care so we can use what God has given us and help others to use their gifts to build up the body of Christ. What a holy and important work it is to then make that offering as part of our entire life, for the sake of Christ in our world.

Thank you, God, for placing within me a holy gift. May I use it to your pleasure and glory; in Jesus' name. Amen.

## Sunday, August 22

# Behavioral Action Goals of Christians

*Romans 12:9-21*

**What would you identify as your "defining motto" in life?**

In the last part of Romans 12, Paul lists a wide range of guiding principles that the church needs to hear. These are not meant to be laws that, if followed, grant us eternal life. Instead, they should be the response of faithful followers to the gracious gift already given to us in Christ. They are down to earth and practical—especially the one that announces, "Don't think that you're so smart" (v. 16).

Perhaps the most compelling one is the last one: "Don't be defeated by evil, but defeat evil with good" (v. 21). We are called in our holy eternal life to be different, and to respond and act in thoughtful and God-centered ways. You could almost add the phrase, "Because you are a cherished child of God . . ." before each one of these sayings. As a child of God, you are claimed, marked, and set loose in this world to transform it, to bring about the infusion of love into loveless places, and to be light and salt so that the world may know the One who has given his life for them.

Think carefully about the words that you use to guide and direct those you care for, or how you are able to influence the thoughts and actions of other you meet through your remarks. How can you change your world today? How can you bring the love of Jesus Christ to others through your own speech?

Speak through me, loving God, and help me to
change my world for you; in Jesus' name. Amen.

## Monday, August 23

# Buried in Baptism, Raised in Christ

### *Colossians 2:6-12*

**What does it mean to you to be "raised in Christ"?**

The Colossians had received the good news of Jesus Christ and had accepted the blessing of being brothers and sisters in Christ as a community. However, after Paul left, some folks within the community began to talk about the need for these new Christians to not only have accepted Christ, but also to take on new philosophies and other rituals, as though living in Christ was not enough. Paul utterly rejects the add-ons to the faith by encouraging them to "live in Christ" as they received him (v. 6). It is by the grace of God that they came to faith, and there was no need to have to add the requirements of receiving the grace.

Unfortunately, we sometimes tend to do that in our churches. We can tell it's happening when we add anything as a necessary requirement for someone to be called a Christian. Any actions for Christ should be expressions of our gratitude to Christ and not a prerequisite for being a Christian. In the end, Paul says, the only thing that matters is that who we used to be was buried in Christ and then raised to new life through God's grace through faith alone!

As you think about your own way of living out your faith, do you see your salvation depending on you doing lots of good things, or simply depending on Christ? I invite you to make a renewed commitment to live holy as a grateful response to what God has done for you.

Dear Lord, allow me to thank you with my
life today; in Jesus' name. Amen.

## Tuesday, August 24

# God's Example in All Relationships

### *Matthew 5:43-48*

**How can you possibly show complete love?**

It would be impossible to name the single most important teaching of Jesus. However, as Jesus preaches about love in the Sermon on the Mount, this teaching comes close! Jesus offers a revolutionary way to view and act in the world. Loving and praying for one's enemies completely upsets the notion of being divided into friends and enemies.

Jesus teaches this as he invites his followers (and us) to be "complete in showing love to everyone" (v. 48) in the manner of God's love toward us. Some translations state "Be perfect," but complete love seems more captivating, and maybe more challenging. How do we offer complete love? Two things must happen at the same time: one, we must shed preferences from our lives of who will receive or not receive our love; and two, we must allow the Spirit to overwhelm our decisions, so that every action we take, and every word we speak, and even every thought we think is molded and filled with the love of God for others. Can we do this? Certainly—it only takes an utter surrender of ourselves to God's will and complete transformation of our hearts. Is it easy? Of course not—but to love consistently requires the muscle of the heart to be as strong and gentle as God has created us to be.

Help me do what seems impossible, gracious God—
let me love in all things; in Jesus' name. Amen.

## Wednesday, August 25

# Life with Christ in the World

*John 17:14-19*

**Why would you want to live in but not of the world?**

Jesus' words today are a prayer to God the Father. He's concerned and wants the best for his disciples, as he knows he will soon have to leave them. His words can help us understand that thin line between diving full speed into what the world wants and does and separating ourselves from anything that might be considered "worldly." This has been the challenge of faithful Christians for centuries.

I think our key verse is verse 15, where Jesus doesn't ask God to take the followers "out of the world," but better, to keep them from the "evil one." That is, it appears that Jesus expects you and me to be engaged in the struggles and the challenges of living fully in the world but to not give ourselves over to a mindless following of the world's seductions and invitations, like drunkenness, sexual immorality, foul language, breaking relationships, violence, and more. Those are not our life's qualities or pursuits. Instead, we who follow Christ are called to use the powerful love of Jesus to change the world in which we find ourselves, and at the same time, not lose our authentic and honest place as a child of God.

What is a part of your life right now that you could and should leave behind in order to live with Christ more fully in our world, and bear that witness of love and holiness?

Help me, O God, to be your child in thought,
word, and deed; in Jesus' name. Amen.

## Thursday, August 26

# Life in the Spirit

*Romans 8:1-11*

**How do you learn to live as righteous and not selfish?**

Paul talks about life in the Spirit in contrast to life based on selfishness. Isn't it interesting that those two images are set up as opposites? That is, if my life is based solely on my own needs, my wants, my perspective on what I should get out of life, then my life becomes disarrayed and, ultimately, a messed-up life. Life in the Spirit, however, demands and offers a different sort of life. The demand is discipline: it's not about me and my particular momentary desires; instead, I place myself under the guidance and direction of God's Spirit. Another word for that ability to have my life corrected and built according to God's purpose is that I become righteous—not because of what I have done or accomplished, but because of what the Spirit does in me. I am led "to life and peace" and I am able to please God (v. 6). Again, not because of how I've built my life, but precisely because I hand over the building of my life to the One who knows better than me the way that leads to life.

The most important thing to realize, however, is that it is your choice. God will not force you to leave your selfishness and take up the Spirit. That's up to you. But if we want that life of abundance and peace, it comes when we live in the Spirit. Are you living in the Spirit? How can you allow God's spirit to live in you today?

Change my heart, O God, and allow it to be forever for you; in Jesus' name. Amen.

## Friday, August 27

# Speak Truthfully Always

### *Ephesians 4:25-30*

**What motivates you to live an honest life?**

Lying exists in many different forms: I say something that's not true, or I refrain from saying something that is true. Lying also happens when we attempt to live a façade that is not honest or valid. Whenever the specter of lying enters the situation, trust, respect, and anything positive breaks down. Any forward movement toward a greater life or relationship with another comes to a complete stop, because any good that someone does is burned away by the acid of the lie.

That's why Paul demands that we tell the truth to our neighbors "because we are parts of each other in the same body" (v. 25). Whatever I do that harms you or our relationship also harms me and diminishes my life, since you are part of me. Beyond lying, we refrain from holding anger or stealing from each other, or even using language that is foul and diminishes our life together. Paul ends by saying, "Don't make the Holy Spirit of God unhappy" (v. 30).

Our actions are never without consequences in our world. If our desire is to make the Spirit happy and grow a stronger body of Christ, then it is up to you, and to me, to be careful and thoughtful about all that we say and do.

What habits are part of your life that may be harmful to the body of Christ? What new ways of working and living with the people in your life and in your church would help grow a stronger, more truthful, and more holy existence?

God of truth and light, help me to imitate you through my words and my actions this day; in Jesus' name. Amen.

## Saturday, August 28

# Replace Anger with Forgiveness

### *Ephesians 4:31–5:2*

**What actions keep you from living a Christlike life?**

When I am running the hectic life, with deadlines and unmet expectations and a host of unresolved issues, they grow and bulge into my heart, and I become frantic in reaction. The ways of acting and speaking that are uncalled for and out of place in the life of a Christian receive a small amount of permission to be unleashed. Bitterness, losing one's temper, and all of the others grow bigger, and the imitation of God in my life becomes dimmer and more blurred. That is, until I meet someone who refuses to let those actions claim them. When I stop—when we stop, perhaps even taking Sabbath, and refusing to compete and strive after all of these things, then the clearer and purer imitation of the love of God can begin to emerge once again. I can learn again to be kind instead of demanding or demeaning. I can forgive instead of holding a grudge. I can live my life with love, following Christ's example to me.

In our world today, a thoughtful and gentle approach to life and those who live with us or who come into contact with us is more critical than ever, as we offer Christ through everything we do. I invite you to take an inventory of ways in which you may want to shed those habits that keep you apart from God. Where will you begin to have God create such a new life in you?

Gracious God, clear my heart of anything but the desire to live for you in all that I am this day; in Jesus' name. Amen.

## Sunday, August 29

# Live the New Life in Christ

### *Colossians 3:1-17*

**How would you like to live a transformed life in Christ?**

These seventeen verses in Colossians are almost self-explanatory. Paul is inviting the church members to be transformed into the revealed, raised children of God. What is stunning is that he uses phrases like "put to death the parts of your life that belong to the earth" (v. 5) or "Take off the old human nature" (v. 9). Paul is calling us to a radical reformation and renovation of who we are, how we think and feel, what we say, and certainly how we act. This isn't just some adjustments or giving up a couple of habits—Paul wants us to put on a "new nature," which means an utter and complete change in who we are (v. 10). That can only happen as we go beyond just getting rid of old things, to the point that we take on and fill our lives with the new life. We are invited and urged to live as thankful people and to do all in the name of the Lord Jesus.

Certainly, this is how we hope to live. This is our desire. What keeps us from doing so? I believe it is because we are comfortable in tolerating those things which do not bring life, and we fear in some ways handing our lives over to be changed in such profound ways. Friend, this is your choice. The way of life is set out carefully before you. Will you allow yourself to be transformed and to live this life that is offered to you today?

Give me the courage and the grace to live for you and to set aside all that would keep me away from you, O God; in Jesus' name. Amen.

## Monday, August 30

# Forgiveness and Healing of the Land

*2 Chronicles 7:12-16*

**Have you experienced God's forgiveness and healing?**

It's interesting, as we read today's Scripture, that the piece often quoted, verse 14, becomes a bit different statement by God when we read the whole paragraph. God was pleased with the temple being established in Jerusalem, and God promised Solomon to listen in that place to the pleas and prayers of the people. When God sent drought, locusts, or plagues on the people of Israel because of their disobedience and sin, when they prayed in the temple, that's where God's "eyes and heart" would be (v. 16). That's probably why so many people feel closer to God in a church building or a chapel. It reflects the same promise of God's presence in the temple: a place where prayers may be heard and answered and forgiveness given.

"Humbly pray, seek my face, and turn from [your] wicked ways" (v. 14). Those are the requirements of having God hear us, forgive us, and heal us. Therefore, our attitude and our approach to our prayer and our penitence make a huge impact on our own lives and the lives of our loved ones. We experience the loving forgiveness and healing of God when we are mindful and aware that God is indeed the One in the universe with the power to offer such gifts.

How can you create that mindfulness and trust in God's healing power for your own life? How will you feel God's love today?

Hear my prayer, O God, as I come before you this day. Heal us, I pray; in Jesus' name. Amen.

## Tuesday, August 31

# Forgiving and Consoling the Offender

### *2 Corinthians 2:5-11*

**What does it take for you to be able to reconcile with someone who has offended you?**

There was someone in the Corinthian church who had acted wickedly. As a result, the congregation banished the person. To try to bring reconciliation, Paul wrote, "This is why you should try your best to forgive and to comfort this person now instead, so that this person isn't overwhelmed by too much sorrow" (v. 7). The church is different from other organizations. Indeed, we have many rules and expectations of behavior, and there are times when we can no longer accept the ongoing bad behavior of someone; so he or she must leave. What Paul offers, however, is the thought that the person must never be lost from our love.

In the church, we are in the forgiveness business. That doesn't mean there are not consequences for our actions. Sometimes, even though we forgive, another must still endure those consequences. But Paul was concerned that we not fall into the trap of banishing someone and then feel self-righteous about it. Instead, he wanted the Corinthians, and us, to recognize that we all are to be forgiving and forgiven.

I need to consider who in my life I may have carelessly cast away when instead I should consider them as precious children of God. I should at least offer an opportunity for reconciliation and forgiveness.

Loving God, teach me to act like you and to forgive
and care for the one person I can't stand. Amen.

# SEPTEMBER

## Contributor:

*Sue Mink*
*September 1–30*

## Wednesday, September 1

# God Blesses Ishmael and his Descendants

### *Genesis 21:8-13; 25:17-18*

**When have you seen unlikely people blessed by God?**

What a shocking and difficult story! Abraham loved his son Ishmael, yet his wife insisted that Abraham disinherit him and send him and his mother out into the desert to die. And even more shocking, God agreed, and Abraham obeyed God. How could this be a story about the father of our faith and our loving and compassionate God?

Ishmael was born because Sarah and Abraham logically worked out an answer to the problem of Abraham's progeny. Sarah thought she was past child-bearing age and offered her maidservant to Abraham, resulting in Ishmael. He was born because of their own effort. Isaac, however, was born to Sarah when motherhood was impossible, a miracle.

God appreciates and blesses our effort, reasoning, and planning to accomplish the divine will. Like Ishmael, the result of our own work in service to God is treasured and honored by God. Even though Ishmael was not the child of the covenant, God still loved Ishmael, and pledged to Abraham, "I will make of your servant's son a great nation too, because he is also your descendent" (v. 13).

The covenant is an astonishing contract of mercy and miracles between God and humanity. Yet God left room, and even blessings, for those who live outside the covenant. Everyone is created by God, and so everyone can be gifted by grace.

Lord, thank you for your amazing grace that
extends to all the people of the world. Amen.

## Thursday, September 2

# Different Traits Rooted in Conception

*Genesis 25:19-34*

**When have you had to wait on God's promises?**

The strange story of Esau selling his birthright reflects badly on both brothers. Jacob took advantage of his brother and his brother's impulsive personality. We know from the prophecy that Jacob would be the dominant brother; but, somehow, it seemed it would be harder than this.

While some commentators suggest that Esau was trading physical comfort for spiritual blessing, this is not entirely true. The birthright entitled him to two thirds of his father's fortune; so, certainly, he was trading away earthly goods. He was also trading present-day comfort for his future. "Since I'm going to die anyway, what good is my birthright to me?" he answered when Jacob offered the trade (v. 32). The promises of his father were inconsequential compared to immediate gain.

In this story, Esau becomes like Sarah and Abraham when they decided that Abraham should have a child by Hagar. They could not wait and trust what was promised to them and, instead, took what they thought they needed for themselves. Esau despised his birthright, not because of what he would gain but because he didn't have what he thought he needed immediately. In the end, Esau gave up everything for a bowl of pottage.

Lord, help me to trust in your promises and
value them over my own solutions. Amen.

## Friday, September 3

# Reject Deceit; Seek God's Face

### *Psalm 24:1-6*

**Who is worthy to seek God?**

Psalm 24 speaks of the requirements for anyone who strives to see the face of God. Verses 1-2 remind us that this is the Creator God who crafted and commands the heavens and the earth. Yet in this psalm, God has become accessible. There are those who can dare to approach the mighty God of all of Creation!

Verse 4 tells us who may presume to seek God's face. They are not kings or high priests but "Only the one with clean hands and a pure heart; / the one who hasn't made false promises, / the one who hasn't sworn dishonestly." Clean hands and a pure heart describe inward motivation and outward actions. This does not mean someone who has a special designation or has gone through ritual purification. Instead, it speaks of the relationship one has with God and how that relationship is manifested toward others.

What motivates a person? One with a pure heart is motivated by God's desires for his or her life. How does that change one's life? It changes it by actions of grace and mercy to others around them, not dirtying their hands with greed or domination of their neighbors. God's name should never be invoked if one is not within God's desires for justice, mercy, and grace for all people. If we promote our own goals or desires, be it as an individual, a community, or a nation, we cannot stand on holy ground and seek God's face.

Lord, may I have a pure heart, clean hands, and a truthful soul, so I may be worthy to seek your face. Amen.

## Saturday, September 4

# Live Openly and Honestly

### *1 Peter 2:18-25*

**How do you respond when you are disrespected?**

This is one of those passages that can be distressing to interpret. As Christians, we are commanded to respect the worth of every person and to strive for justice. Yet here Peter tells slaves to submit to unfair masters who would subvert their human worth and dignity. How can we reconcile the cruelty of slavery with the good news of the gospel?

Because Jesus taught the value and worth of every person, many first-century slaves were Christians, which was a powerful lesson for the enslaved. Here, Peter tells them that Jesus himself suffered unjustly too. Jesus' response to personal injustice was not to repay evil with evil. Instead, he responded even to those who taunted, tortured, and killed him with grace and mercy. Jesus is to be the template for one's response to personal injustice. Submission is not because one does not deserve respect but because as a Christian, one strives to be Christlike.

Notice Peter does not excuse or approve of harsh slave masters, and it is our duty as justice-seekers to protect, support, and uphold those who suffer at the hands of others. This passage does not in any way condone those who oppress others; and if we are to pattern ourselves after Jesus, we are tasked to fight against oppression. Even though others may not see their worth, each Christian should see every person as valued and loved.

Lord, give me the strength to respond to evil
with the same grace that you did. Amen.

## Sunday, September 5

# Water Issues Resolved Peacefully; Peoples Blessed

*Genesis 26:6-22*

**How do you respond to jealousy?**

Isaac was blessed with a beautiful wife, Rebekah. He was concerned that the Philistines would kill him in order to have her. Like his father, Isaac lied and said that Rebekah was his sister, willing to give her up for his own safety. The king found out their ruse before he took Rebekah into his household. The Lord protected the people of the covenant, even when they repeated the mistakes of their parents.

When Isaac planted crops, God blessed him with a huge harvest. He became so wealthy that the Philistines complained that he was getting too powerful, and he quietly packed up his goods and left. He unstopped two former wells of his father, but both times, the Philistines stepped in to claim the water rights. He again packed up and moved on. Finally, he dug a third well that he could use in peace and named it Rehoboth, or "Room," because the Lord had made room for them to flourish. Isaac quietly served the Lord, humbly acquiescing to others because he trusted that God would continue to bless him.

Isaac recognized that others were jealous of him. But instead of asserting himself through his power and wealth, he remained a person of peace. Eventually, even the Philistines realized that this humble man was rich in God's blessings, and they approached him to pledge their goodwill and harmony.

Lord, may I trust in your blessings so that I respond to others in humility and peace. Amen.

## Monday, September 6

# Differences Settled Peacefully

### *Genesis 26:28-33*

**When have others seen God's blessings through you?**

Nowhere in Genesis 26 do we read that Isaac preached to the Philistines. We know he was a servant of God; God spoke to him twice in this short chapter, blessing him and his descendants. He acquiesced to the Philistines when they needed the land he was on or the water he had found. He knew he was blessed, and so he didn't need to fight for survival. The Philistines noticed. They saw that Isaac flourished, despite the fact that he walked away from fertile land and plentiful wells in the desert. They knew that he worshipped a different deity than they did, and they saw that he was blessed. Isaac's life was a witness to God's power and grace.

A God that powerful was not to be ignored, so the Philistines went to Isaac pledging peace. Even though Isaac and the Philistines disagreed on what had transpired up to then in their relationship, they swore an oath that they would not harm one another. God's blessings were so evident, even to nonbelievers, that they had to be reckoned with, so Isaac and his family had the additional blessing of peace.

It is right to praise and thank God for blessings. But even more powerful than talking about how God has changed our lives is living it out in ways that others can recognize. Our quiet lives of service can be a powerful witness to others and a further blessing for ourselves.

Lord, make me a living witness to your love, using not only my words but especially my deeds. Amen.

## Tuesday, September 7

# Isaac Prepares to Bless Esau

### *Genesis 27:1-4*

**When have you been surprised by an unlikely person being blessed?**

Today's reading is the beginning of a story that seems strange to today's culture. The elderly Isaac gave both of his sons blessings, which were actually prophesies that had the power to shape their futures. Like arrows shot from a bow, once uttered, there was no going back, even when Isaac realized that he'd been deceived into giving Jacob the blessing he meant for Esau.

The struggle for contemporary readers is to understand why Isaac's blessing was so important. Certainly, God could have blessed both brothers. But the theme of God blessing the unlikely, and even sometimes the undeserving, is one that runs throughout Scripture.

In God's world, it is not kings or the wealthy who are blessed. It's Joseph, the youngest son sold into slavery; David, the shepherd boy forgotten in the fields; and even the baby born in a stable. God takes those who society would forget and bestows blessings, even as society and tradition prepare to bless those the world has placed first in line. While kings assert their authority, Jesus blesses the poor, the meek, and the mournful. In a stunning reversal that catches the world by surprise, it's those the world would forget who receive God's grace, gifts, and blessings.

Lord, you are a God of surprising reversals! Help me to recognize the worth and importance of those the world passes by, those you choose for your blessings. Amen.

## Wednesday, September 8

# Rebekah Diverts Isaac to Bless Jacob

### *Genesis 27:5-17*

**Why did God choose deceitful people for the covenant?**

This strange and unsettling story continues as Rebekah masterminds a great deception. Scripture doesn't say that Rebekah prayed about her plan; and she never stated that God was guiding her. It was just happenstance that her goals for Jacob aligned with God's. Instead, this is an example of God's plan coming to fruition in spite of the people involved.

If we examine all four people involved in this story, none of them is a good role model. Isaac refused to accept God's prophecy. Esau was impetuous and capricious. Jacob and Rebekah were schemers, willing to cheat other family members for what they wanted. One has to wonder why this would be the family that God chose to carry the covenant. If God is a God of mercy and justice, why did God entrust the story of grace to the ungraceful?

Simply put, because this family is what humanity looks like. God must use unjust, sinful people because that's all there are. So often, we are weak beings who don't trust God when we should, taking matters into our own hands, sometimes with disastrous results. We excuse unethical and deceitful behavior when it achieves our goals. But God uses us, blesses us, and entrusts us with the divine plan anyway. Within this tale of deceitfulness and family dysfunctionality is the story of God's great grace, using flawed human beings to bring the story of light and love to all.

Lord, thank you for your blessings on the
ungraceful, including myself. Amen.

## Thursday, September 9

# Jacob Received Isaac's Blessing Through Deceit

### *Genesis 27:5-10, 18-19, 21-29*

**What would you do to be blessed by God?**

The blessing was not Jacob's. He was second born. But he knew the worth of the blessing. He spent his life reaching for it—by trickery, by lies, and, finally, by wrestling with God. Jacob had a drive, a hunger, that his brother never felt.

Esau had a comfortable life. When he met Jacob years later, he had flocks, wives, and children and was happy in his life. Jacob, on the other hand, was tormented, torn and limping, still reeling from his encounter with God. It would have been so much easier to have been Esau. But this longing, this drive for the blessing, is what drove Jacob's life.

Yes, Jacob stole the blessing. It was deceitful, and he tore apart his family with his actions. But unlike Esau, he knew that his entire identity was defined by this blessing, by his relationship with God. He was banished, exiled, and disdained in his quest for something that Esau traded for a pot of stew. They hungered for different things; and, eventually, they both got what they wanted.

It is difficult to understand why God would allow a blessing on a man who would resort to lies and deceit to get it. But God whispered promises of salvation, even to a thief. Maybe Jacob's unrelenting drive for God's blessings were honored in the end. While God does not condone dishonesty and deceit, Jacob's need to belong to God was what ultimately blessed him.

Lord, feed my hunger for you. May I never stop reaching for your blessings. Amen.

## FRIDAY, SEPTEMBER 10

# Samuel Hears the Voice of God

### *1 Samuel 3:1-9*

**When have you heard God's call?**

In this beloved passage, God calls Samuel, the young apprentice to the head priest Eli, but Samuel doesn't recognize who is calling him. As the message was for Eli, human logic would say that God would talk to Eli directly. But this is often not the case. God surprises people, catching them unaware, at times and in places they least anticipate.

Gideon hid in a threshing room and was astonished by the call to lead his people into battle. Peter the fisherman stood fearfully in his boat. Saul persecuted Christians before his epiphany knocked him off his feet.

God's call is often sudden, unexpected, and demanding. God's call brings something new, for the community and certainly for the person called. It's a drastic change. No wonder we don't always hear the call; sometimes the new beginnings that come with answering God's call can be so challenging that we would rather dismiss it.

Scripture is full of people who tried to run from God's call. It's understandable. There is no instance in Scripture where answering the call was easy. But once we recognize and accept God's demands on us, may we answer God in our entirety, "Here I am."

O Lord, speak! Your servant is listening. Amen.

## Saturday, September 11

# Elijah Meets God's Angel

### *1 Kings 19:4-9*

**Have you ever felt like giving up on your work for the Lord?**

Elijah was completely burned out. He had just orchestrated a showdown at Mount Carmel with Baal worshippers. Queen Jezebel vowed to kill Elijah, so he ran into the desert to save his life. Despite the stunning triumph on Mount Carmel, Elijah was finished with answering the call. "It's more than enough," he cried, "I'm no better than my ancestors" (v. 4). He could be lamenting the prophets who came before him and who were unable to turn the people back to God.

God's answer was simple. God provided the things Elijah needed to keep going: a hot meal and water. God was reminding Elijah that he had not finished his work. The angel urged him to get up and eat, telling him, "You have a difficult road ahead of you" (v. 7). God could have reprimanded Elijah for wanting to abandon the call. After all, God had come through for him at Mount Carmel and had protected him up to that point. Instead, God provided Elijah with what he needed: nourishment and encouragement, reminding him that his call was not over despite his despair.

Perhaps it is comforting to know that even God's great prophets have felt discouraged, but God has been there to encourage and uplift them as they continue to answer their call.

Lord, sustain me as I travel any difficult roads
you've placed in front of me. Amen.

## Sunday, September 12

# The Lord Renews the Weary

### *Isaiah 40:27-31*

**When have you doubted God's power?**

The Hebrews worshipped the Lord, who is the designer of the entire universe, whose ways mere men and women cannot begin to understand. God shakes the very foundations of the earth and deals in the miraculous, in world-changing events that transform all who encounter the divine. So how could the people of Jacob even think that God could not hear them or was incapable of answering their prayers? How could God be drowned out by Babylon?

It was because their fear, their exhaustion with the world, and their sense of defeat kept them from hearing. Even though they knew of God, their challenge was to remember and trust in God's power. Because of God's grace, they could look past Babylon and its soul-crushing oppression to claim the power of the universe and to live a life of hope and new beginnings.

Sometimes the world can be overwhelming, and even as people of faith, we're too weary and feel unable to continue. It is natural to grow tired and discouraged. There is no shame in weakness. Even young men tire and youths will faint. The truth is, we cannot follow God's call on our own.

But those who look to the Lord for their hope will find it. When we feel defeated, God will uplift. When we feel exhausted, God will renew. The promise of our Lord is that there is a reality beyond Babylon that waits for us all.

Lord, be my strength and my encouragement
when I grow weary. Amen.

## Monday, September 13

# A Great Priest for the People

### *Hebrews 10:19-25*

**How do you combat spiritual exhaustion?**

Whoever these "Hebrews" were, they were tired. They were tired of serving God, tired of uninspiring worship, and tired of justifying their faith to themselves and to others. The writer of Hebrews (often referred to as "the preacher") tackled this problem not by introducing exciting new programs or by trying to appeal to the younger crowd. Instead, he revisited the deep theological meaning of Christ's death and resurrection and how profoundly the sacrifice of Jesus Christ affected their lives.

In today's passage, the preacher emphasized that because of the sacrifice of Jesus Christ, all have access to a true and intimate relationship with God. What does that mean for us? First, we are to approach God with an open heart, confident that our baptism and the blood of Christ have made us worthy. Second, we are to cling to hope, because Christ is trustworthy. Third, we are to gather with others and motivate them in good works. To be Christian means to act like Christ and be part of a community dedicated to Christlike action.

The preacher's prescription for spiritual exhaustion, in short, instructs us to confront our faith by deep introspection, draw near to God, trust God's promises, and practice Christlike behavior with others. This is how our faith is refreshed and renewed.

Lord, guide me in a renewal of my passion for you. Amen.

## Tuesday, September 14

# Tithe to Support Levites and Community

*Deuteronomy 14:22-29*

**How do you celebrate thanksgiving?**

This passage describes an annual feast to celebrate a harvest. The people were commanded to set aside a staggering 10 percent of all that their land and livestock produced so that they could celebrate in the presence of the Lord. The harvest feast produced a surplus of food that was then distributed to the Levites, who were the priests and keepers of the temple. They did not own land, so this food was to support them for the year. In addition, food was stored to distribute to those unable to produce their own food—widows, orphans, and immigrants who did not have their own land. Those who could produce were to help those who could not.

Notice how these commands mirror the commands from the Epistle to the Hebrews we read yesterday. The people were called to draw near to God, coming together in worship. They were to become vulnerable by giving God their time and their surplus, therefore trusting in God's promises and provision. And they were to care for others, even those who were unable to produce or were foreigners.

Thanksgiving (the action, not the holiday) is a celebration of God's blessings. We approach God in humble gratitude, trust God enough to become vulnerable, and help others in need. "Do this so that the Lord your God might bless you in everything you do" (v. 29).

Lord, may I respond to you in proper gratitude for all the blessings you have given me. Amen.

## Wednesday, September 15

# Nathanael Will See Greater Things

*John 1:47-51*

**What are your reasons for becoming a disciple of Jesus?**

Nathanael was the first person John writes of who expressed doubts when he heard about Jesus. Yet when invited, he went with Philip to meet Jesus and judge for himself. Jesus responded by calling Nathanael "a genuine Israelite," that is, a righteous man who would engage with his faith enough to wrestle with doubts and skepticism (v. 47). He did not allow his preconceptions to be a roadblock to recognizing Jesus' identity.

While theologians have struggled with the significance of the fig tree, it is clear that Jesus knew things about Nathanael that proved to him that Jesus was extraordinary. That was all it took for Nathanael. But in many minds, the Messiah had been cast as a political figure who would throw off the yoke of Roman oppression and be the new King. Jesus was much more than a political figure, even a sacred political figure sent from God.

In verse 51, Jesus speaks in the plural to all assembled. The image of heaven with ascending and descending angels is reminiscent of Jacob's ladder in Genesis 28:12. What Jesus was saying was that he is the place where heaven and earth meet. He is the conduit between God and humanity and is the lifeline to salvation for all. Following Jesus means proclaiming the miracle of God coming in flesh to earth.

Lord, may I understand who Jesus is so that
I may be a worthy disciple. Amen.

### Thursday, September 16

## Esau Loses Blessing; Exiled

### *Genesis 27:30-40*

**Have you lost out on something you felt you deserved?**

If God is a God of reversals, that's great news for those who are oppressed. But how does God deal with those the world has put first in line when their younger brothers are blessed? If the poor are blessed, what happens to the rich? If the brokenhearted are lifted up, what about those who have no reason to mourn? We love to cheer on the little guy, but many of us are sometimes in the place of the elder brother too. And while society rewards that, it can be an uncomfortable place to stand before God.

Isaac had given the best to Jacob, but he did not send Esau away without a blessing. Despite the violence and exile inherent in his words, there is also a whisper of hope. Esau was not to be the child of promise, but like Ishmael, he would not be forgotten by God. While Esau would be subject to his brother, it would not be a permanent state. His nation, Edom, would not be subservient to Jacob's Israel forever. Remarkably, even those not chosen by God are blessed.

All people are created by God. While history has clear winners and losers, it never means that anyone is outside of God's care. Esau eventually prospered and forgave his brother. His life was not what he had imagined, but it was blessed and protected by God, nevertheless. No one is left out of the care, comfort, and even the miracles of God.

Lord, help me to remember that your blessings
extend to all those throughout the world. Amen.

## Friday, September 17

# Jacob Charged to Marry His Cousin

### *Genesis 27:46-28:5*

**How should Christians strike a balance between spiritual purity and engaging with the world?**

Throughout Scripture, we read about how the Hebrew people struggled with their interactions with other cultures. The Bible often records this through the issue of intermarriage. Apparently, Esau's foreign wives were a source of great stress for Rebekah and Isaac, so they sent Jacob to Paddan-aram to find a wife from Rebekah's family. If Jacob was to be the child of promise, it was crucial, they believed, to protect the covenant from outside influence. Jacob had to turn away from the rest of the world and live among and marry his kin in order to protect the covenant, his parents thought.

We need to be aware of how the surrounding culture can impact our faith. It is important to continually weigh the demands of our commitment to God against the influences of our society. But that commitment is not to abandon those around us. Micah 6:8 tells us what the Lord requires of us: "to do justice, embrace faithful love, and walk humbly with your God." If prevailing cultural values suggest we behave differently than this call from God, then for the sake of our own spiritual health and faithfulness, we need to intentionally turn away from the norms of our society even while testifying to God's blessings with the way we live.

Lord, guide me from any influence that would keep me from living within your blessing. Amen.

## Saturday, September 18

# Transformed by God's Visitation

### *Genesis 28:10-22*

**When have you been given a new direction for your life?**

While we usually refer to this vision as "Jacob's ladder," the Hebrew brings to mind a stairway or a ramp, like a tower reaching into the sky. Because of it, heaven and earth are interconnected, and what happens in one place affects the other. The profound message of this vision is that the Lord God interacted with earth's drama and stood beside the refugee, the shamed man, the cheating liar, and offered presence, protection, and security to the lonely, vulnerable, homeless fugitive sleeping in the desert. By human standards, Jacob's future looked bleak, but God offered him an alternative. He had a hope and a future. Despite all that he had done, he would be blessed.

Jacob awoke from his dream, but the message of his dream became his new reality. He honored the place of his epiphany and blessing and then committed himself to God. While it is true that even then Jacob's response was conditional, his promises reoriented his life. Jacob was pledged to faithfulness, even as God was faithful to him.

God is intimately connected to what happens to us, even those who are outcast, alone, guilty, and rejected. Throughout history, God has lowered Jacob's ladder to earth to stand by, to protect, and to create a home. The greatest example, Jesus Christ, stands as a testament to our divine connection to our Creator and to God's grace and love.

Faithful and loving God, thank you for your presence and protection, and your promise of an eternal home. Amen

## Sunday, September 19

# Jacob Marries Leah and Rachel

### *Genesis 29:15-30*

**When have you felt that God has forgotten a promise?**

Today's passage might well be titled "What Goes Around Comes Around." Jacob, the trickster, was duped by his uncle Laban on his wedding day. Jacob contracted a bride price for Rachel, seven years of labor, and gladly served it. But his former actions would come to haunt him on his wedding day. After the marriage was consummated, Jacob realized he had been tricked into marrying the wrong sister. Laban then offered Rachel as a second bride, with the wedding a week later if Jacob would agree to seven more years of labor. Jacob agreed, binding himself for fourteen years.

One of God's promises at Bethel, where Jacob saw the ramp to the sky, was that God would take him back to that land. Jacob might have been thinking when he was there that he would find a bride and take her back immediately. Instead, it was twenty years before he was back in Bethel.

The promises that Jacob heard in the desert that night probably seemed distant during those years. People are not good at being patient. It's easy to imagine that Jacob began to dismiss his vision at Bethel as the years dragged on.

Today's Scripture reading does not mention God even once. But God did not forget the promises made to Jacob that night at Bethel, even if it would take many years for those promises to come to fruition.

Lord, grant me faithfulness as I wait on you. Amen.

## Monday, September 20

# Leah Gives Birth to Four Sons

### *Genesis 29:31-35*

**How does God respond to people the world rejects?**

In quick succession, Leah gave birth to four sons: Reuben, Simeon, Levi, and Judah. Genesis 29:31 says that God gave Leah children because "the Lord saw that Leah was unloved." The names Reuben and Simeon are related to the Hebrew words for "seeing" and "hearing" because God saw and heard Leah's situation and blessed her by giving her sons. She named her third son Levi, which means "joined," hoping that his birth would join her to Jacob. The name of her fourth son, Judah, means "praise."

These names show Leah's faith and trust in God. Her father manipulated a marriage for her, her sister saw her as an interloper, and her husband did not love her; but God saw her, blessed her, and loved her. She knew that she was not forgotten, even if everyone around her treated her as if she were unimportant. This is the compassionate, remarkable nature of our Lord God.

Throughout the Bible, God always saw and blessed the underdog, the people the world forgot. Every person has worth and value to God, even if others do not recognize it. Our challenge as people of God is to see, hear, and then honor those the world has thrown away. Time and time again, it is exactly those society has deemed of little worth who God raises up, blesses, and gives a significant role in the divine plan.

Lord, help me to see, hear, and honor
the Leahs of this world. Amen.

## Tuesday, September 21

# The God of Jacob Brings Victory

### *Psalm 20*

**Where do you turn in difficult times?**

Psalm 20 is a prayer about battle. The key is verse 7, which states that human solutions cannot be trusted. Our future depends on being faithful and humble servants of God, living within God's will. The psalm repeats three key words to stress this point. The first is *ana*, the Hebrew word for "answer," used in verses 1, 6, and 9. While the people prayed, they were not telling God what to do. Instead, they waited for God's answer so that they could obey.

The second repeating word is translated as "help" or "victory." The Hebrew root of the word is *ys*, which means "saving power," a power that only comes from God. The last word is "name," which is repeated three times and refers to God's character, trustworthy and reliable. The people called out, appealing to God's character for saving power, and waited for an answer so that they could obey.

But the Hebrew people did not win every battle and were even conquered and exiled. This psalm stresses the key element of God's protection: not to follow one's own ambitions and desires but to faithfully turn to and trust in God's response in faithful obedience. To say that "God is on our side" is arrogant. God does not align with sides. Instead, we may choose to align ourselves with God. When we submit to God's will rather than trusting in our own power, we can claim a quiet confidence despite difficult situations.

Lord, may I turn from my own devices
and learn to trust in you. Amen.

## Wednesday, September 22

# Rachel Gives Birth to Two Sons

*Genesis 30:22-24; 35:16-21*

**When has God filled your emptiness?**

Barrenness for a woman was often listed with afflictions such as famine, disease, and drought that signified God's disapproval. Because God was the source of life, an infertile woman was thought to have been forgotten by God. Genesis 30:1-2 is an argument between Rachel and Jacob where she blames him for her infertility, but he directs her to the giver of life, God. It was only when God remembered her (30:22) that she gave birth to a long-awaited son.

God remembering the infertile woman is a theme throughout the Bible. Sarah, Rebekah, Rachel, Hannah, and Elizabeth were all infertile and remembered by God. For every one of them, God demonstrated divine power over emptiness and despair by creating life.

Each of us, at some time in our lives, can experience barrenness, where it seems we are empty and lacking purpose. It is often not a physical barrenness like Rachel's but a spiritual lacking where we are unable to bear fruit. Even though we may struggle and strive to be faithful, it feels as though there is no life inside. We may feel worthless or less of a person because we cannot create that spark in our faith. But creating life is God's work, not ours. Our work is to remain faithful and engaged, confident that God will hear and remember, just as God has heard and remembered throughout the ages.

Lord, create in me a new life, so that I may be filled with the joy of your blessings and bear fruit for you. Amen.

## Thursday, September 23

# Jacob Prospers at Laban's Expense

### *Genesis 30:22-32, 43*

**When have you seen God's will in action?**

Jacob had shown up at Laban's doorstep empty-handed twenty years before, but now he had wives, children, slaves, and large flocks of sheep, goats, camels, and donkeys. It was tempting to believe that all that came from Laban's resources. In reality, God was blessing Jacob.

Jacob's solution to take the black, spotted, and speckled animals was clever. In a tense situation where Jacob was being accused of theft, sorting the animals by color made it obvious which animal belonged to each man. It also was advantageous to Laban, because most of the sheep were white. Yet even when the odds were stacked in Laban's favor, Jacob's flocks continued to grow, due to God's blessing. As Laban did not worship the Lord, he must have deduced that Jacob was somehow cheating him, and their relationship became even more tense.

God made a promise to Jacob twenty years earlier to watch and protect him and bring him home. Jacob accepted that promise and made one of his own to return if God was faithful to him (Genesis 28:20-21). Laban worked for twenty years to thwart that promise, but God and Jacob stood firm. Despite the scheming and dishonesty, God was able to mold events to fulfill promises and create the patriarchs of the nation of Israel and bring them back to their home. God has a plan, even within the deception and unrighteousness of humanity.

Lord God, help me to trust in your promises, even when others are working to keep them from happening. Amen.

## Friday, September 24

# Living Among Wrongdoers

### *Psalm 57*

**When have you seen God's love conquer hatred?**

Psalm 57 speaks of the two worlds that coexist on earth: the kingdom of God and the secular world. The kingdom of God is not yet fully realized, but there is no doubt that God reigns and that ultimately God's vision for the world will come to pass. Sin still exists in the world though; and while those who preach hatred and division may seem strong, the love of God is stronger.

Verses 2-3 describe three ways that God will save and protect. The first way is that God will come through for me. God has a vision for believers that cannot be frustrated. The second is that God will send orders from heaven to save the psalmist. Those who are doing the will of God have the power of the heavens above to protect them. The third is that God will rebuke those who attack them. Those who use their power to harm and destroy will have to answer to the Lord.

And this is why the psalmist can sing and make music in the face of hatred and oppression. Those who claim God as their shelter can sing songs of praise. Verse 9 tells us to sing "among the nations" so that all people see the power of God's love and faithfulness, and no one will call anyone else an enemy again. This song of love and praise is the kingdom of God present on earth. This glorious psalm promises that one day, God's glory will be over all the earth, and all people will join in a hymn of praise, exalting God above the heavens!

Lord, thank you for the hope that enables your people to sing of your love in the face of hatred. Amen.

## Saturday, September 25

# Perfect God's Love Among You

### *1 John 4:7-21*

**When have you drawn on the power of the love of God to counter hostility?**

Sometimes the world can seem a hate-filled and divided place. Our faith calls for us to love all; but in the face of hostility, it seems impossible. Responding in love to hatred goes against all our instincts. This passage tells us that this kind of love isn't natural to humanity.

God's love for us is the source of our ability to love one another. God loves all people, regardless of their worthiness. Sometimes this is difficult for us to accept when we are staring at the faces of unlovable and even hostile people. But this love is God's core nature. This love is how God is revealed to humanity, through the sacrifice of Jesus Christ. And as followers of Jesus Christ, we are to be transformed by this love. When God lives within us, we live in this love, and God enables us to communicate God's love to others.

Simply put, God's love is incompatible with hatred. As recipients of God's love, we then are to see others through God's eyes. We are to be agents of love in an often-hostile world. This is what it means to be transformed by Christ. Those who abide in the love of Jesus Christ become aliens and strangers in the world because Jesus can enable people to live beyond the abilities of natural human compassion. They can become reflections of the love of Christ in a hostile world.

Dear Lord, transform me into an agent of your love. Amen.

## Sunday, September 26

# Jacob Steals His Family from Laban

### *Genesis 31:1-9*

**When have you hedged your bets with God?**

In today's text, Jacob tells his wives that it is time he returned to his native land. Jacob credited God for his remarkable success. He told his wives that it was because God had been watching out for him that he had prospered. Jacob had worked out a deal with Laban, to receive the speckled and spotted of Laban's livestock as payment.

If you go back and read the story of Jacob's prosperous flocks, you will read of two tricksters—Laban and Jacob—working to outsmart one another. Seemingly, Jacob was the cleverer of the two, and his scheme to make the flock bear spotted and speckled young made him rich. It is unclear how much he actually thought the speckled flocks had to do with God and how much they had to do with his scheming. While Jacob gave God the glory for his large flocks, no doubt he was also patting himself on the back for his own efforts.

But we know Jacob's schemes were totally ineffective. Put simply, breeding has to do with genetics, not what the animals are looking at. Jacob might have considered himself clever in acquiring this blessing, but it was really God at work despite Jacob's supposed cleverness.

God can use us to do work for the Kingdom, but life is given, hearts and minds are changed, and new vistas are revealed because of God. While the work we do is important, the power behind it always belongs to the Lord.

Lord, may I always give you the glory for
the blessings in my life. Amen.

## Monday, September 27

# Jacob and Laban Make Peace

### *Genesis 31:43-50*

**When have you ended a relationship because it stood in the way of following God's will?**

For twenty years, Jacob was trapped with his conniving father-in-law, first working for his wives and then for flocks. When he left, Laban chased after him to take back what Jacob had taken. Laban had been warned by God in a dream not to say anything to Jacob, good or bad. Presumably, this was why he capitulated, even though he felt that Jacob was running off with wives, children, and flocks that belonged to him. He proposed a monument to witness their uneasy truce, saying, "The Lord will observe both of us when we are separated from each other" (v. 49).

This truce, far from being a sentiment of friendship, was one of mistrust. It called on God to make sure that each of them lived up to the pledge they just made to one another and that Laban and Jacob would be accountable to God if they did harm to one another. The monument would serve as a border between them, and they each promised not to pass beyond it. Warily, they left one another's lives for good, trusting that God would protect them from one another.

As Christians, we try to mend broken relationships and heal divisions. But, sometimes, the best choice is to end a damaging relationship. Laban was preventing Jacob from following the call of God. His best choice was to leave his connection with Laban behind.

Lord, help me to recognize when I should walk away from a relationship that is hindering my service to you. Amen.

## Tuesday, September 28

# Jacob and Esau Reconcile; Families Blessed

### *Genesis 33:4-11*

**When have you seen God in the forgiveness of others?**

Worried about seeing his brother, whom he had wronged, for the first time in years, Jacob did his best to stack the deck in his favor. But, remarkably, all that was unnecessary. Esau, the wronged brother, ran out to greet Jacob, hugging and kissing him. Jacob was still recovering from another profound encounter. Just the night before, he had struggled with an angel, an embodiment of God (Genesis 32:22-32). On the banks of the river, he confronted his fears and his sins, dealing with the way he had responded not only to his family but to the call of God in his life. He left that encounter humbled and empowered, secure in his relationship with God but chastised and chastened.

Our relationship with God affects our relationships with others. Jacob saw the same grace in his brother that he had felt the night before, telling Esau that seeing his face was like seeing the face of God. Our ability to accept the forgiveness and grace of our Creator and therefore forgive and accept ourselves also allows us to forgive and accept one another and to respond in grace and gratitude when we are forgiven.

We often speak of the need to forgive, but this story reminds us also of accepting forgiveness when others offer it to us. If we cannot accept forgiveness from God, it is difficult for us to accept it from others, making it impossible for relationships to heal.

Lord, thank you for your blessing of forgiveness from you and from others I have wronged. Amen.

## Wednesday, September 29

# Too Late for Repentance

### *Hebrews 12:14-17*

**How much do you value your place in the family of God?**

The author of Hebrews used Esau as an example of what can happen when people are distracted from their greatest life work: being a disciple. Esau sold his birthright to his brother, Jacob, for a bowl of lentil stew. Esau's birthright was being the keeper of the covenant with God. Thus, Esau's story is one that is repeated over and over in our society today: the trading of simple earthly needs and desires for the most profoundly important aspect of our lives, a deep and life-changing relationship with God.

Esau became distracted from what was important by what was easy and comfortable. He did not have the spiritual endurance to remain as the keeper of the covenant and, instead, traded it for something inconsequential. When he realized what he had done, his place with God was gone. Hebrews 12:17 tells us, "He couldn't find a way to change his heart and life, though he looked for it with tears."

This passage brings to mind a great group of disciples, moving toward the shining light of holiness. When one stumbles, another reaches out his hand. When someone is lured from the goal, another calls them back. While we all carry elements of Esau within us, it is our responsibility to one another to support and strengthen one another so that we all can strive to see God's face.

Lord, strengthen my endurance as your disciple,
and allow me to be strong to help others. Amen.

## Thursday, September 30

# Commit to God's Love and Justice

### *Hosea 12:2-6*

**How would your life change if you struggled with God?**

Jacob had carried the covenant and hadn't lived up to the responsibilities of the covenant he had with God. Yet God met Jacob, and the two struggled at Bethel. It was a mysterious and terrifying encounter; and Jacob left a different man. No wonder the writer of Hosea used Jacob as an example to call the wayward Hebrews back to God. They were also the keepers of God's holy covenant and, like Jacob, they were turning their backs on the greatest responsibility in the world. They needed their own epiphany, their own struggle on the banks of the river.

Hosea 12:6 is the prophet's fervent cry to his people: "But you! Return to your God / with faithful love and justice"! Their encounter with God would be difficult and painful and would change them profoundly. But to shy away from that meeting would ultimately destroy them.

Every one of us has a riverbank where God waits for us. If we call ourselves Christians, we have a profound responsibility to live as faithful servants to God instead of chasing idols and living by deceit.

Coming face-to-face with our Creator, and acknowledging our shortcomings, is painful and difficult. But without that struggle, without that epiphany, we turn away from the only hope we have to be convicted of our sins and to be transformed into a true person of God.

Lord, convict me! May I serve you with faithful
love and justice all of my days. Amen.

# OCTOBER

**Contributor:**

*Sue Mink*
*October 1–31*

## Friday, October 1

# Perseverance

## *Acts 14:21-27*

**How did Paul respond to rejection of the Word?**

When the apostle Paul went to Lystra, he was attacked, stoned, and left for dead (Acts 14:19). Yet this passage says that soon after he recovered, he returned there. He went to minister to those who had tried to kill him and "strengthened the disciples and urged them to remain firm in the faith" (v. 22). Their persecution only helped in the growth of the faith. Paul didn't allow even attempted murder to stop him in his quest to make new disciples for Jesus Christ.

Boldness for Jesus Christ can be dangerous. Thankfully it's not often life-threatening, but Jesus spoke a countercultural message that challenges the ways of life of many who hear it: Love your neighbor, and even your enemy! Blessed are the poor! Turn the other cheek! It's not the way people naturally live, and truly living by these words can disturb the status quo. But God blesses those who live by the words of Christ.

The story of Jesus was so important that Paul could not leave others without it. His return with a message of love and forgiveness, even after being persecuted, must have done much to turn the hearts of those who heard him. His boldness for Jesus Christ brought others to salvation. May our churches remain bold in speaking of the radical love of Jesus Christ for all!

Lord, give me the courage to be persistent for you,
even in the face of suffering and difficulty. Amen.

## Saturday, October 2

# Strengthening the Faith Community

### *Hebrews 10:19-25*

**How can a church maintain a healthy congregation?**

This passage in Hebrews speaks of three things that the congregation had to do to strengthen their faith. The first thing was to draw near to God. Because of the sacrifice of Christ, we all have been made pure and clean enough to make a home in God's personal space because we are part of the family of God, called to be in the very presence of the Lord. The second thing was to hold on to hope. Christians can be certain that every promise made by Christ is true. This was especially important for those who were becoming impatient for Christ's return and beginning to doubt. The third instruction for this church was to motivate each other in love and good deeds. Often we think about what we do wrong, but this reminds us that not doing right when God gives us the opportunity can be just as bad.

These instructions are very relevant for the church of today. Drawing near to God means that we are active in worship, prayer, and study, always nurturing our relationship with the Lord. Holding on to hope means that we keep confidence in our faith. And motivating one another in love and good deeds means that we are built to do God's work on earth. When we become deaf to God's call to strengthen and serve others, we lose our purpose as people of God. How can we do anything less? May we value Christ's love for us with passion in our worship, prayer, and service.

Lord, help my church to draw near to you, to keep our confidence in you, and to always serve you. Amen.

## Sunday, October 3

# Changing the World

### *Acts 2:37-47*

**How did the early church grow strong so quickly?**

When the people heard Peter, they cried out, "What should we do?" (v. 37). Peter told them to repent and be baptized. They were to turn from their old ways of life and commit themselves to living by the Spirit and the Word.

To follow Christ meant that they would live their lives with a totally different focus. This was not just a religion but a radical new lifestyle.

Sharing of possessions in the early church gets a lot of attention today because it's so radical, but even more important are the other ways they grew in faith together. They "devoted themselves to the apostles' teaching" and focused on learning the true word and how it would impact their lives (v. 42). They became a community, breaking bread together despite social conventions and barriers between different economic classes. They prayed together, making their relationship with God their priority. God was not just an occasional duty for them but instead they were bonded to the Lord, empowered by the Spirit to become an authentic image of Christ in the community.

How can we apply this to our churches today? Life in the Spirit is not another thing to add to our to-do list but is a way to be. It is a commitment to both the community and to God that directs and focuses our entire lives.

Lord, may your Spirit permeate our congregations and strengthen our bonds with one another and with you. Amen.

## Monday, October 4

# The Power of a Community

### *Ecclesiastes 4:9-12*

**Why is it important to be part of a community of faith?**

My hobby is fiber arts. I love to knit and weave on my loom. Through the years I've learned a lot about fiber and especially different kinds of yarns. Most yarns are plyed. This means that there are at least two strands of yarn that are twisted together. Unplyed yarns, which are only one strand, are very fragile and therefore can't be used for many things. But by twisting two or more strands of yarns together, they become much stronger and therefore much more useful.

This short passage in Ecclesiastes applies this same concept to people. Two people working as a team can accomplish much more together than alone. When one tires or is injured, the other can pick up the slack. One person's knowledge, skills, and abilities can augment those of the other person. It's certainly not difficult to apply this concept of companionship and support to the church. We can each go our own way in our faith, but in difficult times it is crucial to have another to offer their hand to raise us back up again. God gave us one another for a reason.

I can't warp my loom with one ply yarn. The yarn needs to be in tension to get a good weave, and one ply will pull apart under that stress. We live in a world full of tension and stress, so as a church, we need to depend on one another to keep our faith, our commitment, and our works in the Lord strong.

Lord, help our church to rely on both your power and the power of the community you create for us. Amen.

## Tuesday, October 5

# Encouraging One Another in Faith

### *Romans 1:11-12*

**What can others teach us about our own faith?**

Consider Paul's situation. Paul did not start the church in Rome. Although a pillar of the new church, he was a Jew, a former Pharisee, writing to Gentiles who were struggling with their relationship with Jews. He had much to teach this new congregation. Yet he made sure that they knew that he was open to instruction and encouragement by them. It was to be a mutually supportive relationship, and he respected the faith that they had already demonstrated. He wanted to spend time with them to encourage their faith and teach them but also hoped that they could encourage him as well.

God enriches each of us with different strengths in our faith. I enjoy scholarship and like to teach others about the meaning, history, and background of the Word. Other people's faith is more heavily steeped in service or in deep prayer or a pure and simple trust in the care of the Lord. Spending time with people God has enriched in other ways is deeply encouraging to my faith as well. When Paul visited these fledgling churches, he could not only instruct them but could also experience the different ways the Spirit was working in their lives. I think that this would be an important thing for him to point out to a church that was struggling with division. Each person in the church, despite their differences, could encourage and strengthen the faith of another by working together and learning from each other.

Lord, may my heart be open to the faith of others so that
I may learn from and be encouraged by them. Amen.

## Wednesday, October 6

# Everyone's Contribution

*Romans 12:3-8*

**Why is it important to be a vibrant member of the church?**

Paul wrote this passage to a church that was struggling with incorporating diverse members. Paul reminded them that their strength came not from their similarity, but from their diversity of gifts and abilities. If they all contributed their God-given talents, together they could build something that would nourish their faith and the faith of others. Paul was asking them to respond in grace with their talents and abilities that came from God in the service of God. It was and still is the way that grace should be evident in the daily lives of Christians. Using the gifts that God has given us, we are to nourish the world with our service.

Except for prophecy, most of the gifts listed here are "ordinary" gifts that we generally don't think take extraordinary talents. I think his point is that everyone can contribute. There is a job for everyone, and no one should think too highly of any ability they might have that would elevate them above anyone else.

Paul even said that each one of us is part of Christ's body. Every Christian is intimately connected to Christ but also connected to every other Christian. We think of being members of a church, but Paul speaks of members as being part of a body, where everyone is crucial to the health of the whole. Each one of us is necessary to the well-being and strength of the body of Christ, his church.

Lord, guide me to my place within your church so
I can be a valued part of your body. Amen.

## Thursday, October 7

# Carrying Burdens Together

### *Galatians 6:1-5*

**What are our responsibilities to others in our church?**

Paul told the Galatians that as a community of faith, they were responsible for the well-being of each other. It was their responsibility to guide one another back into obedience and to help heal rifts or transgressions when they saw them happening. Each person in the church has a duty to take care of their congregation's spiritual life. But couldn't that cause trouble? I'm sure that many people would say to mind your own business. Paul explained that the only way to counsel another was in a spirit of gentleness and humility, knowing that everyone needs some correction now and again. Giving counsel was not to be an act of superiority but of taking up the burden of another, just as Christ took up our burdens.

Verses 4 and 5 might seem at first to contradict what the previous verses said. However, they are talking about ultimate responsibility. Each one of us must one day stand before the Lord's judgment for our own works and our own misdeeds. While we are to help our faith communities grow and flourish by routing out sin and offenses, in the end each one of us must personally answer to the Lord for our own actions. No one then can take our place. But in the meantime, if we are to live as Christ, then we have the responsibility not only to offer counsel but to take counsel from others so that everyone in the community of God can grow and mature into true disciples of Jesus Christ.

Lord, give me and those in my church the proper discernment to counsel one other in our growth. Amen.

## Friday, October 8

# Caring for the Sick

*James 5:13-18*

**How does the church care for those who are suffering?**

Much has been written about this particular passage because of the way that James writes about the power of prayer to heal. But what are our responsibilities to those who are weak, suffering, and alone?

Notice that the sick person is instructed to call together the community of the church for solace, and the church is instructed to respond. There are many diseases or conditions that are isolating. Mental illness is especially segregating. Those with dementia are often forgotten in nursing homes. Yet in this passage, the sick were not forgotten. They were still members of the church and were comforted with care, prayers, and spiritual nourishment.

As members of a Christian community, this passage is reminding us that we have a responsibility to our members who need care, be it physical, emotional, or spiritual. As we surround them in love, God becomes active in our involvement, offering whatever healing is appropriate for the situation. The strength of God's care is reflected in the power of the community of faith and all are able to draw upon it. By caring for those who are weak and suffering, we as a church have the chance to heal along with those who need healing and to see God at work, in whatever way God chooses to act in each situation.

Lord, help my church to care for those who are suffering,
and open our eyes to your many ways of healing. Amen.

## Saturday, October 9

# All Baptized into One Body

### *1 Corinthians 12:12-13*

**How does discord in the church harm Christ's work?**

By being baptized, each individual joined into the body of Christ, becoming a part of the whole. Their individual differences were no longer of any importance. This was a radical thought in Corinth. Corinth was a melting pot of many different cultures and many who were newly rich. They were very concerned about advancing up through the social structure, so they were very careful to be seen with the "right people." For Paul to tell them that there was no difference between a slave or a free person, for example, would have been shocking.

If having the spirit of Jesus Christ within them made them into one being, infighting and contention among members was as damaging as if a body part decided to rebel against the body. It's significant that Paul only used this analogy of the body with congregations who were having difficulties within themselves. He was reminding them that their discord was damaging the very body of Christ.

The health of any church depends on the unity among members. Perhaps that is why, sadly, many churches today are made up of people who are similar. If we are to truly be the body of Christ, then every person who "drinks of the Spirit" is an important member of the family of God and should be a welcome member of any congregation.

Lord, may our church truly reflect a
healthy body of Christ. Amen.

## Sunday, October 10

# Honoring Every Part of the Body

*1 Corinthians 12:14-31*

**Who are the unsung members of your church?**

Each person in the church, although with different talents and abilities, is important. Paul compares the church to a body. Eyes, ears, hands, feet—all of these body parts get a lot of attention and are considered essential. Likewise, those in the church who are visible and accomplish high profile things probably seemed to be more valuable.

But notice that Paul didn't write this passage to the powerful members telling them that they weren't as important as they thought. Paul wrote this passage to the whole church, including those who were behind the scenes. They could be thought of as the spleens, toes, gall bladders, and the like who didn't see their own importance. Yet the spleen helps fight infections, toes help us keep our balance, and gall bladders aid in digestion. All these things allow the body to maintain itself in health. Those who pray for the church to keep it in harmony, who help the church to balance its priorities or mitigate dissention in the congregation, are allowing the church to maintain its health too. No one is unimportant to the body of Christ.

Paul reminded the Corinthians that God put their church together. By valuing every member and bringing them into the life of the church, congregations benefit from a diversity of talents, gifts, and abilities.

Lord, thank you for every member of our congregation. Help me to appreciate what each person brings to our community. Amen.

## Monday, October 11

# Discernment and Wisdom

### *Proverbs 18:15-17*

**Why is it important to be able to change our minds?**

People have been spreading misinformation since the beginning of time. In order to be wise, we have to be discerning, double-checking information and determining where that information came from. Verse 16, which talks about gifts, seems a little out of place in a discussion about discernment and wisdom. But the writer here was warning against the use of material gifts for deceptive purposes. Discernment means looking for the truth, and sometimes people work to keep the truth hidden. To that end, verse 17 tells of a trial where a witness presented a strong case that sounded reasonable, until cross-examination steps in. By listening to a second witness, another opinion, or conflicting information and considering it carefully, a person comes closer to gaining true knowledge. Quickly rejecting another point of view because it does not match our own doesn't lead to wisdom.

It can be a difficult thing to reexamine long-held beliefs or question biases we may have about others or other viewpoints, but this passage tells us that a sincere desire to know all the facts is a key to wisdom. Being aware of our biases is the first step. Being open to change our minds is true wisdom.

Lord, teach me to be open to new knowledge and understanding, and to be discerning of what I hear. Amen.

## Tuesday, October 12

# Test the Spirits

### *1 John 4:1-6*

**How can you know if your spiritual beliefs are being improperly influenced?**

How do we know if we're being influenced to follow false beliefs? John was clear that there were those who taught as though they were Christian who were not. He wrote that God was within the hearts of true believers and that they could be guided by God's spirit to know the truth. The spirit of truth will guide believers through prayer, study, and discernment.

A very effective way to discern truth is by observing how others respect Christ's teachings. Those who are open to the way of Jesus will respect it when they hear it. Those who are not will not listen. There are basic tenets of Jesus Christ: to love God, to love and care for our neighbor, and to value our relationship with God above all others. Anyone who rejects those beliefs cannot be trusted, even if they say they are a believer. Anyone who actually knows God will resonate with those beliefs, not only in their words but in their actions.

The key of John's teaching is that God guides the maturity and growth of believers, and God is the one who is worthy of trusting with our spiritual lives. It's easy to be swayed by the crowd and to be led into false beliefs. But because God is within every believer, there is a spirit that can be both tested and trusted. Often the way of Christ clashes with culture, but by devoting ourselves to the Lord, we can rest assured that God will not lead us astray.

Lord, protect my faith and teach me to recognize
your guidance as I mature spiritually. Amen.

## Wednesday, October 13

# Growing Toward Maturity

### *Hebrews 5:11-14*

**Why should we challenge ourselves to grow in faith?**

Apparently, the readers of Hebrews were not progressing and becoming strong Christians. Clearly, the writer of Hebrews was frustrated with them. By this time, they should have been teaching others and bringing them into the faith, but it wasn't happening. This passage was a challenge to them to "step it up" and prove to him that they could shake off their spiritual laziness and mature further in the faith. Spiritual maturity takes work, and to grow we must take our faith seriously. It takes wisdom and maturity to discern between good and evil. Following God's will takes not only the desire to do it, but the wisdom to know what God desires.

That wisdom comes from practice. Even mature Christians can sometimes fail in their discernment, but they try again, using prayer and study to guide themselves. This helps them grow, but if they don't practice the faith, they don't become strong and secure in their discernment. This is what the writer meant when he wrote that the readers weren't ready for solid food. Because they hadn't worked toward spiritual maturity, they were still "babies" in the faith (v. 13) when it came to following the will of God. Far from being a warning not to get in too deep, this passage is a challenge to push ourselves further and grow in faith. Through practicing our faith in these ways, we grow to full maturity in Christ.

Lord, help me to grow in spiritual maturity so that
my service to you may please you. Amen.

## Thursday, October 14

# Understanding God's Commandments

*John 7:19-24*

**How could misunderstanding God's laws thwart God's work in the world?**

John 5 recounts Jesus healing a man on the Sabbath. Jesus responded to the man in the way that God would have desired, but the religious authorities condemned him because he had violated their tangle of Sabbath rules. They were actually using the Sabbath commandment to keep people from serving God, the very opposite of its intent.

Jesus pointed out their hypocrisy. They needed to look at the law differently, responding to its intent as a call to serve God. They needed to take a step back from their rules and regulations, asking themselves what were God's true desires and how could they be served.

God's desires are for us to love and serve God and to love our fellow human beings as ourselves. What misunderstandings of religious law today stand in the way of us fulfilling those desires? Are there any people we exclude from the love of God because we don't feel they qualify? Jesus told us not to judge according to appearances, but with the desires of God in mind. Faithful living challenges us to see the world through God's eyes, rejecting anything that stands in the way of serving God, holding the love of the Lord and of neighbor paramount to anything else.

Lord, open my eyes to your desires and
help me to fulfill them. Amen.

## Friday, October 15

# Wisdom and Discernment

### *Hosea 14:8-9*

**How can we learn to discern the path of righteousness?**

Verse 9 in today's reading, the final verse of Hosea, is a summary of the lesson of the entire book. It sounds like a verse out of Proverbs, seeped in the wisdom tradition. It tells us that those who walk in the ways of the Lord, obeying God's commandments and being faithful to God, are upright and righteous. Those who are not will stumble.

This makes it sound like doing the right thing is the easy thing, but we all know that it is not. Even the righteous often stumble on the path of obedience to God. Sometimes it's not even clear what the right thing is! That's where discernment comes in. The beginning of verse 9 tells us that the wise and discerning can know what is right. Discernment takes maturity and the ability to see things for what they really are, not what we want them to be. Discernment asks that we are honest with ourselves and aware of how our actions or beliefs are affecting us and others around us. That's often more than we're able to do, so that's why we're instructed to pray.

Conversations with God can be our most trusted means of discernment if we're open to often uncomfortable or unwelcome truths that God tells us. But it doesn't end on just knowing the right path. To be righteous means that we commit ourselves to following the path that God has shown us. Those who do can find life in the shelter of the Lord.

Lord, teach me the difficult task of discernment.
May I always listen to your guidance. Amen.

## Saturday, October 16

# Seeking Connection with Others

### *Proverbs 18:1-2*

**Why is it important to listen to those you disagree with?**

Those who isolate themselves, either from others or just from disparate viewpoints, can become indulgent and selfish, refusing to consider the thoughts or needs of others. True wisdom, today's verses tell us, comes from being in community and being open to listening to everyone. In order to be wise, we must have the capacity to understand others, even if we don't agree. The ability to empathize with others, even in controversial situations, can work toward achieving sound solutions to contentious problems.

If your opinions keep you from considering the situations of other people, if you refuse to consider another person's point of view, these verses serve as a warning. Verse 2 says, "Fools find no pleasure in understanding," which implies that wise people enjoy understanding the viewpoints of others. Understanding *why* others believe what they believe can't help but foster harmony because that understanding is a search for common ground. It's respecting others enough to hear their stories.

And isn't that what Jesus did? Jesus ate and drank with those whom others rejected. He listened to their stories and sought to understand their hearts. It didn't mean that he had to agree with them, but it meant that he cared enough to find a place of connection with them. Seeking that place of connection is not only wise, it is the way of Christ.

Lord, open my mind to really hear the thoughts of others
so that we may find a place of connection. Amen.

## SUNDAY, OCTOBER 17

# Discerning Jesus

### *Matthew 16:13-19*

**Who do you say that Jesus is?**

"Who is Jesus?" is a question that is still controversial over 2,000 years after he walked the earth. When Jesus asked his disciples who people said he was, they named prophets from the past. When Jesus asked them who they say he was, however, Peter responded, "You are the Christ, the Son of the living God" (v. 16). Peter knew this not because anyone told him, but because God had revealed it to him.

This is how any of us comes to faith. We may think we know who Jesus is, calling him a great teacher, a social reformer, a healer, a revolutionary or a humanitarian. All have a kernel of truth, but to limit him to any or even all of these descriptions is to try to conform him to human understanding. We finally learn who Jesus is not by watching or even studying him but by knowing him. We come to know Jesus by entering into a relationship with him, a relationship that is initiated by invitation only.

This relationship is the basis of the church. Christ told Peter that he would build his church on "this rock" (v. 18). There have long been arguments over whether "this rock" meant Peter or Peter's confession, but consider: without the bedrock that Jesus is the Christ, the Son of the living God, our faith would have nothing to stand on.

Lord, thank you for your invitation for a relationship with you. May I truly know you and in so doing, know who you are. Amen.

## Monday, October 18

# Guarding God's Words

### *Proverbs 4:20-23*

**How do God's words impact your life?**

Some translations use the word "heart" in verses 21 and 23 of today's passage, while others use the word "mind." In our modern way of thinking, "heart" indicates your emotional center, while "mind" means your reasoning side. So, which understanding is correct? Actually, the Hebrew word used in these verses, *lebab,* has connotations of both heart and mind. The *lebab* held a person's true inclinations toward God on both a conscious and subconscious level. A good or strong *lebab* would hold the basis of a person's wisdom or righteousness. It would be where one's actions would originate, both reasoned and spontaneous. To guard one's *lebab* would mean to nurture right thinking, right inclinations, and a right moral code.

This passage instructs us to hear and to see. People can often become so focused on unimportant things that they lose awareness of what is happening around them. God may be whispering to them but they don't hear God's call.

Therefore, we are to keep ourselves alert and aware for the movement and impact of God in our lives. When we recognize God's work, we are to open our hearts and minds to bring God into the center of our being, allowing God to be the driving force in our lives, both consciously and in our spontaneous actions.

Lord, open my eyes and ears so that my heart
and mind will belong to you. Amen.

## Tuesday, October 19

# Joy within Repentance

### *Nehemiah 8:9-12*

**Why would someone celebrate when they became aware of sin in their life?**

The books of Ezra and Nehemiah tell of the Israelites' return home and their rebuilding the temple and city walls after the Babylonian exile. These books also tell of rebuilding their community of faith in the Lord. Today's passage picks up after Ezra has read the rediscovered book of law (likely Deuteronomy) to the returned exiles. They are heartsick to realize how far they have strayed from God's commands. However, Ezra told the people not to mourn. He designated the day as holy and told them to celebrate!

That's because while God's word lays bare our sin, it also offers us the solution. Repentance is followed by commitment to a new way of life. God's law outlines the remedy. It also makes us aware of how our lifestyle affects others. The true test of faith is not what we know, but what we do with what we know.

Faced with the tragedy of their sin, Ezra told them not to be sad because "the joy from the Lord is your strength!" (v. 10). They were rescued by God, ushered into a new way of life, and promised God's steadfast love. Although our failures are often difficult to deal with, we can rest in the assurance that God is there to lead us out of the messes we've often created for ourselves. Awareness is the first step toward joy in a new life of righteousness!

Lord, thank you for your grace, which allows
a new life for every sinner. Amen.

## Wednesday, October 20

# New Cloth and Wineskins

### *Matthew 9:16-17*

**How do Jesus' teachings integrate the old and the new?**

In Matthew 5:17, Jesus said, "Don't even begin to think that I have come to do away with the Law and the Prophets. I haven't come to do away with them but to fulfill them." He didn't come to discard the old, but to show how the new realized those laws and prophecies in ways that ripped open old ideas, like a new cloth patch tearing an old garment. They were fresh ways of seeing things that didn't fit into the confined thinking of conventional religion. Trying to force Jesus' new vision of the kingdom of God into rigid and unyielding religious practices would be like putting new wine into old wineskins that would burst under the pressure. Jesus was telling his disciples that nothing could contain what he had come to do!

Following Jesus means we must think big and outside of the box. Jesus showed humanity new ways of responding to the call of the Lord. Following the law meant an eye for an eye was acceptable, but in the more expansive way of Christ, turning the other cheek fulfilled the law of love. The law said to love your neighbor, but Jesus taught to love your enemies because your enemies are your neighbors. The love of God that Jesus taught about was not limited to only what had to be done. Jesus went beyond, into a new way of completeness, of showing God's love to all.

Lord, help me to live beyond the limits of the law and into your vision of the kingdom of heaven here on earth. Amen.

## Thursday, October 21

# Love–Genuine!

### *Romans 12:9-13*

**How do Christians live out God's love within their community?**

In the Greek, verse 9 of today's passage begins with the simple command, "Love–Genuine!" After that, Paul listed ways in which the family of Christ shows genuine love to each other and to others outside the family. We should hate that which is evil and hurts others. This is the basis for all the other commands. Love is unhypocritical and will always consider the good of others, so if we let love guide our actions and completely reject evil, then the details of proper behavior probably don't have to be spelled out. Love like this results in a natural behavior born of living within the Holy Spirit.

If a church demonstrated a love like that to its members, its elderly would truly be cared for. So would its children, its struggling parents, and its needy. All of the members would be eagerly and enthusiastically looking for ways to demonstrate God's love to one another. Our everyday lives would demonstrate the love and grace of Jesus Christ.

Just as Jesus defeated death on the cross by demonstrating the greatest love of all, our call as Christians is to harness the power of goodness and grace and to demonstrate it to our own community and then out into the world. They will know we are Christians by our love!

Lord, may my life reflect your grace and love! Amen.

## Friday, October 22

# Joining Together in Obedience

### *Haggai 1:12-15*

**Why would you obey a God you barely knew?**

After several decades of being in Babylon, the Israelites who returned to Jerusalem had great difficulties. The people were frustrated and struggling to survive in a ruined city. But through Haggai, the people heard that the Lord was with them, and God "moved the spirit" of the leaders and of the rest of the people (v. 14). Together they joined one another to work on rebuilding the temple, even in the face of their own devastation.

God sent the people a prophet to deliver God's divine message. We don't know how God moved or stirred the spirit of the people, but they responded. Verse 12 says that they "feared the Lord" and so obeyed.

Obeying someone in fear sounds terrible, but the meaning of "fear" here is closer to awe and wonder. The people weren't cowering before God, obeying because they were terrified of what God would do to them if they didn't. Instead, as they learned about the Lord, they became amazed that such a glorious and powerful God would choose to be with them, and they responded in gratitude to please God. Instead of a fear that diminished them, God's power empowered them. God's inspiration caught up the entire community, and they worked together to rebuild their temple.

Lord, stir the spirit of my faith community so that
we will work together to do your will. Amen.

## Saturday, October 23

# Building up the Community

### *1 Corinthians 14:6-12*

**How do spiritual gifts strengthen the church?**

Showing off our wisdom and ability is often a temptation, even in church. In today's passage, Paul is not writing against the use of one particular spiritual gift—in this case, speaking in tongues—so much as warning against pride and showing off in church. In the example Paul gives, speaking in tongues without anyone to interpret what's being said does nothing to build up the church.

Paul instead praised prophecy. Prophecy in this case was not an ability to tell the future but to speak words that everyone could understand and that were inspired by the Holy Spirit. The authority in true prophecy was because of the Spirit inspiring the words, not in who was speaking.

Local church prophecy of this sort didn't have the same authority as Scripture, and it needed to be considered, weighed, and judged. But it could work to build up the church. And isn't that the goal of everything we should be doing for our faith community?

Paul certainly wasn't upset with people having spiritual gifts, but he was concerned with how they were being used. When we think about gifts or abilities we offer to the church, we should assess them on their value to the faith community, not on how they make us appear to others.

Lord, thank you for the spiritual gifts you have given my congregation. Guide us to use them to strengthen our community. Amen.

## Sunday, October 24

# Spiritual Malaise

### *Revelation 3:1-6, 14-20*

**What are some of the dangers that can destroy a community of faith?**

Sardis was a city in decline. Like the city, the church was dying. They had reverted to worshipping idols and false images of Jesus and their once white robes, symbols of their faith, were ruined. Jesus called on them to repent and turn back to him. Laodicea, in contrast, was a wealthy, thriving city. This church felt totally self-sufficient and thought that they didn't really need Jesus in their lives. Jesus called to them with a broken heart, asking them to repent. He was knocking at their door, waiting for an answer so that he could come and fellowship with him.

Both of these churches had turned away from the true meaning of Jesus Christ. Sardis had perverted his word until who they worshipped was merely an idol. When we read the Gospels, are we shocked and surprised by the demands that Jesus makes on people of faith? If so, perhaps we have made Jesus into something easier. Like the church in Laodicea, do we depend on ourselves and our own resources instead of calling out to the Lord? Perhaps our faith has become lukewarm. The wonderful message of these passages, though, is, despite our failings, Jesus waits at the door, asking to be let into our hearts.

Lord, open my heart to who you truly are! May you be my strength and my rock. Amen.

## Monday, October 25

# Revere and Serve the Lord

### *Joshua 24:14-15*

**Why is a choice to revere and serve God a daily decision?**

Shechem was where Jacob told his family to "Get rid of the foreign gods you have with you" (Genesis 35:2). Jacob held a ceremony in Shechem where his family buried their idols and left them forever. And so it was fitting that Joshua asked the Hebrew people to consider their own loyalty to God at Shechem (Joshua 24:1). His call to faithfulness was focused on two words: "revere" (or "fear" in some translations) and "serve" (Joshua 24:14). Joshua told the people that proper reverence to the Lord was devotion that recognized the full power and majesty of God. It meant taking their commitment to God seriously. This would absolutely prohibit sharing any devotion between the Lord and any other deity. "Serve" in this passage has the same root as "slave" or "servant" and means exclusive, wholehearted commitment. Joshua announced to the people that while they had the choice of whom they would serve, he and his family were committing themselves to the Lord. A choice to serve the Lord isn't made once and then forgotten. Instead, it's an active, ongoing choice to be faithful to God every moment of every day.

The world will compete for our loyalty, but God demands to be first priority. This commitment is at the very heart of our faith. Every new day is a new commitment to revere and serve the Lord for the faithful.

As for me and my house, I will serve you, O Lord. Amen.

## Tuesday, October 26

# Serving a Demanding God

### *Joshua 24:16-18*

**How can we meet the challenge of reverence and service that God demands?**

Joshua challenged the Hebrew people at Shechem to make a decision about whom they would worship and told them that following the Lord would demand reverence and service. Immediately the people responded as a force that they would choose to follow the Lord.

Although they were a generation removed from those who experienced the Exodus, they remembered God's grace and protection for their forebearers who were rescued from Egypt and made the harrowing journey. They were grateful to God for driving out their enemies from the Promised Land. They had heard of God's mighty works and they were thankful. They unambiguously declared their devotion and chose to worship the Lord.

Every congregation and every individual in every congregation needs to ask themselves how committed they really are to the Lord. Reverence and service on the scale required by God is constant and demanding. Failure means disrespecting the Creator of the cosmos. Committing ourselves to God isn't just following a code of ethics and going to weekly worship. It's entering into a relationship that demands daily connection with God's guidance through prayer and seeking God's will in everything we do.

Lord, may I listen to your voice. Guide
me in your love. Amen.

## Wednesday, October 27

# Reminders of the Lord

### *Joshua 24:25-28*

**What reminds you of your commitment to God?**

Many people have physical objects to remind them of their commitment to God. Maybe it's a cross to wear or a picture on the wall. In this passage in Joshua, the people pledged themselves to the Lord, and to remind them of that pledge, Joshua placed a large stone under an oak tree in God's holy place. Every time they saw the stone, they would recall the pledge they made to revere and serve only the Lord. It was the symbol of their covenant with God.

The nature of human beings is to become distracted by the minutia of our lives. Before I get up each morning, I think through what is scheduled each day and what I need to get done—the minutia of the day. A better priority would be to focus on God and say a prayer of praise before I even put my feet on the floor. Like the ancient Hebrews on this occasion, I am trying to have reminders throughout my home and daily routine to break through my thoughts to remind me of my commitment to the Lord.

If we have chosen to revere and serve God, then we need to structure our lives to reflect that. God needs to be able to intrude on us at any time, and we must arrange our lives to allow that. That also means listening for God's word throughout the day, open to God's call. God wants a relationship, and that doesn't happen when we don't hear God. May we always be ready to hear God calling!

Lord, help me to establish daily routines that
remind me of my commitment to you. Amen.

## Thursday, October 28

# A Covenant of Peace

### *Ezekiel 37:24-28*

**How realistic are the promises in Scripture?**

It's important to remember that today's passage was written in the darkest days of ancient Israel's history. Imagine how the Hebrew people reacted when they heard this hopeful prophecy! When things look bad, it can be difficult to believe that life will ever be joyful again. Ezekiel never saw the return of his people to Israel. But even if he had, this prophecy still seems too good to be true. Read it again, with the eyes of an exiled person.

Ezekiel's vision was eschatological, speaking of the final climax of history when God will come to dwell on earth with God's people. Even today, that vision of a healed, whole earth seems difficult to believe. Hunger, wars, disease, destruction of the environment—so many things currently work against this vision. How can we trust that there will be a future where the world is peaceful, restored, and in accordance with God's holy will?

But Jesus taught us to pray, "Bring in your kingdom / so that your will is done on earth as it's done in heaven" (Matthew 6:10). Ezekiel's vision is exactly what we pray for when we pray the Lord's Prayer. The kingdom of God come to earth was the promise of Ezekiel, just as it was the promise of Jesus Christ. It's the hope for the future of humanity, and because it is a hope that runs throughout Scripture, it's a promise we can trust.

Lord, may your kingdom come and your will be
done on earth just as it is in heaven! Amen.

## Friday, October 29

# A Second Chance

### *Jeremiah 31:31-34*

**What does "a new covenant" mean in Jeremiah?**

The Hebrew people had broken their covenant with God, despite God's love and care. They didn't have the ability to remain faithful and devoted. God gave them a second chance to develop a relationship with God. But first, God had to teach them how to be successful in a covenant relationship. God had to change their hearts so that they were able to take advantage of their second chance.

This new covenant was not new law, but a second chance at keeping the law, this time with a God-inspired attitude toward obedience. God began the process of reconciliation by forgiving them and bringing them back into God's care. This time God would change their hearts and motivate them to obedience. God promised to turn them toward God's self when they could not do it themselves.

As Christians, we equate the new covenant with Jesus Christ. Jesus' dramatic destruction of the hold of sin and death on us all surely was a radical re-creation of the relationship between God and humanity. But it is important to realize that all throughout history, God redefined the relationship with God's people to enable a new understanding, new healing, and new connection. God was and always has longed to repair broken relationships with those whom God loves.

Lord God, thank you for your amazing,
everlasting love, and your desire to heal broken
relationships with your people. Amen

## Saturday, October 30

# A New Relationship

### *Hebrews 12:22-24*

**How did the relationship we are able to have with God change through the sacrifice of Jesus?**

In today's passage, the writer of Hebrews described the relationship the Hebrew people had had with God, and then how it had changed once Jesus instituted the new covenant. Hebrews 12:18-21 depicts Mount Sinai. While it was a good place, the site of the giving of the law, it was also a place of fear that emphasized human unworthiness before God.

Although God had forgiven the people over and over again for their sins, it took Jesus Christ to change the basis of their relationship with the Lord. So, in verses 22-24, instead of Mount Sinai, the people were called to "Mount Zion, the city of the living God, heavenly Jerusalem" (v. 22). This is the site of grace and peace. To enter this city of joy, one has to pass through the gateway of the righteous, but it's guarded by our Advocate and Savior, Jesus Christ. The blood of Christ purifies all who approach him. Instead of a covenant of law, he has instituted a covenant of forgiveness and mercy. Our relationship with our God is not one of fear and unworthiness, but of love and delight in one another.

Those of us who follow the Lord are blessed by the guidelines and structure of the law. That has not changed. But Jesus takes us beyond the law to a new realization of grace and forgiveness.

Lord Jesus, thank you for your sacrifice, the way
of entry into the holy city of Zion. Amen.

## Sunday, October 31

# Rehearsing the Covenant

### *Deuteronomy 29:10-29*

**Why did Moses have the people recommit to the covenant before entering the Promised Land?**

In this passage, Moses and the Hebrew people were poised at the entrance to the Promised Land. Moses paused to speak to them about what they needed to do to make their lives with God in their new home successful. He reiterated the covenant that they had made with the Lord, rehearsing the promises that they had made to be faithful. He wanted to cement those oaths in their mind before they proceeded.

Notice that everyone was included in this covenant, not only the elite or the decision-makers. Children, immigrants, and servants were asked to swear the oath. Verse 15 even included those who weren't present. This covenant would include future generations and encompass every last person, even those who were hanging back in their own hearts. It was impossible to excuse yourself. If you were part of the community, you were part of the covenant.

It takes courage and hope to stand at the edge of a new endeavor, especially when you have failed before. By reviewing the covenant with the people, Moses caused them to rehearse the importance of their relationship with the Lord as they began a new stage of their lives. Moses' rehearsal of the people's covenant with God is a powerful tool that we can use for keeping our relationship strong when we face new events in our lives.

Lord, prod me to pause and recommit myself to you,
especially when there is change in my life. Amen

# NOVEMBER

## CONTRIBUTORS:

*Greg Weeks*
*November 1–28*

*Randy Cross*
*November 29–30*

## Monday, November 1

# Why 99-Year-Olds Run

### *Genesis 18:1-15*

**What moves you to act in a generous manner?**

You don't ordinarily imagine someone almost 100 years old lacing up their athletic shoes and running as fast as they can. The opening verses of Genesis 18, though, paint such a picture. Why the hurry and the extravagance? There is no indication that Abraham knew the strangers had divine roots, nor that he was seeking a favor. Perhaps the reason behind Abraham's urgent generosity lay in the kinship he felt with the strangers. He knew what it was like being a wanderer. So, he was overjoyed at the opportunity to care for these men.

All strangers have the potential to be bearers of God's presence. We may fear them, since they are different from us. But Abraham's joy at the possibility of serving unknown aliens is foundational. It has been, and continues to be, the model for people of faith: "Don't neglect to open up your homes to guests, because by doing this some have been hosts to angels without knowing it" (Hebrews 13:2).

Like Abraham, the abundance of our hospitality is in direct proportion to the joy we have in serving the visitor. In the process, although we don't seek it, we receive a blessing in return. In our welcoming the stranger, we receive new perspectives, possibilities, and relationships. Through sharing our abundance, God's dreams for the future unfold.

Lord, give me eyes to see you in the faces of others, a heart to bless them, and feet to serve them! Amen.

## Tuesday, November 2

# The Tension Between Taking and Giving

### *Deuteronomy 23:24-25*

**How do you balance taking care of your needs while being considerate of the needs of others?**

Today's verses anticipate a fellow Israelite going into a neighbor's vineyard or grain field. Moses' counsel is that the person may take and eat, but just enough for his immediate needs. No basket for additional grapes and no sickle for more grain.

Two principles lie behind this. The first is affirming abundance for all. A hungry person may go into someone else's field since the fruits of the earth are God's unrestricted gifts. The owner of the land is simply a steward and must, accordingly, welcome a hungry brother or sister. The second principle is showing respect for the provider. The hungry person must consider the needs and rights of the field's owner. If the person takes too much, and others do as well, then the owner and his family may be in need. This would then be the same as stealing.

Ultimately, personal habits should reflect communal responsibility. Mutuality ensures that everyone has enough. When both parties respect the needs of others, then abundance is assured. The "What's in it for me?" mentality undercuts God's vision for the community. It gives rise to withholding from the needy out of greed and fear. Likewise, taking without gratitude and respect is also sinful.

God, thank you for the gifts from the land that sustain me,
and for those who generously share those gifts. Amen.

## Wednesday, November 3

# A Miracle's Difficult Lesson

*Mark 8:1-10*

**How do you get an outlook that seeks abundance for all?**

While all four Gospels include the story of Jesus feeding the 5,000, only Mark and Matthew (15:32-39) describe a later, subsequent time when he fed 4,000. Comparing the two feeding miracles in Mark points to a way Christians can move ahead more faithfully. In both accounts (Mark 6:34, 8:2), Jesus initiated the miracles because of compassion. When the disciples allowed themselves to be moved as forcefully by compassion as the Master was, they would be able to anticipate abundant possibilities instead of being restricted by a scarcity mentality.

The importance of compassion is underscored by the setting for today's event. When Jesus fed the 5,000, he was ministering in an area close to his home; his audience was Jewish. In today's text, though, he was traveling in the region of the "Ten Cities" (Mark 7:31), a predominantly Gentile area. Jesus' compassion knows no human distinction. The needs of both Jew and non-Jew alike moved him equally as well and as deeply.

When we love beyond human distinction, we will be well on our way to developing the habit of trusting in God's abundance. As a result, miracles will happen.

Jesus, I pray for a heart that is moved by the needs of others. Encourage me to act on their behalf. Amen.

## THURSDAY, NOVEMBER 4

# The Joy of Sharing

### *Acts 4:32-37*

**How do you find freedom from being married to your possessions?**

Being "one in heart and mind" conveys the sense of sharing the same feelings and thoughts (v. 32). Such cohesion drives out a divisive, "This is mine" mentality. The early church could live in this amazing way because their experience of the Holy Spirit validated what they'd witnessed. Christ is really present, right here and right now. They had seen him heal a lame man and give confidence to the apostles. Consequently, when those leaders preached the Resurrection, it became a lived reality.

It was impossible to separate being united with Christ from being united with one another. The earthly Jesus had felt the hunger, pain, and loneliness of people. His compassion compelled him to address such need wherever he found it. Consequently, his followers shared the same compulsion. It would have been an insult to his presence if anyone in the fellowship lacked anything. The early believers did whatever it took to ensure there were no needy people in their midst. Following Jesus' example, they would love others so much that giving to them became more important than keeping from them. Through such compelling love, they demonstrated that there is abundance for all.

Lord, thank you for loving me so extravagantly!
Touched by your presence, inspire me to
love others just as generously. Amen.

## Friday, November 5

# Developing a "Good Eye"

### *Proverbs 22:7-9*

**How do you find happiness in life?**

Today's passage contains both a warning and a promise regarding a person's relationship with wealth. Verses 7-8 warn of the misuse of power associated with money. The foundation of a happy life regarding money, by contrast, is to be "generous" (v. 9). The literal meaning of the Hebrew is "to have a good eye." A person with healthy eyes sees God's abundance everywhere and delights in sharing instead of hoarding. He or she will seek ways to help others with what they've been given. They are compelled by a spirit of generous compassion.

The surest sign of such a happy person is how they relate to the poor. The Proverbs writer goes so far as to say they're happy *because* they give food to the hungry. This differs from the spirit of the wealthy young man in the New Testament, who went away sad because Jesus invited him to give generously to the impoverished (Matthew 19:16-22).

Giving food to the poor is more personal than simply giving money. Providing a meal, in addition to addressing a physical need, also provides an opportunity for connecting. Sharing food breaks down barriers and promotes justice, a key theme running throughout Scripture. Discipleship requires good eyesight. Ordering our lives along the lines of generous kindness ensures that there will be enough for all of God's people.

Lord of compassion and generosity, open my eyes to see the good waiting to be done all around me today. Amen.

## Saturday, November 6

# John's Last Word

*John 21:9-19*

**If you summed up your mission, what would you write?**

John 21 forms an epilogue. It presents the remarkable scene of Jesus inviting the apostles to breakfast. This meal reflects earlier moments of Jesus' life and ministry, including the feeding of the 5,000 and the Last Supper. The message Jesus conveyed comes home in the verse following the breakfast scene: "When they finished eating, Jesus asked Simon Peter, 'Simon son of John, do you love me more than these?' Simon replied, 'Yes, Lord, you know I love you.' Jesus said to him, 'Feed my lambs'" (John 21:15).

Just as Jesus had fed them, so now were they to go and feed others. They were to do so with Jesus' gentle spirit. They were his "children," and they would feed his "lambs." From now on, they would provide an abundant meal to all who gathered in his name.

The early Christians would have witnessed how this mission unfolded. No one was hungry or in need within their fellowship. Hearts touched by Jesus' love generously shared what they had. They made sure that everyone had a place at the table, and that the table overflowed with food.

It's good that John included an epilogue. He leaves us with a question that should focus our discipleship: How are we tending to Jesus' lambs?

Master, you call me your child and lovingly provide for me. Similarly, give me grace to care for your lambs, whoever and wherever they are. Amen.

## SUNDAY, NOVEMBER 7

# Phrases Jesus Never Used

### *John 6:1-15*

**Do you live with an outlook of scarcity or abundance?**

Jesus feeding 5,000 is the only miracle recorded in all four Gospels. John interprets Jesus' question to Philip as a "test" (v. 6). Philip and Andrew both expressed pessimistic outlook on the possibilities. The rest of the story teaches that "just a little bit" (v. 7) and "what good is that?" (v. 9) were never in Jesus' vocabulary.

The remainder of the narrative relates what happens when even a small gift is placed in Jesus' hands. In contrast to each person not even having a little bit, everyone had "as much as they wanted" (v. 11). When Jesus assigned the Twelve to pick up the leftovers, it's as if he wanted to impress this lesson upon them. Filling so many baskets, when they had started with not enough food for even one, would cause them to think twice before answering any future question from Jesus!

The challenge is trusting in a power greater than our own. If we think it is all up to us and our meager resources, then we will paralyze ourselves with, "But what good is that?" The image of baskets overflowing with food should be enough for us never to withhold a possible miracle because of fear. In those situations in which we assume scarcity, Jesus sees abundance. Will we be Philip and Andrew, or the young person with barley loaves and fish?

Master, you took the small and humble and nourished
thousands. Open my heart and eyes, so that you
may continue filling baskets today. Amen.

## Monday, November 8

# Compassion That Transcends Differences

### *1 Samuel 28:20-25*

**When have you been surprised by unexpected kindness?**

Witchcraft was common in the nations Israel encountered as it moved into Canaan. It was also strictly prohibited for Jews since they viewed it as a lack of trust in God (Deuteronomy 18:14-15). King Saul's journey to see the medium shows Saul's desperation. Traveling to En-dor would have been risky, requiring a clandestine trip around the encamped Philistine forces.

Our passage today begins with the natural outcome of Saul's hearing the pronouncement of death in battle the next day: He collapsed. It was at this point, though, that the medium, remarkably, offered a meal. She didn't have to do it. Her obligation was only a business deal. It would have been in her best interest for him to leave as soon as possible. Saul was also a Hebrew while she was a Canaanite. They shared neither the same culture nor the same deity. And she did it lavishly, offering a fattened calf and kneading fresh bread.

The takeaway is that mercy transcends our differences. Regardless of political, religious, or other distinctions, a person's suffering can move strangers to act as friends. The medium's persistence in offering the meal serves as a model of compassion. Perhaps the sincerity and intensity behind the offer were more important than the food itself.

Lord, thank you for the witness of this
woman. Grant me grace to show kindness
with extravagance and intensity. Amen.

## Tuesday, November 9

# The Surprising Harvest of Compassion

*Ruth 2:14-16*

**When have you seen an act of kindness produce unexpected results?**

Like many immigrants, Ruth found herself in a vulnerable position. She became a "gleaner," meaning that she followed those who harvested barley, picking up the droppings. Her decision to accompany Naomi left her desperate. Yet her compassion was noticed and elicited compassion as well.

Today's text finds Boaz going well beyond providing only food. He gave Ruth the status of equality by insisting that she sit with the harvesters as she dined. Such an act transcended the socioeconomic prejudice of a lower-class gleaner sitting with the harvesters. Also, more importantly, it transcended the prejudice against Gentiles.

The story reveals that the consequences of compassion run deep. Even though Ruth may have had fearful moments, her unwavering support of Naomi touched her neighbors. Boaz modeled this, looking past her immigrant status and welcoming her fully.

God works through people moved by such compassion. The union of Ruth and Boaz affected Israel's history. She would become the great grandmother of King David. She would also be honored as one of only four women mentioned in Jesus' lineage (Matthew 1:5).

Lord, thank you for compassionate people like
Ruth and Boaz. Help me notice them, honor
them, and learn from them. Amen.

## Wednesday, November 10

# Loving Even When You Don't Feel Like It

*Proverbs 25:8-22*

**Why should you show kindness to your enemies?**

Jesus taught that words are an indicator of what's in the heart (Matthew 15:18), and James instructed us to "tame" the tongue (James 3:1-12). Similarly, the Proverbs writer says that right words are "gold apples in a silver setting" (Proverbs 25:11). He wrote from a practical standpoint. The proper choice of words mends relationships and provides insight. How much better for words to be used instead of swords, since a "tender tongue can break a bone" (v. 15).

Proper speech, though, must be backed up by proper actions. In contrast to an ancient world where retribution was often the norm (Deuteronomy 19:21), the writer closed by focusing on kindness. Giving an enemy food and drink is a concrete way of obeying Jesus' command to love your foe. Showing such compassion invites healing in the relationship.

There is, of course, no guarantee of resolution. Regardless, like choosing not to use antagonizing words, the offer of food and drink undercuts the defenses of an enemy. That person must decide whether to pursue a zero-sum game of win/lose, or to let the person's kindness open the door for understanding and reconciliation. Offering food and drink to an enemy shows that we are serious in being "complete in showing love to everyone" just like our heavenly Father (Matthew 5:48).

Master, thank you for showing me the higher path of love. Help me reach out to those who, at first, may seem unlovable. Amen.

## Thursday, November 11

# The Key to Peaceful Living

### *Romans 12:9-21*

**What must happen for you to live peacefully with others?**

Leading up to instructing us to not repay evil with evil, Paul defined humility: "Consider everyone as equal, and don't think that you're better than anyone else" (v. 16). Such an inner quality is a nonnegotiable prerequisite for everything he wrote in today's text. A humble person refrains from hurting an enemy.

Such a person will "show respect for what everyone else believes is good" (v. 17). Such "good" builds up the community and seeks an inclusive fellowship; this contrasts with the ego-driven duality of friend/foe. The positive qualities he listed in verses 9-15 take root only in a humble heart. Humility leaves room for God to be the judge. If there is to be "wrath," it must come from one who judges better than we do.

Better than prideful vengeance is humble kindness. Paul appropriately quoted Proverbs 25:21-22. The "burning coals" image refers to burning off impurities, as in refining silver. Showing consideration for an enemy may result in that person's transformation, along with the transformation of the relationship. That, in turn, will truly enable an open table fellowship to flourish. He concluded the section with the call to overcome evil with good. Humble people will do that, and thus inherit the earth by treating enemies as friends.

Master, as you walked among us with
gentleness and kindness to all, so also may my
steps be measured with yours. Amen.

## Friday, November 12

# The Reward of Loving Enemies

### *1 Peter 3:8-9*

**How do you feel when you show undeserved kindness?**

Peter wrote this letter to a church that was being mistreated by society. Peter reminded them of how Jesus handled his persecution: "When he was insulted, he did not reply with insults. When he suffered, he did not threaten revenge. Instead, he entrusted himself to the one who judges justly" (1 Peter 2:23). It was essential for the Christians to demonstrate this, first, with each other. The beginning of this is to be "of one mind" in Christian fellowship, as Peter stated in 3:8. He listed the qualities of such an intimate fellowship. Anchored in humility, they reflect how Jesus lived.

In verse 9, Peter said that this type of living will carry over to the very people who were hurting and killing them. Persecution comes in both deed ("evil") and word ("insult"). Regardless, the believer's response is to give a blessing. The Greek word for blessing literally means, "a good word." For the Christian, a good word is that which expresses sincere concern for the enemy. It's praying for them, wishing them well, advocating for them, forgiving them, and not letting them anger you.

While Peter's words are in the form of instruction, we should view them as an invitation. He invites us to live a life that transcends present difficulties. Gently blessing leads to fully living.

Lord, move my heart so that I love my enemy because
I want to, not because you told me to. Amen.

## Saturday, November 13

# The Mission of Surprising Grace

### *Luke 19:1-10*

**How can you surprise "sinners" with unconditional love?**

This story of Zacchaeus sees the "ruler among tax collectors" (v. 2) move from curiosity to shocked happiness, and finally a changed heart. Throughout this encounter, Jesus added to the drama by focusing on Zacchaeus. When he invited himself to the tax collector's house, he ignored the hostile crowd, where "everyone" grumbled (v. 7). When he proclaimed Zacchaeus to be a valued son of Abraham, he addressed the audience but remained looking at him (v. 9).

While this dramatic passage shows the transformation that happens when someone encounters unconditional love, it ultimately points to the mission of Jesus and his church. His calling to seek and save the lost connects to what he said to the Pharisees in an earlier incident involving a tax collector. "I didn't come to call righteous people but sinners to change their hearts and lives" (Luke 5:32).

Other religious leaders viewed people like Zacchaeus as sinners and ignored them. Jesus saw them as beloved children of his Father and reached out to them. The church he would form would be that of the reconciled sitting around a table filled with respect and friendship. For many, that would start with a surprising encounter of grace.

Lord, thank you for inviting yourself into my life.
Help me surprise others with your invitation,
welcoming them as brothers and sisters. Amen.

## Sunday, November 14

# A Blueprint for Being a Peacemaker

*1 Samuel 25:2-39*

**How do you help people resolve a conflict peacefully?**

The dispute started with Nabal rejecting David's request for food. David reacted by declaring war. Rage blinded his thinking, leading to a nonsensical vow to avenge a verbal insult by murderous action. Abigail prevented this calamity in an amazing way. She teaches us how to make peace.

Abigail saw the situation clearly and took a risk. She was undercutting what her husband had done and doing so secretly. She offered an abundance of food to David. The humble way in which she addressed him underscores this. Such generosity softened David's emotions, opening him to hearing Abigail's wise counsel.

In today's culture of social media that fan the flames of emotions and encourage conflicts, peacemakers are needed more than ever. Abigail's model is extremely timely, but also difficult to follow. People who strive to see things clearly, who are willing to take risks, and who respond generously to others may feel as if they are outsiders. Yet, in the process, they will discover a deeper fulfillment than that which passes for happiness today.

Jesus had the Abigails of this world in mind when he said, "Happy are people who make peace, because they will be called God's children" (Matthew 5:9).

Lord, let your peace flow through me, and let the happiness with which you bless me bless all I meet. Amen.

## Monday, November 15

# What Makes the New Covenant New?

### *Luke 22:14-20*

**When you take Communion, what are you affirming?**

Jesus, at the end of his ministry, talked of a new covenant. He used the setting of the Passover meal as a way to both explain and commemorate it. The consecration of the cup contains the key phrase, "new covenant by my blood" (v. 20). As the blood of a special lamb was used in the first Passover (Exodus 12:3-7), so would Jesus' sacrifice be central to the new one.

The Lord's bond with us through Moses entailed *our* obedience to laws and rituals. But the new covenant is based on faith in *Jesus'* obedience. He obeyed in a way that we cannot. As Paul said later, "he humbled himself by becoming obedient to the point of death, / even death on a cross" (Philippians 2:8).

In trusting in what he did, not in what we try to do, we experience a new intimacy with God. Faith in Jesus' obedience fulfills Jeremiah's prophecy (Jeremiah 31:31-34), where God's words are engraved upon people's hearts.

Because of the new covenant, our obedience now comes from a desire to honor God. Taking Communion is a way of expressing our gratitude. It is also a way of embodying a new, inclusive kingdom. As we sit at the table, we affirm our commitment to love God completely and to love our neighbor as ourselves.

Master, accept my life in gratitude for your sacrifice. As you love me so amazingly, so also will I love others. Amen.

## Tuesday, November 16

# The Power of "One Loaf of Bread"

### *1 Corinthians 10:14-17*

**Does Communion affect your relationship with others?**

When the Corinthians came together to worship and celebrate the Lord's Supper, Paul pointed to the wine, symbolic of Christ's sacrifice for us. Instead of it being part of a meal people offered to gods to solicit favors, it is a meal in which believers offer gratitude to Christ for what he did for us on the cross. His unconditional, sacrificial love symbolized in the blood of the new covenant has already blessed us. He's already given us all we need for fullness of life, with God and with one another. Such worship, focused on gratitude, shapes the Christian fellowship differently when compared to its pagan counterpart. Christian worship, results in bonding together the entire fellowship.

Paul mentioned a "loaf of bread" three times in these verses. The visual of a single loaf being passed, with each taking a piece, conveys a powerful meaning. The bread, representative of Christ's body, also symbolizes that we are all connected together to his body. We're not individuals seeking our own desires. Instead, we are brothers and sisters to Christ and, like him, ultimately concerned about others' needs first.

Lord, thank you for this family meal. When I take Communion, make me sensitive to the needs of my brothers and sisters around me. Amen.

## Wednesday, November 17

# Remembering and Reliving Through a Meal

### *Exodus 12:1-14*

**What makes a meal truly memorable for you?**

Today's text contains a mix of instructions for both the first Passover and the annual celebration of it. Verse 14 summarizes the purpose of these instructions. The celebration of Passover is remembering and reliving.

The Jews remember that God hears their cries and intercedes powerfully. Their rituals for families to follow in eating the meal (the "Seder") help them relive the Lord's saving action on the night preceding the Exodus. Throughout the millennia of their history, this remembering and reliving has served as a source of hope for the Jewish people. Similarly, the celebrating of the Lord's Supper fulfills this same purpose for Christians.

Rituals that have developed around Communion center on Jesus' words, "Do this in remembrance of me" (Luke 22:19). Taking the bread and cup, like the Jews taking the lamb and the unleavened bread, is a way of reliving that night. It also joins us to generations of believers who've lived the faith before us.

For both Jew and Christian, our respective ceremonies must continue "forever." The lure of the gods of Egypt, and their modern counterparts, is ever-present. By remembering and reliving, we proclaim our hope in the God who parts seas and opens tombs.

Master, thank you for inviting me to your table. Each time I take the bread and cup, I will remember and be grateful. Amen.

## Thursday, November 18

# The Challenge of Trusting God

### *Exodus 23:23-25*

**How do you demonstrate trust in God during a crisis?**

Our text is in a section of Exodus called the "Covenant Code." It contains material gathered over a long period of time in Israel's history. The destruction of the Canaanite nations in Exodus 23:23 is linked to the destruction of idols in verse 24. Such violence sounds foreign to us. It expresses, though, the passion of the writer in ridding the land of idols. He viewed turning to these gods as an insult to the God who had liberated and cared for the Hebrews. This faithlessness revealed a desire to manipulate these idols instead of trusting in God's love and care.

By contrast, continuing to trust in God's goodness and protection, and consequently obeying the covenant laws, would mean fullness of life. The ground would be as fertile as the sky was when it rained manna and quail. People would be healthy, raise children, and live to an old age.

Unfortunately, Israel did not heed Moses' command to trust and obey. Throughout its history, the prophets would continually call the people to abandon idolatry and renew their covenant with God. The Lord would continue caring, even in the midst of their turning away. Providing food and water was a tangible sign of a faithful love. Ultimately, God will provide a banquet that will celebrate a new covenant that will be written on their hearts.

God, thank you for being faithful even when I haven't been. Please empower me to trust you more when I face the unknown. Amen.

## FRIDAY, NOVEMBER 19

# When a Meal Forms a Nation

### *Deuteronomy 12:1-7*

**When has a meal helped you find common ground with strangers?**

Today's Scripture begins a section where Moses instructs the Hebrews as to what they must do once they settle in the Promised Land. They are about to end their wilderness journey and become an established nation. How will their relationship with the Lord and with one another change?

The feasts Moses described would serve three functions.

The first is to unify the people in their worship of the LORD, as Moses instructed them to not only destroy the idols but even the very places where the idols stood. Abundant food and drink would characterize these gatherings. The offerings people provided show their desire to share with one another and to praise God for fertile land. Finally, an important part of the banquets would be inclusivity. They would not only be for those who could provide for the banquet, but for everyone, including foreigners, strangers, and the poor.

This inclusion would be central to Israel's identity. It must share God's compassion for those in need. Christians reading this passage see the connection with the Lord's Supper. As with our Jewish ancestors, we experience the power that comes from joining with fellow believers around a common table. Unity, celebration, and inclusion form our witness to God's continuing involvement in the world.

Lord, thank you for a church that knows no boundaries. Let my life celebrate your unconditional, inclusive love. Amen.

## Saturday, November 20

# Communion Isn't About Us

### *Matthew 26:26-30*

**What makes the Lord's Supper special for you?**

Matthew's is the only Gospel where, when Jesus passed the cup, he said that his blood will be poured out "for many *so that their sins may be forgiven*" (v. 28, italics added). Jesus' blood fulfilled the intent of the covenant God made through Moses. After the Israelites agreed to obey God, Moses took a sacrificed ox's blood and sprinkled it upon the people. He said, "This is the blood of the covenant that the Lord now makes with you on the basis of all these words" (Exodus 24:8).

Jesus fulfilled what Moses couldn't. He takes away our sins, reconciling us to the Lord. Additionally, the covenant will be sustained by him. Jesus said that he wouldn't drink from the cup again until he did it "with you" (v. 29). This phrase is unique to Matthew, connecting with the Master's final words: "I myself will be with you every day until the end of this present age" (Matthew 28:20). There is an intimacy between Jesus and his followers.

Finally, Matthew notes that at the conclusion of the meal, before they left for Gethsemane, Jesus and the disciples sang "songs of praise" (v. 30). The early church incorporated singing into worship and daily life. Their songs of praise would give thanks for the love of Christ, who laid down his life so the covenant would be established forever.

Master, you invite me to your table out of love.
As you gave yourself for me, so do I give myself to
you in receiving your bread and cup. Amen.

## Sunday, November 21

# Testing Yourself Before Receiving Communion

### *1 Corinthians 11:17-34*

**How aware are you of the needs of those around you during Communion?**

Since Corinth was a prosperous center of trade, the church had wealthy members as well as impoverished ones. Communion took place as part of a larger potluck-style fellowship meal. Since the wealthier members could provide more and better food, they felt entitled to eat that, taking as much as they wanted. It was easy for them to treat this as a private occasion, oblivious to the needs of the poorer participants.

This was so blatantly opposed to the gospel that Paul said it was "necessary" (v. 19) such a division existed, so as to contrast it with a genuine Christian spirit. Paul emphasized that the whole meal is sacred, and how we eat it "broadcasts" Jesus' sacrifice (v. 26). He died so that *all* may be reconciled to God and to one another.

What Paul says in this passage provided a real-life situation where Christ's love could be put into action. He challenged a fellowship to transcend socioeconomic differences by coming together as a united family around the Lord's Table.

The apostle's words, written almost 2,000 years ago, speak to the church today. We can celebrate Communion inclusively only when we believe that of all the Christian virtues, "the greatest of these is love" (1 Corinthians 13:13).

Lord, please show me how to honor you by honoring those with whom I share your bread and cup. Amen.

## Monday, November 22

# The Joy of a Large Guest List

*Luke 14:12-15*

**If you received a surprise invitation to a big event, how would you feel?**

When Jesus instructed his host to invite the "poor, crippled, lame, and blind" (v. 13) to a banquet, he expanded what it means to love your neighbor. God yearns that all, regardless of status, enjoy fullness of life. The marginalized can be overlooked, but not by God. Anyone showing such care for the vulnerable will be repaid with the joy of God. Jesus said we will be "blessed" when we extend such an invitation (v. 14).

Jesus connected this blessing to a future happiness as well. He emphasized that what we do today has consequences tomorrow. The link between the present and the future is the banquet table. A disciple's happiness comes from ensuring that the guest list for today's festival mirrors that for the heavenly one. Practically speaking, today's congregation must resemble tomorrow's.

Early church leaders mandated that all should be warmly invited to the fellowship table. Such non-partial welcoming was for them, as for us, a way to obey Jesus' teaching in the Sermon on the Mount: "If you love only those who love you, what reward do you have?" (Matthew 5:46).

Our purest form of joy comes from loving as God loves. It's what happens when we expand our guest list and not expect anything in return but a "Yes, I'll come!" response.

Lord, you love beyond human standards. Following your example, empower me to expand my guest list. Amen.

## Tuesday, November 23

# Hungering for Justice and Righteousness

### *Isaiah 1:18-20*

**What are the characteristics of a life devoted to justice and righteousness?**

Today's passage reveals both divine frustration and hope. The verses begin with legal language. It's time to "settle" things (v. 18). There will be no more claiming to be God's children without acting like it. Verse 19 outlines the path to redemption: "If you agree and obey." "Agree" conveys the sincere desire to pursue a more mature relationship with God. It's seeking a righteousness characterized by concrete obedience.

This new relationship with God will result in a blessing of the land. When the people hunger for justice and righteousness, the land will be fertile again and they will eat abundantly. Verse 20, however, outlines consequences if they continue giving lip service to God while ignoring covenantal requirements. As they would eat of the land's bounty, so would they be devoured by invaders.

Isaiah, though, also foresaw a time when God's grace would triumph. "Look! I'm creating a new heaven and a new earth: / past events won't be remembered; / they won't come to mind. . . . / Before they call, I will answer; / while they are still speaking, I will hear" (Isaiah 65:17, 24). Anyone with an appetite for a compassionate and just world welcomes such a time.

Holy God, guide my feet, that I may walk in the way of righteousness and along the paths of justice. Amen.

## Wednesday, November 24

# Hope During a Time of Despair

### *Joel 2:23-26*

**In what ways may a crisis help you discover God's redeeming presence?**

Joel wrote during a time of national peril. Relentless swarms of differing types of locusts (Joel 1:4; 2:25) had invaded the entire land: "Like blackness spread out upon the mountains, / a great and powerful army comes, / unlike any that has ever come before them, / or will come after them in centuries ahead" (2:2b). The ensuing wasteland devastated the agricultural nation. It was so complete that the land mourned and the animals groaned (Joel 1:10, 18). It was a portrait of the "Day of the Lord," God's judgment upon the people.

Against this bleak backdrop, Joel dared to make a case for hope. Today's text reflects this through a complete reversal of the devastation. A new era will begin. With the plague lifted and the land becoming fertile, the people will eat abundantly once again. Such fullness of life signifies God's presence. The Day of the Lord, once a label for judgment, will become a day of redemption and reconciliation. God will have "poured out my spirit on everyone" (2:28) as lavishly as water, wine, and olive oil were poured.

Christians see this culminating in God pouring the Holy Spirit onto the church at Pentecost. It's a reminder that a Day of the Lord event is a call for us to open ourselves to the redeeming work of the God who's already here.

Lord, thank you for your faithful love. In
times of uncertainty, make me a witness to
your abundant, unfailing grace. Amen.

## Thursday, November 25

# A Thanksgiving Homecoming

### *Revelation 7:9-17*

**What are your memories of being welcomed home?**

Some who celebrate Thanksgiving today will be opening their doors to family and friends. Smiling faces and the aroma of a banquet will greet the guests. When John wrote Revelation, he was trying to strengthen the first-century Christians who were enduring relentless persecution in the Roman Empire. He wrote today's passage in an effort to lift their eyes from their present suffering and see a future scene of a joyful homecoming.

The elder's description in verses 15-17 relies heavily on images from Isaiah. These Christians survived the time of hardship only because of the Lamb. His saving work turned their scarlet clothes to pure white (Isaiah 1:18). From now on they will be sheltered by God and never hunger or thirst again (Isaiah 49:10). The result will be God drying every tear, because even death has been defeated (Isaiah 25:8).

Such prophetic imagery shows that God's redemptive work is now complete. All the promises made throughout Israel's history have been accomplished through Jesus. The new Passover Lamb has fulfilled the intention of the first one.

As you give thanks today, remember this scene from Revelation. It is John's portrait of the time when we will hear from the throne, "Welcome home!" What greater reason for Thanksgiving can we have than this?

Lord, thank you for your faithfulness. Help me trust you to dry every tear and encourage every heart. Amen.

## Friday, November 26

# A Dramatic Invitation

## *John 7:37-39*

**How do you know that Jesus is your Messiah?**

Jesus was in Jerusalem as part of a religious festival. One of the rituals that day would have included the ceremonial drawing of water from the nearby pool of Siloam and pouring it in a basin near the altar. This symbolized Moses' striking a rock, with a resulting flood of water that sustained both the community and the livestock (Numbers 20:11).

Perhaps seeing this, Jesus, in a loud voice, linked himself to this water. His audience would have heard his speech as a Messianic reference. It closely resembles Isaiah's invitation to God's banquet: "All of you who are thirsty, come to the water!" (Isaiah 55:1). Additionally, the disciples would have remembered Jesus offering "a spring of water that bubbles up into eternal life" the drama with the Samaritan woman (John 4:13-15).

Jesus invited people to "believe" in him and drink (John 7:38). It goes beyond an intellectual assent to doctrine. Rather, it conveys a sense of trusting, of having confidence in. Listening to Jesus with an open mind and heart will result in new life. The drama painted in today's passage invites each of us to join the crowd in asking, "Is Jesus the Christ?" Accepting his invitation to trust him, even with our lives, quenches the thirst in our hearts. The waters of life will become a living reality.

Indeed, who else has the words of eternal life (John 6:68)?

Lord, you call me out and offer me living
water. Thank you for the chance to trust you
in the daily scenes of my life. Amen.

## Saturday, November 27

# A Banquet That Gives Hope

### *Isaiah 25:6-10a*

**How do you find strength to deal with difficult times?**

Isaiah praised God's saving work. The LORD will overthrow tyrants and care for the poor, needy, and homeless. Then, Isaiah describes a lavish banquet God will host in their honor. Its extravagance reflects God's heart. Moved by compassion, the Lord will spare no expense in welcoming the people to a land of renewed peace and prosperity. The Lord's presence will return. The disgrace the Israelites had felt at seemingly being abandoned will be replaced by joy in God's saving action.

This grace, though, will be extended beyond the Israelites. The prophet noted that God will prepare the feast "for all peoples" (v. 6). Israel will fulfill its destiny of being a light to the world (Isaiah 42:6). This complete picture, with all people on earth gathered around the banquet table in Jerusalem, puts the difficulties of the present time into perspective. There's no way of knowing when such a vision will become a reality. Just because we hurt today, though, doesn't mean that God isn't working to vanquish suffering and death, dry every tear, and make a home for all.

The vision of the future banquet proves God's work on behalf of those who suffer. Jesus, the one who invites all to his table, is the greatest proof.

Dear God, thank you for tirelessly working
behind the scenes. Open my eyes, and I will
praise your name forever! Amen.

## Sunday, November 28

# A Different Type of Birthday Party

### *Isaiah 55:1-3*

**What does an invitation to a banquet reveal about God?**

Today's passage conveys an invitation that would be both joyous and surprising to the Israelites. Our three verses today convey the excitement and passion behind the invitation to this feast. The Lord says "Listen!" twice (vv. 2 and 3) and "Come!" three times (vv. 1 and 3).

However, this invitation is not to an ordinary celebration.

First, there is diversity and equality among the invited guests. Regardless of whether or not you have money, you are invited. Oppression of the poor by the rich, including misconduct by those in power, had been a recurring sin in Israel. Such oppression will now end, because no one can buy a preferred place at God's table. Indeed, the impoverished themselves will have reserved seats.

Second, guests must bring a gift of repentance. Verse 2 implies that people have misplaced their priorities, spending on things that don't promote what's essential for life. Accepting the invitation means prioritizing God's desire for justice and righteousness.

God's invitation points to the dawn of an age when we will connect with God in a new, more intimate way. This will ultimately happen in a Bethlehem stable. When we celebrate Jesus' birth in a few weeks, we will be celebrating a love that will do anything possible to welcome us to the banquet table.

Lord, thank you for your relentless love. As I accept your invitation, I bring my life as a gift, yielded to you. Amen.

## Monday, November 29

# Forgive One Another's Complaints

### *Colossians 3:12-17*

**What does tolerance mean to you?**

In the letter to the Colossians, Paul says that all actions must be preceded by the incorporation of important perspectives and practices: compassion, kindness, humility, gentleness, and patience. These are born out of love and of our understanding that we are the chosen, holy, and loved ones of God. When we start from that perspective instead of the point of view that I'm always right and you are only right when you act and talk like me, then we have the ability to carry the particular rules of life with loose hands.

We indeed can tolerate different actions and points of view, not because we are beneficent, but because we don't own the world to start with! We can forgive one another because arising out of the relationship with God, we know we have first been forgiven ourselves.

Life becomes far more enjoyable and living with others far more bearable when we act less out of judgment and more out of mercy, which includes room for others to live as they best see fit within God's overall love and care for us all.

What irks you in your life? How could you approach that particular thing differently if you were to live out of the perspective of God's acceptance and care for you as you are? How will you act in the name of Christ today?

God, sometimes it's hard to live together! Give me grace and tolerance for others today; in Jesus' name. Amen.

## Tuesday, November 30

# Keep Forgiving One Another

*Luke 17:1-4*

**What is your capacity to forgive?**

In Luke 17, Jesus is not concerned about someone being sorry so much as he is concerned about our behavior when it comes to accepting and embracing the request to be forgiven from another. In an effort to keep someone from falling into sin and the danger that goes along with it, Jesus made sure to instruct the disciples in the fine art of forgiveness. If someone changes his or her heart, forgive that person (v. 3). If someone sins against you seven times in a day and asks forgiveness, forgive that person (v. 4).

That's tough! Sometimes I don't feel so inclined to forgive someone who has done wrong against me. Sometimes the offense just plain hurts, and I can't muster up whatever it takes to cover the pain. Sometimes, what that person has done is so terrible that even if he or she were to apologize, I wouldn't believe that the person was sorry.

Jesus says that's fine, but it doesn't matter. If we are to be like Christ, in the image of the God of love, then we are in the forgiveness business. We don't have time to create narrow paths of justice. Jesus says we have forgiving to do. Remember all the past sins we have committed have been forgiven by the loving gift of Christ for us. How can you begin to turn offense into forgiveness in your life? What can you give away in order to simply love and forgive?

As you have forgiven me, O God, give me the strength to forgive someone else today; in Jesus' name. Amen.

# DECEMBER

**CONTRIBUTOR:**

*Randy Cross*
*December 1–31*

## Wednesday, December 1

# The Most Important Instruction

### *Matthew 22:37-40*

**What is your core responsibility as a faithful person?**

Our Scripture today may be Jesus' greatest teaching. He was able to distill the entire law of Moses and the teachings of the prophets of Israel into the single commandment to love God and love neighbor. Every faithful Christian has been called to consider this commandment as he or she lives out the daily life. All of our words, our actions, and even our thoughts should be wrapped up in this critically important responsibility as the followers of Christ.

But it is amazing how distracted we can become, even as we follow Christ. We often demand consideration from others for our own lives, as though others exist to take care of us. We may even ignore or set aside the needs of others, who indeed are our neighbors. It is almost as if we have heard the commandment to say, "Make sure God and your neighbor love you as you love yourself!"

That's why prayer and the Sabbath are so critical for our lives. They become time that is set apart to refocus and reorient our important faithful work. When we are exhausted and distracted, how can we possibly stay fully aware of what God commands us, invites us, creates us to do?

How could you change parts of your life to make love of God and neighbor your core?

Dear God, help me to love you and your
children more dearly. Amen.

## Thursday, December 2

# Treat Your Neighbors Justly

### *Leviticus 19:13-18*

**What does it mean to be a good neighbor?**

Our Scripture reading for today has a lot to say to the Israelites, and to us, about basic good behavior toward those persons who are connected to us in a community. The instructions appear to be divided into two lists: not harming (stealing, lying, insulting, slandering), and making sure to care for those persons in a loving and open manner. Things like standing around watching a neighbor's blood be shed or simply hating a neighbor run contrary to what the Lord expects, requires, and even demands of us.

God calls us to be the good neighbor, to invest ourselves in loving and protecting those persons who are around us. Beyond avoiding doing bad stuff, it means we honestly take on Scripture and John Wesley's three simple rules: Do no harm, do good, stay in love with God (and neighbor).

Being a follower of Christ means something. It means that your life and mine are only fully lived out in the context of loving others, however that may look. Although today's reading is one in which the Lord speaks to Moses, we can hear Christ speaking to us in the same words.

Will we have the strength and intention to listen to Christ today and heed these words in a way that changes our neighbors' lives for the good? Will we be good neighbors?

Come, Lord Jesus, and show me how to love;
in the name of Christ, I pray. Amen.

## Friday, December 3

# Fulfilling the Royal Law

*James 2:8-13*

**How do you keep the Law as a follower of Christ?**

The Old Testament contains, at most counts, 613 different laws that cover diet, hygiene, community welfare, and worship. Given all of this, how can we possibly keep the law? This is what James talks about in his letter. It becomes akin to chasing after one's tail to try to keep every law at every moment. Even more, James makes it clear that if we break one law, it's the same as breaking any law (v. 11).

The good news, however, comes in the theme that James follows throughout his letter: the law of freedom, or the law of liberty. For us as Christians, those who follow Christ, we are called to follow the Great Commandment of loving God and loving neighbor. Christ has gone through the incredible work of crucifixion and then resurrection to ensure that our place in eternal life is secure, by grace through faith in him.

The law of freedom or liberty doesn't mean that we are free to do whatever we want without any consequences! It means we live by loving God and loving neighbor as a continual grateful response to God for the gracious gift of Christ. That foundation reforms our way of thinking and acting, so that we desire to fulfill the Law, but even more, to love without ceasing. Can you imagine your life lived this way, so that out of freedom we find our path and our grateful heart ready to serve as a follower of Christ?

Lord, free me to follow you and to be
bound to a new way of living. Amen.

## Saturday, December 4

# Don't Forget the Lord

### *Deuteronomy 6:10-15*

**How do you live as someone who is always aware of God?**

Moses tried to predict the future for the Israelites. When they finally were able to go into the land promised to them for centuries, and they got fat and happy with "money in the bank," Moses wanted them not to forget what they needed to remember. All of this had come by God's hand, and they needed to remember God in all they did. The worst thing the people could do, and that we can do, is to forget, or diminish, or somehow set aside the core call to live as grateful people, aware that we are grateful to the One who provides it all.

Simply, God is eager to bless and provide wonderful lives for us and, even more, God promises to always be with us wherever we go. In return, it is for us to not leave God, but instead to remember and keep at the front of our minds the love and the grace of the One who brought us life and gives us the opportunity to experience life.

As we are enjoying our lives, let us remember to be thankful continually for God's continual love for us. Let's make sure there is no room for the worship of other gods, even those of our own making.

What discipline could you use to make sure that you also remember God continually in your life? Prayer? Study? Worship? Spending time with others who also want to remember God?

O God, I am thankful for your blessings. Gently work in me so that I am always aware of you. Amen.

## Sunday, December 5

# Do What Is Right and Good

### *Deuteronomy 6:16-19*

**What does God promise if you follow with your whole life?**

Moses told the Israelites as they prepared to live in the Promised Land, "You must carefully follow the Lord your God's commands" (v. 17). If the nation of Israel did so, then things would go well for them (v. 18). Even though it sounds as if God would bless or curse them, depending on their actions, I have to wonder if the greater truth is whether their right and good and faithful actions would simply bear the good fruit and help them avoid a bad future.

We can think about the directions God offers to us in our lives today. They are similar, almost the same as God gave to the people back then. Follow God's commands, do what is right and good, and don't test God. Don't frustrate God with self-centered desires and actions that indeed may go counter to what brings life and peace.

We wonder sometimes, when it seems our lives are a big mess, if we have messed up or have taken the path that doesn't bring light and life. When we realize we are the cause of some undesired effects, we must stop where we are and look for God or at least look for where God has been. Then we need to find that new path, that new behavior, that new commitment to love and follow in the way that will ensure things go well with us in this land in which we dwell.

Guide my path, loving God, and help me
walk with you; in Jesus' name. Amen.

## Monday, December 6

# Fear the Lord and Live Rightly

### *Deuteronomy 6:20-25*

**What story are you telling with your life?**

I love today's Scripture: "In the future, your children will ask you . . ." (v. 20). Every Israelite needed to be ready to answer their question with a family history, which of course is woven into God's sacred history. Once we were slaves, but God brought us out! More importantly, the explanation describes even deeper purposes. It's not that God "brought us out," but it was done *so that* God could "bring us in" (v. 23). Of course, that refers to God taking the Israelites into the land of Canaan, the land blessed for their ancestors. And God commanded them to keep the regulations and revere God so that things would go well (v. 24).

What stories have we heard in our lives, or what stories are we telling to those who follow us, that help to inform the "why" of the present day, and the hope for the future? The story we share should always explain the why of the happening, whether we have done it or a long-ago ancestor has done it. Even the story of salvation becomes brand-new and empowered with a current urgency to tell and hear when we know the "why." I follow Jesus today in my life because the truth of God's love for me is seen so clearly in what Jesus did, and I dare not miss a moment of life with God!

Lord, open my mouth and heart to tell of
your story in my own life today. Amen.

## Tuesday, December 7

# Multiply God's Gifts

*Matthew 25:14-30*

**How do you use what God has given you?**

A master leaves three different servants in charge of part of his possessions, and two of the three do a pretty good job of turning a profit. One, however, decides that it is best just to preserve and not use the money, so he buries it and gives it back to his master when he returns. The master is angry, of course, and orders this servant to be thrown outside in the darkness for not even doing the minimum to earn something.

We must translate this a bit and think more broadly than just money. As we understand stewardship in our lives, we come to know that all we have and all we are is a gift to be used in this world to further God's love. Imagine if I could take all the gifts and abilities God has given me and double all of that in terms of the love I share on this earth.

However, if I become a miser in terms of using God's love and gifts, if I bury them so that no one benefits, and I offer no hope and grace through them, if I choose not to share love, can I possibly believe that God will bless that way of living? Or would I instead be correct to expect that I had wasted my life, and in a real sense, wasted God's investment in me?

If we allow fear of what might be to rule our behavior and our choices, it's possible that we will miss out on the beautiful gift of loving in this world. Living intentionally aware of what God wants us to do is to live a life of blessing.

How will you invest in God's gifts in your life?

Allow me, dear God, to fill this world with
your love through my life. Amen.

## Wednesday, December 8

# The Lord Is God Alone

### *Deuteronomy 6:1-9*

**How have you been able to fill your life with the truth that the Lord is God alone?**

The nine verses of today's Scripture reading are dense with meaning and direction. The overall powerful message, of course, is that God's people must follow these words, these laws, with their entire lives—themselves and their entire families—so that things will go well, they will multiply, they will live long lives, and they will live in peace. Beyond that, the commandment was to be a teaching tool for the children and the family. These verses are an intense and overwhelming instruction, designed to make sure everyone everywhere knows that the Lord is God alone.

Does that happen in your life? What actions or reminders do you include in your life so that there is a constant affirmation that Jesus Christ is Lord of your life? How often in a day do you discuss this critical truth with those around you? Have you told your children or grandchildren about Jesus? Part of the challenge of the Christian faith today is that so many of us know the truth but have not shared it or demonstrated it to anyone else. As that happens, soon it becomes private and then silent and then gone for another generation.

Who needs to know what you know? What greater joy might you feel if you were able to fill your own life with the call to love the Lord with all you are? Can you begin today?

Show me better how to love you, Lord, and
how to share that love with others. Amen.

## Wednesday, December 9

# Rules on People Relating to God

### *Exodus 20:1-11*

**What's the best way to show how you love God?**

Love for another is lived out in the respect you give others. Today's Scripture is quite well known: the first four of the Ten Commandments. I'd like for you to consider today, however, that instead of these being commandments or rules that we have to follow in our lives, this expression of God's will and intention for us is more about love.

Love is indeed a feeling, but it only comes alive through our actions and our lived-out intentions. So if I indeed love God, I will keep God first, having no other gods before God. Loving God means not only that I will keep God first; it also means that I will not worship other things in my life, no idols of any sort.

Even more fascinating is the way the Common English Bible states the next way for us to love God: "Do not use the Lord your God's name as if it were of no significance" (v. 7). We love God as we respect even God's name and no longer trivialize it as a profanity or an exclamation point to our statements.

In a real sense, as a child of God, I show my love in my respect, my honor, and my willingness to live differently before God than the rest of the world. Can you take on that important love in your life? Can you form your life around the God who has loved you?

O God, allow me to show my love for you
through the actions of my life. Amen.

## Thursday, December 10

# Rules on People Relating to People

### *Exodus 20:12-17*

**What's the best way to show love for your neighbor?**

Commandments 5-10 give us a path to the love and cherishing of the rest of the world, especially those who are connected to us in some way in a community. These six commandments radiate out from the center in how we live out cherishing others.

First, is how we care for and respect our parents. Respect and deference are how we best show our love.

The next three are rapid fire: Don't kill, don't steal, don't disrespect the vows that you or another has made with another person by committing adultery. Can you hear the call to basic respect in these commandments?

The next commandment invites us to cherish not only our neighbor but our society, as we are called to tell the truth, especially as we recount the actions of others. Finally, our love and cherishing for our entire community comes as we take on the discipline of refusing to consider whether the property or the relationships of a neighbor are indeed something we think we should have instead.

Everything goes back to how we express and live out feelings found in a loving relationship and also how we protect, respect, and hold dear the lives and loves of others. Can you imagine how much stronger and more blessed our communities would be if we all loved and cherished one another in these ways?

God, guide me to begin the work of caring
for my neighbor today. Amen.

## Friday, December 11

# Keep the Faith and Live

### *Joshua 23:2-6, 14-16*

**What can you expect from God?**

We read in today's Scripture that Joshua was old and wanted to once again tell the nation of the blessing they were living in at that moment. In the midst of this good news and evidence of God's love, Joshua offered a warning: All of this had happened because of God's love. If the people decided to break the covenant that God had made with them, God would be "furious" and cause them to "quickly vanish from the fertile land" God had given them (v. 16).

Yikes! Why would Joshua, and God, threaten the people this way? The answer carries us back to God's covenant that Abram's family would be a blessing to the world; and through Abram's people, the world would come to know God in a more fully revealed way. However, if Abram's people decided to ignore God's claim on them and the relationship made with them, it would only make sense that God would set them aside and raise up a new way of blessing the world.

If we act in a way that proves that we could care less for any relationship with God in Christ, why would we then expect to receive a blessing and place in the Kingdom? Isn't God simply taking our desire into account, that if we don't care for God, God will not make us enjoy the blessing of eternal life and love?

How can you prove your love for God today through your own life?

As you have blessed me this day, O Lord,
let me love the blessing. Amen.

## Saturday, December 12

# Rescued From Egypt, Settled in Canaan

*Joshua 24:4-12*

**What reminds you to be grateful?**

Joshua 24 is a final "state of the union" address by the leader of the nation of Israel, years after they crossed the Jordan and entered the Promised Land. Today's Scripture records how Joshua helped the people recall where they had been and what had happened to them, and he reminded them of who it was who had made this all happen. The entire journey occurred through the will and hand of God.

It was a critical and wonderful part of the heritage and faith of the Israelites. They were God's people, chosen through Abraham and led through each ancestor and finally led out of slavery and into the new land they now occupied. We, too, need to have reminders of the reason for our own gratitude to God.

What's yours? Maybe it's the face of a grandchild, a home, or some other kind of touchstone that helps you remember and moves you deeper into God's ongoing story. The more often we can recover and uncover those events or tangible things that call us to thank God for our lives, our life's path, and ultimately our salvation in Christ, the more joyful a life we can live.

Joy begins with gratitude, a grateful response for the gracious gift given. How do you find that path to gratitude in your own life, as you worship God? How do you help others to find their point of gratitude as their own worship of God?

Gracious God, grant me the privilege of
saying "Thank you" today. Amen.

## Sunday, December 13

# We Promise to Serve God

### *Joshua 24:16-21*

**What does it take for you to keep an important promise?**

Joshua completed his address to the people of Israel, and their response was to make an enthusiastic promise to serve the Lord in all the ways they could. They echoed Joshua's speech and recounted all of the marvelous things that had happened to them and credited God for the blessings they now lived with. Why would they not serve God? The people pledged to keep their most important promise: to follow God. History will tell us not how well they made the promise but how well they kept it.

What are the important promises you have made that remain in place today? Certainly, ones involving relationships have to be on the list. Perhaps a promise to live a certain way or to protect and care for something of great value is on the list. My promise list is different from yours, but the common thread is how we care for them and keep them in our lives. These promises shape us and our behavior in many ways. We can't make an important promise and not be altered by the meaning of it. It's tragic at times when we fail, and the finest offering of grace comes when we are given the opportunity to start anew and our failure is not held against us.

Be sure, however, to always know: We are known by our promises of value and our willingness to live with them. What promise do you struggle with in your life today?

O Lord, enable me to keep my promise to be
faithful to you for my whole life. Amen.

## Monday, December 14

# Covenant with God Confirmed

### *Joshua 24:25-28*

**What covenant signs do you recognize in your life today?**

After all of the speeches and affirmations to stay faithful to God and be God's people, finally Joshua seemed convinced that the nation of Israel wanted to try. So, he took a large stone, put it up "under the oak in the sanctuary of the Lord," and announced that this now was the witness, the sign, the reminder of the intention of God's people to be and remain faithful from this time forth (vv. 26-27).

You probably can't take more than two steps in all of Israel and not hit a stone! It's a rocky land! Joshua took the most common item in all the land to be the sign of the covenant. It was a powerful symbol, because the people would be reminded by every stone they saw of their calling to be faithful and to be the blessing God offered to the world.

As you walk through your life seeking to be faithful yourself and holding your own covenants intact by your best efforts, perhaps you'd like to find even those everyday items that can become holy when we use them as signs of the covenant. A tree, a rock, a coin, even a paper clip, if it reminds you of God's love for you and your love for God, is worth keeping in front of your eyes and in the front of your mind. What covenant have you made or you are about to make that deserves a special sign or witness of its own? Will you take the time to pray over the sign and allow the power of God's love to shine through it?

Holy God, receive my offering to you this
day as a sign of my love. Amen.

## Tuesday, December 15

# Choose to Love and Serve God

### *Joshua 24:1-3, 13-15, 21-24*

**What makes you want to choose to serve God?**

The first task in any choice is deciding to choose. Think about it for a minute. We first must make the conscious decision that we are going to take part in a selection of some group of things, or else the choice is completely empty.

Before we can choose to serve God, we have to make the choice to serve anything or anyone besides ourselves. We have to intend that we will place our lives in another's hands, our heart's devotion in another's care. Only then can we begin the task of choosing the focus of our devotion.

After Joshua's speech, the Israelites chose to choose. It was the important work of choosing between so many different foreign gods offered to them. At least with their voice, they did choose the Lord (v. 24).

The question still falls before each of us. Do we even want to choose to follow any god at all? We have many from which to choose once we make that first decision! Hundreds of things in this world can steal our devotion, even our love. From pleasures to goals to those things that are just plain horrible for us, still, we can choose. What a pity it would be if God were not on the list! If God were not known or someone did not have the opportunity to choose God to love and follow, that would be tragic.

Today, as you make your choice to serve God, will you also choose to make sure that others have the opportunity to make the same choice? Who will you tell about God today?

Give me a voice to share your love this day, O God. Amen.

## Wednesday, December 16

# Nothing Separates Us from God's Love

*Romans 8:31-39*

**How deeply do you trust God?**

For me, today's Scripture carries enormous power and grace and support for my life. "If God is for us, who is against us?" should ring in our ears every day as we get up and begin to face whatever it is that the day brings, whether that's a challenge at work, with our health, in a relationship, with our finances, or any number of other things (v. 31). We're not asked to believe that nothing will go wrong in our lives. Instead, Scripture assures us that it doesn't matter in the end what happens to us, because in all of it and through all of it, God is for us; and, indeed, nothing will or can separate us from the love of Christ.

A few years back a saying was making the rounds that asked, "What would you do today if you knew you could not fail?" In a sense, this Scripture goes even further, as it basically asks, "What will you no longer fear in your life, because you know God is with you?"

Whatever challenges or tragedies or problems descend on you or the ones you love, you can carry the root promise for your life that you don't have to go it alone. Wherever you find yourself, even in the direst situation, you can repeat the words: "If God is for me, who is against me?" And with that, you can follow the Leader safely in your own life.

What looms in your life today that you know God won't make you face alone?

I thank you, God, for your loving care
each day of my life. Amen.

## Thursday, December 17

# An Answer in Time of Trouble

### *Psalm 86:1-7*

**How do you know that God will care for you?**

In today's Scripture, the writer turns the question around and tries to answer the "why" of God's actions, even if God didn't need to know! Six times in seven verses, the writer feels the need to reinforce the call for God's care with a "because." Why should God listen, guard, save, have mercy, make life happy, and listen again? Because I'm poor, I'm in need, I'm faithful, I cry out to you, I've given my life to you, I trust you, you are good, you are forgiving, you are full of love, and you will answer me. Granted, it includes praise of divine acts and approach to someone in need. Isn't it strange, though, how the writer needed to tell God of divine qualities?

Yet that's what we do. Often, our prayers end up something like, "I know you'll do this for me because," and we compliment or somehow believe we can make God keep that holy word and take care of us. The truth is much simpler. We don't have to beg or convince God to act in ways that are consistent with the divine character. God is already all of the things the psalmist described and has already acted to respond to our needs and to even go before the needs arise, to sustain our life in peace and in trouble. Imagine how more powerful a prayer we might offer if instead of giving God the "why" answers, we simply brought our need and our hope and placed them into God's hands, knowing divine care is there for us always.

Loving God, you have already told me why you love me,
and for that I thank you with all my heart. Amen.

## Friday, December 18

# Psalm 86:8-13

### *Let Me Walk in Your Truth*

**What is your core prayer for your life today?**

Today's Scripture begins with a wonderful song of praise to God. No one and nothing compares to who God is! Psalm 86:10 is clear: "You are awesome. . . . You are God. Just you." I suppose we should begin there. It's only as we realize and fully accept God's wonderful and awesome nature that we can begin to move forward and think about what our best response can be with that knowledge. The psalmist offers us an equally deep and challenging prayer to God as a way toward the next step of living in God's presence: "Teach me your way, Lord, / so that I can walk in your truth. / Make my heart focused / only on honoring your name" (v. 11).

If you strip away all the distractions and contingencies in your life and are focusing on learning God's way and focusing your heart on honoring God, then, with that focus, you can live the purest abundant life of walking in God's truth. All of the frantic large and small concerns, all of the battles with family and friends and enemies, even all of the opinions and positions we take about things we have no control over, but what guides our loves and our hates—all of those things drop away, and we wait to be taught God's way and to walk in the truth alone. The truth, of course, arises out of God's love for us and for our neighbor, as our love should also grow. Once we make that the core, then all the rest of our lives come into harmony with God and the entire world God has created.

Let me see you today, O God, with all of my heart. Amen.

## Saturday, December 19

# Acts of God's Steadfast Love

### *Nehemiah 9:16-21*

**Can you recall a time when God treated you better than you deserved?**

You probably know the story of the children of Israel and their forty years of wandering in the wilderness. Over and over, instead of gratitude and worship, they treated the God who brought them out of slavery like an irritation and wished they could live differently. In today's Scripture, we read how God responded to that arrogant disrespect: God loved the Israelites and guided and protected them and gave them food and water. They "lacked nothing in the wilderness" except for thankful hearts (v. 21).

Why would God act in such a caring way toward a people who were a giant pain in the neck? At the same time, when we stop for a moment and think of the times in which we have ignored or disobeyed or outright defied God by our own actions, we could and should ask the same question of our own lives: Why? The answer is powerfully simple: God loved Israel and created a special people. Despite the Israelites' best efforts to destroy that relationship, God remained faithful and loving at every turn, just as God does for us.

Perhaps it is time for us to recount and ask God's forgiveness for our seasons of rebellion and self-centered hearts and express gratitude for the incredible, holy, and gracious gift of God's love for us. How might you ask for that forgiveness today?

Thank you, O God, for loving me more
than I could ever love you. Amen.

## Sunday, December 20

# God Abounds in Steadfast Love

*Exodus 34:1-7*

**How profound is God's love for you?**

The Israelites not only understood that their God's power was not limited to any geographical area; they also came to know that God actually was for the people of Israel, wanted the best for them, and wanted a loving relationship with them. All of this in spite of the fact that the Israelites themselves continually broke God's commandments.

But in today's reading, we find the Lord, in a cloud, talking to Moses and self-identifying the qualities that we would hope and pray would be God's self-revelation! Compassionate, merciful, patient, full of loyalty and faithfulness, and forgiving—this is the God we know. But God is clear that there are consequences for bad behavior. Even that punishment is limited, but God's love is not!

Later in our faith history, we are blessed to experience God's fullest self-revelation, showing even more clearly all of those qualities and intentions of God for this world. God's actual Word is made flesh and comes to live among us. In Jesus, we see the full revelation of God. In Christ's death and resurrection, as in Christ's incarnation that we celebrate in a few days, we are given the privilege of witnessing who God is, full of grace and love.

In the face of such profound love and amazing grace, how might you respond with the actions, thoughts, and feelings in your own life?

Lord, I thank you for your holy love for me. Help me follow you with all of my heart. Amen.

## Monday, December 21

# God Forgives and Loves People

### *Numbers 14:13-20*

**Can you remember a time when you experienced God's forgiveness and love?**

Today's Scripture is a peculiar reading. God was so angry with the people due to their grumbling, lack of respect, and lack of trust that God's first reaction was a plan to strike them down with a plague and start over. But Moses asked God to forgive the people, not because of what they had repented of doing, since they hadn't, but because of God's loyalty and patience in dealing with such a stubborn people.

I'm sure each of us can remember a time when we were on the receiving end of the gracious gift of forgiveness, even when we didn't deserve it. Hopefully, each of us can recall the experience of offering forgiveness when it wasn't deserved or even asked for. It's important always to remember that it is God's nature to forgive and to love, even when there is no reason to do so.

At the same time, one of the greatest things we can do in our lives is to forgive because we have the power to do so and not because someone has earned that forgiveness. As you can tell from reading the biblical account, there were still consequences, and it was not all perfect. But when forgiveness is in charge, there we see the face of God.

Who needs the gift not of making everything perfect but of forgiveness that you can offer from your heart today? How will you act in the image of God?

Forgiving God, teach me how to be like you. Amen.

## Tuesday, December 22

# The People Bless the Lord

### *Psalm 103:1-17, 21-22*

**How do you bless God through your own life?**

Today's psalm is a world-class psalm of praise and thanksgiving to God. It begins with the psalmist asking that his whole being be given over to blessing the Lord. God has acted and acts in extraordinary ways to show love and care. Justice, compassion, mercy, patience, healing, and more are all attributed to God. Everything the psalmist says is not new. It is the foundational fact of our relationship with God and God's relationship with all the world for all time.

All God's creatures are invited to join in this universal time of blessing God. Among humans, we often ask God to confer blessings of grace and love on us, others, the food we eat, and so forth. But when we bless God, we exalt, praise, and worship the very Source of all blessing.

Apart from times of worship or devotion and prayer, it becomes difficult to continually speak words of blessing to God, even if the psalmist aspires to do so with his whole being. One way we may bless God continually is to be always mindful of God's presence and act and speak as though we are standing before the throne of God ourselves. I'm sure we can immediately recall our actions that we hope God might not be aware of! We also recognize that we often fall short of blessing God with everything we are. That's why we are called to continue to grow in our faith.

How might you find a new way to bless God this day?

Bless you, Lord, for all that you are. Amen.

## Wednesday, December 23

# The Birth of John Promised

### *Luke 1:11-16*

**What long-time promise has God fulfilled in your life?**

We know the story of a priest and his wife, praying for years that God indeed would be gracious and give them a child. Now, when both of them were old and their prayer was equally old, an angel greeted Zechariah as he was serving the special role in the Holy of Holies, offering incense to God on behalf of the entire nation of Israel. The angel told the old priest that he and his wife would have a son; that he should name him John; and that he indeed would be special and would bring people to God.

But why be so surprised? Wasn't this the prayer that these faithful people had prayed their whole lives? But how often do we offer up sincere prayers for God to act on our behalf, and then we put time restraints and particular conditions on how the prayer is to be answered? Are we surprised, or maybe even disappointed, when we are blessed as God will bless and not as we demand or dictate?

I wonder, as I read this story, if the prayers that I offer up to God may be too small themselves. Do I ever ask God to use me to change this world, to turn the face of the world to the face of God? Do I let my prayers be a vision for the future, or do I just ask for crumbs or junk food instead of the bread of life?

I thank you, O God, for the miracles you bring.
Let me be part of a miracle today. Amen.

## Thursday, December 24

# Live by Faith

### *Habakkuk 1:2-4; 2:1-4*

**What are things you trust about the future?**

The prophet Habakkuk is clear: This world is a mess. His first words in his dialogue with God were words of complaint: God was not listening! Have you ever felt that way? The words flowed out of Habakkuk: injustice, anguish, devastation, violence, strife, conflict. And nothing, not even justice, could break the grip of the wicked on this earth. Isn't that gloomy? This is why it's so hard to read this on Christmas Eve, but let's not give up. The fact is as much as our culture and even our church has created a gentle, bright-star-and-cattle-lowing image for us of Christmas, Habakkuk reminds us of a deeper truth: This world is lost without Jesus.

Then God answered Habakkuk. The answer was simple: Hope for the future. Write the vision of what has not yet come to be. There is an appointed time, God said (Habakkuk 2:3), and it will not be late; but it also will not come simply because we want it to be here right now, like Christmas morning.

The time when the kingdoms of this world will become the kingdom of our Lord and of Christ is soon to come! Our task as God's children and the followers of Christ today is to continue to hold that light of hope, even when it is gloomy and feeling hopeless. We are to be the witnesses of what is yet to be and what has already been accomplished in the salvation of the world.

Will you claim this Christmas story today?

God of light, guide me in hope this day. Amen.

## Friday, December 25

# Rewards for Hospitality

### *Matthew 10:40-42*

**How do you make room for Jesus today?**

Merry Christmas! By the way, do you know why we say "Merry Christmas" in the first place? When we break down the phrase, it's important for us to realize that "happy" is an emotion we carry, but "merry" is a behavior. We "make merry," which means we treat others and the day as a different type of experience than that of a normal day.

The idea that our Christian faith is a behavior rather than just a feeling is the key to living a vital and deeply spiritual faith. Beyond what I feel about Jesus, his life, ministry, teachings, sacrifice, and resurrection, how I behave and respond to that reality makes the difference in the type of faith I have. Indeed, our Christian lives should always be grateful response to the gracious gift. I do more than feel the faith; I must live it out in a daily manner. In a real sense, each day we are called to make merry, to love one another, and to live holy lives. That's why in today's reading Jesus talks about behavior toward others. Beyond the desire we might have of receiving Jesus into our lives and into our homes, Jesus said that the way in which we welcome those who come into our lives makes a huge statement about our commitment to act like followers of Christ and not just give lip service to the idea. We make room for Jesus when we make room for all who need the gifts and love we can offer.

Lord, help me to make room for you and welcome you with all my heart this day. Amen.

## Saturday, December 26

# The Lord Was with John

### *Luke 1:57-66*

**Do you know your own name's meaning? Does it carry a sense of power for you?**

In a miraculous turn of events, two old people were given the gift of a child. And since the father, Zechariah, a priest, could not believe it would happen, he was made mute until the baby was born.

*Zechariah* should have been the name of the firstborn son of the couple, as a tradition, like Junior. However, Elizabeth, the mother, was firm that the baby would be called John. Now, for some reason, as it always happens, everyone else believed they had the right to have input into that decision. But finally, they asked the mute Zechariah, and he indicated that indeed the boy's name would be John. The name means "God is gracious"—gracious to grant them a child; gracious to pave the way for the coming of the Messiah in a few years.

John received the power to prepare the way of the Lord and to ensure that the minds and hearts of many were ready to understand that the world was about to change with the coming of Jesus. It's critical to understand, however, that all of this happened not because he was named John. It was because he was filled with the Holy Spirit.

When you think of your life, what role has God played in establishing who you are? What has determined your role in this world? How will you claim that as your own birthright today? How will you live out your own name in this life?

Lord of life, guide and direct my path
so that I may serve you. Amen.

## Sunday, December 27

# Let It Be According to Your Word

### *Luke 1:32-38*

**How willing are you to live as a servant?**

In first-century Israel, what would have been the greatest and worst change that could come to a teenage girl? Most likely, it would have been to become pregnant without being married and without having a father identified. Yet that was precisely what came to Mary that day when Gabriel announced that God was going to change her life and change the world at the same moment. After being confused and questioning the angel, this young woman responded, probably gulping at the same time, with the words that echo our life's call: "I am the Lord's servant. Let it be with me just as you have said" (Luke 1:38). And the world was transformed.

Could you respond like Mary? Was it faith that brought that response? I expect that it came to her as a holy gift, as a holy conversation, and she received from God at the same moment the freedom and the courage to become a great servant of God.

What is God asking you to do this day? What have you been delaying saying yes to? Where does God want you to bring new life, new hope, transformation? The most awesome thing about this story is that all that was required of Mary was her obedience and willingness to become what God wanted her to be. Can you find that same willingness in your heart today?

Lord of life, grant me the privilege of
serving you today. Amen.

## MONDAY, DECEMBER 28

# Joseph Obeys the Lord

*Matthew 1:18-25*

**What's the worst thing you might have to do in your life?**

Joseph was in a horrible place. He found out that his betrothed, Mary, was pregnant. By Jewish law, he had two choices: He could take her before the elders and accuse her of adultery, and she would be stoned to death. Or he could simply give her back to her parents as "damaged goods."

Ready to hand Mary back, Joseph had the dream in which he was commanded to assume the position of being an unrighteous person who had broken Jewish law by getting Mary pregnant. Yet he was told, "Don't be afraid to take Mary as your wife, because the child she carries was conceived by the Holy Spirit" (v. 20). It was a terrible decision to make, to be seen by everyone he knew as someone without integrity and honor.

However, he did just that, because his righteousness called him to honor God and not the Law. His obedience is one of the more powerful images of someone who said yes to God; but in the eyes of his contemporaries, he became less honorable because of it.

We all have hard things to do in life, and some are dreadful. However, gauging what we do by our attempt to be obedient to God is the best measure of honor and faith, even if it is a terrible thing to go through.

God of grace, help me to obey you before
and beyond all else. Amen.

## Tuesday, December 29

# Anna Speaks of the Child Jesus

### *Luke 2:36-38*

**What would you say about the baby Jesus?**

It's interesting to find Anna in the temple in today's reading. Eighty-four years old, a long-time widow, she spent her time fasting and praying. Luke calls her a prophet, which meant she must have displayed some sort of power or ability to speak God's message. Mary and Joseph and the baby Jesus were in the temple, and Scripture tells us that Anna found them and began to prophesy about this Baby and the redemption of Jerusalem.

Most people probably long for some sort of signs about where the future is headed and how we should live. Throughout the Bible, we find examples of persons empowered to speak of God's future with us and what God intends.

You may not have the gift of prophecy like Anna, but you do have opportunities to speak about Jesus. You have opportunities to offer words of peace, hope, grace, and comfort. Many of us may hold back from offering those words and insights. But what if, like Anna, we choose to speak a word about the future that helps another person trust God with the future? When we spend time in prayer and study and in opening ourselves to God's inspiration, we need to be ready to hear and then to share at least the hint of a future that is in God's hands, in order to bring some redemption to our part of the world.

O God of the future, open my heart to
listen to you this day. Amen.

## Wednesday, December 30

# Angels Announce Good News to Shepherds

*Luke 2:8-14*

**What have you heard from God lately?**

Have you ever noticed that usually when angels appear in the Bible to make an announcement, they do so alone? But not in today's reading. The scene begins with one angel who shares the news with the shepherds, the incredible news that the Savior has been born to them and to the world. After this angel shared the news, the visitation was not yet over, because "suddenly" there was "a great assembly of the heavenly forces" (v. 13), a multitude that broke out in a chorus of praise to God.

Isn't it marvelous that the announcement was an opportunity for joy and good news? Though prophets were sent to call the people of God to task and to bring them back into a relationship with God, when angels were deployed, it was to celebrate and bring hope and newness and great change and joy to this world.

Here's the fact: God loves this world, and God loves you. God has done and will continue to do all possible to shower the love upon you and call you and me and this world back into a holy, grace-filled, and loving relationship. When we listen for God's word in our lives, it should be with the ear of anticipating a celebration, even a celebration of being able to return home and be reconciled, or a celebration of being sent to a manger to see the future of God's world.

O God of good news, open my ears to hear of
your love and grace this wonderful day! Amen.

## Thursday, December 31

# Inherit the Kingdom

### *Matthew 25:31-46*

**What does God expect of you?**

Today's Scripture reminds us that if we are going to live on this earth and enjoy God's blessings of life and love knowing that God claims and cherishes us, there are some basic things God expects us to do. Maybe the first should be, "Stop whining." Stop complaining; stop bullying; stop being a pain in the neck. But the second is as important: Take care of those who are hungry or thirsty, those who are strangers, those who do not have the basic necessities of life. Take notice of those who are in terrible situations.

These things that the sheep in this Scripture do so well but the goats do not do are not heroic measures! They are commonsense ways for us to bless the world, to love one another, to love neighbor, and to care for others as God has first cared for us. Some people may be shocked to know that God blesses them when all they have done is what is basic: loving others. What is sadder is when people are shocked that God is displeased when their callous and selfish ways of living exclude those who need their love and care.

Perhaps each of us should take time to think about how we might more intentionally, simply, and from our hearts share the love that God has first given us. It's there that we inherit the kingdom of God. Whom do you know who needs the love of God that can be expressed through your actions, your words, your blessed life?

O God of love, let me love this world as well. Amen.

# NOTES

# NOTES

# NOTES

# NOTES

# NOTES

# NOTES

# NOTES

# NOTES

# NOTES

# NOTES

# NOTES

# NOTES